COLD WAR FEMME

....

COLD WAR FEMME

LESBIANISM, NATIONAL IDENTITY,

AND HOLLYWOOD CINEMA

ROBERT J. CORBER

Duke University Press

Durham and London

2011

© 2011 Duke University Press
All rights reserved
Printed in the United States
of America on acid-free paper ∞
Designed by Amy Ruth Buchanan
Typeset in Carter & Cone Galliard
by Tseng Information Systems, Inc.
Library of Congress Cataloging-
in-Publication Data appear on the
last printed page of this book.

An earlier version of chapter 1 appeared
in *GLQ* 11, no. 1 (2005). A portion of chapter 4
appeared in *Camera Obscura* 21, no. 2 (2006).

For Kent

"right as rain"

CONTENTS

....

ACKNOWLEDGMENTS

This book has taken a long time to write, and I owe special thanks to Steve Valocchi and Robyn Wiegman for all their support and encouragement. They not only provided a constant sounding board for my ideas but also read most of the manuscript, sometimes in multiple drafts. I am extremely grateful for their friendship and salutary influence over the years. Lauren Berlant also provided much-welcome emotional and intellectual support. Her incisive comments on several chapters provoked me to think more deeply about the project and to complicate my arguments. I have learned a great deal from her. At a crucial stage two anonymous readers for Duke University Press reminded me of what was most interesting and important about the project. I hope it will be apparent to them how much I benefited from their astute readings of the manuscript, which helped me to hone and strengthen it. For important conversations that contributed to my thinking, I want to thank Zayde Antrim, Jonathan Arac, George Chauncey, Carolyn Dinshaw, Inderpal Grewal, Judith Halberstam, David Halperin, Joan Hedrick, Annamarie Jagose, Janet Jakobsen, Amy Kaplan, Mai Ngai, Beth Notar, Ellen Schrecker, Marilyn Schuster, Barbara Sicherman, Chris Straayer, Susan Van Dyne, Amy Villarejo, and Patricia White. I also want to thank Reynolds Smith and Sharon Torian at Duke University Press for all their hard work and enthusiasm. Reynolds has been everything one could possibly want in an editor. His comments on an early draft of the manuscript helped me to clarify its focus, and his commitment to my work beginning with my first book has meant a great deal to me. I am also grateful to Courtney Berger and Jade Brooks for their patience and astute editorial guidance. I also want to acknowledge the late Gillian Brown, who on a cold and dreary afternoon in Salt Lake City many years ago cheered me up when she planted the seed for this project by encouraging me to write about Joan Crawford. I miss you, Gillian! Finally, I want to dedicate the book to Kent Sargent. Kent shares my love of classical Hollywood cinema, and he watched and discussed with me every movie examined in the book; he was also usually my first reader. His love and support going on thirty years now has sustained me in ways I cannot adequately acknowledge here.

RECLAIMING THE "LOST SEX"

The Lesbian in Cold War Culture

In 1962, Jess Stearn, an associate editor of *Newsweek*, received an invitation from the Daughters of Bilitis, a lesbian civil-rights organization founded in 1955, to participate in its upcoming national convention in Los Angeles.[1] Stearn had authored a bestselling book about male homosexuality, *The Sixth Man: A Startling Investigation of the Spread of Homosexuality in America*, and the Daughters of Bilitis, alarmed by the book's sensationalistic approach, hoped that by participating in the convention the journalist would gain a more objective view of homosexuality. The invitation described the Daughters of Bilitis as an organization of lesbians who had made "the adjustment to the social system" and who in learning "self-acceptance" wanted to provide "assistance" to other women who faced similar problems.[2] The invitation also assured Stearn that the organization did not adhere "to any particular point of view" (15) but sought to strengthen "the bond between the homosexual and society" by engaging in outreach to sociologists, psychologists, and other experts on lesbianism. Stearn suspected that lesbianism was "just as rampant as male homosexuality, only far more secretive" (9), and he had been toying with the idea of writing a book on the topic as a follow-up to *The Sixth Man*. While researching *The Sixth Man*, he consulted several experts who believed that the social upheavals caused by two world wars, combined with women's increasing demands for social and economic equality, had given lesbianism "a strong forward thrust" (14). The invitation from the Daughters of Bilitis confirmed his suspicion that lesbianism was on the rise in American society, and he embarked on an investigation of the lesbian subculture, visiting bars and restaurants in New York and Los Angeles that catered to lesbians, interviewing lesbian couples, as well as "bachelor girls," or femmes who preferred to remain single because of their unhappy domestic experiences with butches, and consulting psychologists, sociologists, and criminologists who studied the causes of lesbianism. *The Grapevine: A Report on the Secret World of the Lesbian*, the bestselling book, published in 1965, that resulted from Stearn's investigation, supposedly provided an even more "startling" view of American society than *The Sixth Man*. Stearn described *The Grapevine* as his "most unique assignment in twenty-five years of reporting the unique" (15).

As its title suggests, Stearn intended *The Grapevine* to shock, titillate, and alarm readers unfamiliar with the lesbian subculture. The journalist claimed that before he began his investigation, like many Americans he thought of lesbians in terms of the stereotype of the butch, a "harshly hostile figure with a short masculine haircut, coarse skin, nasty vocabulary, and rough male clothing" (10). But he quickly discovered that "some of the loveliest women in the world were lesbians, and were, ironically, appealing sex symbols on stage and screen to millions of unsuspecting males who didn't even begin to realize they were worshiping at a false shrine" (10). Indeed, most lesbians were indistinguishable from other women, which enabled them to mingle "congenially in conventional society" (19). Stearn also discovered that a woman's marital status did not necessarily indicate her sexual identity and claimed that many lesbians married: "As the passive partner in matrimony, they can easily disguise their indifference. And staying home all day, they can make friends among other housewives without stirring suspicion" (19). Lesbians supposedly could preserve the secrecy of their identities more easily than gay men could because "nobody thought anything of two women kissing, embracing, or dancing together" (10). As a result, husbands could not always tell whether their wives' affection for other women masked a lesbian identity. Underscoring the threat lesbianism supposedly posed to the institutions of heterosexuality, Stearn insisted that because they had the ability to disguise their aberrant sexuality, lesbians participated in a "vast, sprawling grapevine, with a secret code of [its] own" (12). Indeed, lesbians had an "almost radar-like communication with each other, and seemed able to spot, not only other lesbians on sight, but potential lesbians as well" (315). Moreover, because of their ability to pass as "normally sexed" (10) women, lesbians could supposedly carry on the "bittersweet work" (14) of converting other women to lesbianism without arousing suspicion. Emphasizing the porous boundary between female homosocial desire and lesbian identity, Stearn quoted one of his informants, who told him that lesbianism was "often only an extension of women's natural affection" (12) for other women.

Undermining his objectivity as a journalist, Stearn glossed over the patriarchal social and economic arrangements that lesbians had to negotiate as women and that underlay the aspects of their world that most alarmed him, its secrecy and invisibility. Stearn claimed that the lesbian had "a greater instinct for self-preservation than the male homosexual, and will often zealously protect her job and professional status" (18). Such a claim overlooked the difficulty that even white middle-class women had in achieving economic independence. Moreover, although he acknowledged that lesbians needed to disguise their identities, Stearn derided informants who complained about the homophobia of American society as immature and "maladjusted." He asserted that like the male homosexual, "the lesbian was often a heavy drinker, insecure emotionally, and quick to blame society for her insecurity" (13). He also complained that despite their racial, class, and religious differences, lesbians shared a "morbid preoccupation with their own homosexuality" (311) and that he could not recall meeting "a single lesbian who thought of the male as the superior sex" (317). In providing this view of the lesbian's "secret world," Stearn overlooked evidence that pointed to an alternative construction of lesbian identity, one that did not recycle homophobic stereotypes. He acknowledged that he had met many "well-adjusted" (12) lesbians who had maintained long-term relationships with other women, his own measure of emotional and sexual maturity. But he continued to incorporate a psychoanalytic discourse that attributed lesbian desire to an arrested sexual development.[3] Contradicting his own evidence, Stearn asserted that lesbians shunned the "emotional demands of making a home" (316), and he quoted several experts who insisted that lesbians "generally fly from a mature relationship" (317).

The Grapevine exemplified the homophobic discourse of female homosexuality that circulated in American society during the Cold War era.[4] This discourse fostered lesbian panic by claiming that the lesbian posed an "invisible" threat to the nation; because she could pass as "normal," the lesbian could participate in the nation's social and economic institutions without arousing suspicion. Stearn's publisher promoted *The Grapevine* by promising that the book would provide an answer to one of the most urgent questions that Americans allegedly faced: "How can you recognize homosexuality?"[5] By learning how to identify the lesbian, Americans could prevent her from spreading her "unnatural" sexuality throughout society. An effect of this construction was to link the lesbian to the communist "conspiracy" that purportedly threatened American democracy. The belief in the need to expose the lesbian so she could no longer seduce impressionable and emotionally vulnerable women unaware of her abnormal sexuality uncannily recalled the hysteria produced by the McCarthy witch hunts, which reflected the fear that communists had infiltrated the nation's political and social institutions, and were secretly conspiring to overthrow them by recruiting naïve and unsuspecting Americans to their cause.[6] Thus in 1946 George Kennan, one of the architects of the Cold War, warned that "world communism is like a malignant parasite which feeds only on diseased tissue."[7] In echoing this language, Cold War homophobia positioned lesbians as un-American. Like the communist, the lesbian allegedly threatened the American way of life.

Cold War Femme examines this discourse and its relation to the construction of normative femininity in postwar American society. Recent scholarship has shown that Cold War homophobia accelerated the consolidation of the hetero-homosexual binary by underwriting a psychoanalytic model of sexual desire that privileged object choice over gender identity.[8] One result of the Cold War construction of the homosexual was the disarticulation of gender and sexual nonconformity, with gender presentation increasingly functioning as an unstable signifier of sexual identity. Although this scholarship has clarified the role of Cold War homophobia in the reorganization of sexuality, it has focused almost exclusively on gay men and tended to assume that its conclusions apply equally to lesbians.[9] *Cold War Femme* seeks to rectify this imbalance by showing how Cold War homophobia transformed the category of the lesbian. As Stearn's book indicates, in the Cold War era the femme displaced the butch as the lesbian whose perverse sexuality posed the greatest threat to American society. Unlike the femme, the butch was easily identified by her cross-gender identification, which prevented her from participating in mainstream American society and from recruiting other women to the "secret world" of lesbianism as easily as the femme could. In this respect, the Cold War discourse of homosexuality marked a significant shift in the homophobic deployment of the category of the lesbian in American society. Earlier in the century, medical professionals had treated the feminine woman who made a lesbian object choice as less "abnormal" than the masculine woman who did so and argued that she had the capacity to realign her desire with the institutions of heterosexuality.[10] By contrast, the Cold War discourse of female homosexuality stabilized the femme's relation to lesbian identity and represented her as a threat to the institutions of heterosexuality.

To elaborate this argument, I examine the representation of lesbianism in Cold War Hollywood cinema. Although competition from television and other forms of mass media had led to a steady decline in audience attendance, Hollywood cinema remained one of the most powerful ideological apparatuses in American society for reproducing normative gender and sexual identities.[11] Indeed, it played a central role in the circulation of the Cold War construction of the lesbian by providing audiences with narratives of perverse female desire that incorporated the new model of sexuality.[12] But Hollywood was not a monolithic institution, and one of my goals in focusing on its representation of lesbian identity is to elucidate the tensions and contradictions in the homophobic deployment of the category of the lesbian.[13] Movies continued to draw on an older model of sexuality that linked gender and sexual nonconformity, even as they underwrote the Cold War construction of the lesbian. The Production Code, which regulated Hollywood's treatment of male and female sexuality, stated that "sex perversion or any inference to it is forbidden."[14] How could movies mark the femme as a lesbian without violating this prohibition? Since its introduction in 1934, Hollywood had circumvented the Code by deploying a set of visual and narrative strategies that indirectly identified characters as lesbians.[15] These strategies relied on the association of lesbianism with an inverted gender identity, an association rendered outmoded by the new system of sexual classification. Although the femme's threat to American society reflected her invisibility, Hollywood continued to rely on these strategies, even as it developed new ones for rendering her sexual nonconformity visible to audiences. As a result, the older model of sexuality never wholly disappeared but continued to shape popular conceptions of perverse female desire. One consequence of the circulation of two conflicting discourses of lesbianism in Hollywood movies was that female femininity emerged as a powerfully ambiguous signifier of sexual identity.

THE COLD WAR CRISIS OF THE HOUSEWIFE

In 1955, Adlai Stevenson, the governor of Illinois and the former Democratic presidential nominee, notoriously urged the graduating class of Smith College to help the nation resolve "our crisis in the humble role of housewife."[16] Stevenson realized that many college-educated women felt frustrated as wives and mothers. Domestic life seemed far removed from "the great issues and stirring debates for which their education has given them understanding and relish" (31). Thus they experienced a "sense of contraction, of closing horizons and lost opportunities" (31) when they married. His goal in addressing the graduating class of the elite women's college was to convince them that the role of housewife was crucial to the survival of American democracy, which the emergence of mass society supposedly threatened. Echoing the concerns of the sociologists William Whyte, C. Wright Mills, and David Riesman, who associated mass society with totalitarianism and the reification of experience, Stevenson reminded his audience that "to create a free society is at all times a precarious and audacious experiment" (30) and warned that mass society had reduced man "once again to subordinate status, limiting his range of choice, abrogating his responsibility and returning him to his primitive status of anonymity in the social group" (30).[17] In this respect, American society threatened to become like its political other, the Soviet Union. For Stevenson, women had the capacity, as wives and mothers, to counteract this danger by keeping their husbands "Western" (31). He explained that one of the housewife's primary responsibilities was to "frustrate the crushing and corrupting effects of specialization, to integrate means and ends, to develop that balanced tension of mind and spirit which can be properly called 'integrity'" (31). In other words, domestic life was not so far removed from the "great issues" of the Cold War era as the housewife may have assumed. He assured his audience that college-educated women in particular had "a unique opportunity to influence us, man and boy, and to play a direct part in the unfolding drama of our society" (31). One of the implications of this analysis was that women needed to sacrifice their individualism so that their husbands and sons could preserve theirs. Whereas men violated their identities by assuming a "subordinate status," women realized theirs in doing so, and once married Stevenson's audience would have the "unique opportunity" to protect their husbands and sons from mass society's assault on their masculinity.

Stevenson's belief that the role of the housewife in American society was in crisis was widely shared and underlay the lesbian panic of the Cold War era. In insisting that the housewife had the capacity to reinvigorate American democracy, Stevenson echoed social scientists who worried that women with college degrees would reject marriage and motherhood as aspirations, as they could support themselves economically and had no need to marry. Experts claimed that the importance of marriage and motherhood had declined in the face of women's social and economic gains since the 1920s. They were concerned especially about the companionate model of marriage, which had emerged in the 1920s as a strategy for preserving the institution of marriage by deemphasizing its religious, economic, and reproductive functions.[18] In the companionate marriage, women supposedly did not have to sacrifice their freedom and autonomy, as the bond between husbands and wives depended on emotional and sexual intimacy rather than on procreation. In this respect, the model reflected the increasing acceptance of women as sexual subjects, even as it avoided reducing women to their roles as wives and mothers and promised them a more equal relationship with their husbands. But a growing chorus of experts claimed that in reforming the institution of marriage so that it accommodated women's increasing demands for social and economic equality, social progressives had precipitated a crisis, for women's dissatisfaction with their traditional roles had in fact intensified. For example, in their bestselling book, *Modern Woman: The Lost Sex* (1947), Ferdinand Lundberg and Marynia Farnham argued that women's greater autonomy in marriage had led to a dramatic increase in cases of frigidity. For them, no woman could enjoy sexual relations unless she possessed a "willingness to accept dependence without fear or resentment, with a deep inwardness and readiness for the final goal of sexual life—impregnation."[19] In this way, the authors not only reasserted women's subordination but reinstalled motherhood as the only acceptable goal of female sexual activity. In their view, women's sexual desire was inextricably tied to procreation.

The subtitle of Lundberg's and Farnham's book reflected their disapproval of contemporary American women. They argued that women's social and economic gains had worsened rather than improved their condition in society, that the feminist movement had cut women adrift. In the wake of feminism's successes, women's femaleness had emerged as "a coincidence, an unfortunate complication" (10), rather than as an essential aspect of their identities. Moreover, women were buffeted by conflicting demands and expectations. They felt pressure to pursue a career, but in doing so they sacrificed the "instinctual strivings" (11) that stemmed from their capacity to bear children. Nor could they derive satisfaction from fulfilling those "strivings." Influenced by the women's movement, society no longer valued marriage and motherhood as aspirations for women. Lundberg and Farnham did not deny that society continued to emphasize the "supreme importance" (124) of motherhood, but they believed that it now carried few "concrete benefits" (124) for women. As a result, it was no longer central to their psychological well-being. Rather, women increasingly measured their value in terms of their ability to compete with men. According to Lundberg and Farnham, the feminist movement, despite its pathological hatred of men, had a single objective: "the achievement of maleness by the female, or the nearest approach to it" (167). But women could never derive satisfaction from emulating men or following the same route of achievement, for in doing so, they violated their femaleness. In other words, only marriage and motherhood could restore women's self-esteem. Anticipating Stevenson's graduation address, Lundberg and Farnham urged greater public recognition of the "powerful role and special importance of mothers as transmitting agents, good or bad, of feelings, personality and character" (356). As mothers, women bore responsibility for the psychological development of the nation's future citizens.

Lundberg and Farnham emphasized in particular women's relationships with their daughters. In their view, women had an obligation to provide their daughters with a "design for femininity" (228) so they could negotiate successfully the conflicts they would later experience as adults. Glossing over the enormous pressures to marry and bear children that women continued to face, the authors argued that because girls received the same education as their brothers, they too expected to eventually pursue careers that reflected their "inclination and training" (232). They also argued that girls grew up believing that they had an "inalienable right" to sexual pleasure and that, once they gained access to contraception, they could exercise this right without consequences. Nevertheless, women's basic need for satisfaction inevitably led them "in the direction of marriage and children inside the home" (233), thus precipitating the crisis that Lundberg and Farnham believed defined modern womanhood. Women who were raised to believe that they were men's equals could never fulfill their needs and desires through marriage and motherhood. According to Lundberg and Farnham, this aspect of modern womanhood rendered the relationship between mother and daughter especially fraught. Only the woman who found "complete satisfaction, without conflict or anxiety, in living out her role as wife and mother" (228) could provide her daughters with a model of femininity that would enable them to adjust to their identities as women. Her daughters would grow up valuing their femininity instead of experiencing it as an "unfortunate complication."

Modern Woman's emphasis on the importance of the mother's relationship with her daughter marked a shift in the momist discourse of motherhood initiated by the publication of Philip Wylie's enormously popular book *Generation of Vipers* in 1942.[20] By 1955, the year Stevenson delivered his graduation address, Wylie's book had gone through twenty printings and been selected by the American Library Association as one of the most important nonfiction books of the first half of the twentieth century.[21] Anticipating many of Lundberg's and Farnham's arguments, Wylie warned readers about women's growing freedom and autonomy, which he believed allowed them to dominate the domestic sphere. In hyperbolic prose, he complained that women were "taking over male functions and interpreting those functions in female terms," as well as inverting gender relations by donning "the breeches of Uncle Sam."[22] But unlike Lundberg and Farnham, Wylie focused on women's relationships with their sons. According to him, mothers could not bear any sign of independence in their sons and smothered them with love so they would remain attached to them even in adulthood. In so doing, they cushioned their sons "against any major step in [their] progress toward maturity" (208). Wylie condemned the appellation "mom," which he argued betokened men's dependence on their mothers, as well as their identities as "neuters" (200) incapable of protecting the nation from its enemies. In other words, mothers had robbed their sons of their masculinity, thereby rendering American society vulnerable and exposed. In shifting the focus of this discourse away from the mother's relationship with her son to that with her daughter, Lundberg and Farnham suggested that the reproduction of normative femininity was equally important to the survival of the nation's democratic institutions: daughters who grew up with an appreciation of their femaleness would pass it on to their own daughters, thus resolving the crisis of American womanhood.

In *Their Mothers' Daughters*, which appeared in 1956, Edward Strecker and Vincent Lathbury, both psychologists, rendered explicit the connection between citizenship and gender and sexual conformity underlying momist discourse. Like Lundberg and Farnham, Strecker and Lathbury wanted to focus attention on the importance of the mother's relationship with her daughters. The author of *Their Mothers' Sons*, which appeared in 1947, Strecker regretted that he had not published *Their Mothers' Daughters* first, for he now believed that "without the right kind of mature mothers and daughters, there cannot be produced the right kind of mature sons."[23] But unlike Lundberg and Farnham, Strecker and

Lathbury did not disapprove of women pursuing careers, so long as their careers were in fields like nursing, education, and social work, where they could indirectly express their maternal instincts. Moreover, the authors recognized that many women had no choice but to work, either because they had never married, had divorced, or were widowed. They cited the example of one of their patients, Mrs. B, who they felt had successfully negotiated the demands of a career in a "masculine" field while preserving her femininity. When her husband died, Mrs. B took over the management of his business. Although she was "all business, pleasant enough but briskly efficient" (31) while at the factory, she was "strictly feminine" (31) while at home with her two daughters. She supposedly looked forward to the day her daughters married so that one of her sons-in-law could take over the business: "Then I can go back to being a housewife. In fact I never stopped being one. It is my vocation. The factory is my avocation" (31). In other words, unlike Wylie, Strecker and Lathbury did not question women's equality or their ability to succeed in traditionally masculine pursuits. Mrs. B's "briskly efficient" management of her husband's business showed that she was just as competent as he was. But like Lundberg and Farnham, Strecker and Lathbury did not feel that women could satisfy their needs and desires by following the same route to achievement as men. Instead, they stated even more bluntly that "the main function of women is to give birth to children and 'make' a home in which they may be reared" (29).

Strecker's and Lathbury's analysis reflected the emergence of psychoanalysis as the dominant approach to the study of gender and sexuality in postwar American society.[24] Like Lundberg and Farnham, Strecker and Lathbury emphasized the need for mothers to instill in their daughters an appreciation of their femaleness so that they would accept their biological "mandate" to bear children. They focused on the obstacles that girls in particular had to overcome on the path to a normal, healthy adulthood. Girls frequently developed feelings of "insufficiency and inadequacy" in relation to boys. Strecker and Lathbury argued that unless girls saw their mothers as worthy of emulation, such difficulties might cause them to take the path to feminism, which the authors understood as a form of neurosis, or they might develop penis envy and never adapt to their future roles as wives and mothers. Indeed, girls were at constant risk of developing an inferiority complex in relation to boys. Ignoring the social arrangements that privileged fathers and sons over mothers and daughters, the authors attributed this risk to the *physical* differences between girls and boys. For example, they warned that if girls played with their brothers or other boys, they might come to envy their superior strength and athletic ability (147). Mothers had a responsibility to prevent these impediments from interfering with their daughters' ability to negotiate the Oedipus complex by conveying the importance of their femaleness. Strecker and Lathbury also emphasized the mother's responsibility for her daughter's sexual development. Like Lundberg and Farnham, they believed that frigidity was on the rise, warning that many women had "never had an orgasm, or at most a very fragmentary one" (129). But unlike Lundberg and Farnham, they accepted women as sexual subjects and avoided reducing their sexuality to a maternal drive. They blamed women's increasing frigidity on mothers who regarded sexual intercourse "gloomily and referred to it as unclean and sinful" (131) and urged mothers to instill in their daughters "healthy" attitudes about sexuality.

Strecker and Lathbury reinforced the significance of motherhood by linking it directly to the preservation of American democracy: "No other nation faces as great a danger of failing to resolve the mother-child relationship as the United States. No nation has a higher stake in it than we have. The stake is democratic survival" (40). Along with Stevenson, the authors wanted to persuade women that their roles as wives and mothers would expand rather than contract their horizons, that they had the capacity to foster the values and beliefs necessary for counteracting the threat mass society posed American democracy. As mothers, women had the "unique opportunity" to rear children who would develop the emotional maturity to exercise their citizenship responsibly. "The capacity to live democratically and constructively can be acquired only in childhood" (213), the authors argued, and mothers alone could teach children "these democratic lessons and permit them to practice them in their relations with other children" (213). In this way, Strecker and Lathbury attempted to reclaim what Stevenson had called the "humble" role of the housewife in American society, with their analysis suggesting that girls had no reason to grow up with an inferiority complex. As adults, women could contribute to American society in ways no less important than those of their fathers and brothers, for they would have the responsibility of nurturing in their children the capacity for sustaining American democracy. At the same time, however, to make this contribution, they would necessarily have to accede to a normative construction of womanhood. To play the same role in their daughters' lives as their mothers had in theirs, they would have to sacrifice their ambition to succeed in the public sphere, for such an ambition would prevent them from providing their daughters with an appropriate role model. And it followed that women who failed to instill in their daughters a desire to marry and bear children weakened the nation's ability to defeat totalitarianism. For the authors, the very survival of American democracy depended on the reproduction of normative gender and sexual identities.

LESBIANISM AND NATIONAL IDENTITY

In this context, lesbianism emerged as a perceived threat to American democracy. For many experts, lesbianism provided a troubling sign of women's growing freedom and autonomy. It showed that they no longer needed men sexually or economically. For example, in *The Grapevine* Stearn contended that the increase in lesbianism represented "only one phase of the continuing drive of women all over to share a place in the sun with the male" (308). Sociologists and psychologists saw the femme as especially threatening. Unlike the butch, she did not appear to emulate men or to reject her femaleness as a mark of her inferiority as a woman. Thus experts could not attribute her perverse sexuality to penis envy. Among the functions of the Cold War construction of the lesbian was to pathologize, and thereby contain, alternative narratives of womanhood that did not culminate in marriage and motherhood. Even women who had made a heterosexual object choice were considered "sick" and latently lesbian if they transgressed the dominant construction of femininity. Strecker and Lathbury, for example, ascribed lesbianism to "undissolved and unfulfilled mother-daughter relationships" (160). According to this logic, girls derived their femininity from a wish to be like their mothers, and they were therefore at risk of developing lesbian identities if their mothers failed to provide them with a compelling role model. Strecker and Lathbury argued that the mother "must seem to be important enough and loved by others so that there is in sight a worthwhile reward for being like her—a woman" (161). As this analysis indicates, the psychoanalytic discourse that circulated in postwar American society tended to desexualize lesbian identities. Women supposedly became lesbians not because they desired other women, but because they had rejected their femaleness in childhood and wanted to be men. Strecker and Lathbury declared lesbianism "biological and psychological treason" (158), a form of mental illness in which women turned against their own natures.

This construction of lesbianism bore a striking resemblance to

Strecker's and Lathbury's analysis of feminism, which they associated with a masculinization of female identity. In an uncharacteristically direct passage, the authors enjoined their female readers, "Do not become a feminist. Children recoil from masculinity in a mother, in dress or attitude. Or daughters may imitate it, which puts their future emotional life in jeopardy" (71). Strecker and Lathbury refused to acknowledge the patriarchal social and economic arrangements that underlay women's demands for equality. Indeed, like Lundberg and Farnham, they assumed that women had already achieved social and economic equality, which rendered feminism outmoded. They interpreted feminism as "the deep wish to compete with men, not because it may be necessary or the circumstances of life demand it, but prompted by the desire to prove the male is inferior to the female" (144). Rather than reflecting a justifiable resistance to women's subordination, feminism expressed "dissatisfaction with being a woman and some degree of hostility toward men" (144). Like the lesbian, the feminist experienced an "unfulfilled" relationship with her mother. As a girl, she developed penis envy and fantasized about becoming a boy. As an adult, she either pursued a career to prove that she could be as successful as any man and thus deserved her mother's love, or she married and, resenting her domestic responsibilities, turned into a "possessive, dominating, and devouring" (152) wife and mother. In other words, feminism represented a "biological rejection" (144) that reflected the girl's pathological identification with her father. Unlike the lesbian, however, the feminist could overcome her masculinity complex. Strecker and Lathbury cited as an example one of their female patients, a "pronounced feminist" (150), who had renounced her masculinity after undergoing psychotherapy: "Her dress, her manner and attitude toward males have become gratifyingly feminine. She is almost a woman" (150).

In associating feminism with lesbianism, Cold War homophobia participated in a protracted ideological struggle in American society over women's demands for social and political equality. Since the 1890s, the homophobic deployment of the category of the lesbian had played a central role in this struggle.[25] Influenced by a sexological understanding of female sexuality, social reformers increasingly warned about the pernicious impact on American society of the alternative institutions created by white middle-class professional women to sustain their independence from patriarchal social and economic arrangements, institutions such as women's colleges, settlement houses, feminist political organizations, and Boston marriages, in which two women shared an intimate domestic relationship.[26] For example, Floyd Dell believed that American society treated lesbian activity as less threatening to the social order than heterosexual experiment, and in *Love in the Machine Age*, a study of the need for sexual reform, published in 1930, he complained that "homosexual 'crushes' are conventionally ignored, particularly in girls' schools."[27] In attacking female homosocial institutions and practices, social reformers echoed the sexologist Havelock Ellis's work on sexual inversion, which emphasized the porous boundary between female homosocial desire and lesbian identity. Ellis identified two types of women who made a lesbian object choice: "congenital inverts," or women whose gender and sexual nonconformity were hereditary and irreversible; and women who had inherited a predisposition or weakness for the sexual advances of other women. For such women lesbianism represented an "artificial" or acquired characteristic.[28] Families could supposedly prevent such women from developing lesbian identities by segregating them from female homosocial institutions, where they might fall prey to the blandishments of a congenital invert. Anticipating Dell's analysis, Ellis argued that such institutions promoted "passionate friendships, of a more or less unconsciously sexual character," and thus were particularly dangerous for women prone to "artificial" homosexual attachments.[29] Moreover, although he tended to take a progressive stance on social issues, Ellis also claimed that the feminist movement had led to a rise in female homosexuality: "Having been taught independence of men and disdain for the old theory which placed women in the moated grange of the home to sigh for a man who comes, a tendency develops for women to carry this independence still further and to find love where they find work."[30]

The flapper's emergence in the 1920s as a model of modern American womanhood reinforced this backlash against what the historian Carroll Smith-Rosenberg has called "the female world of love and ritual."[31] The flapper's identity reflected a new emphasis in American society on consumption, leisure, pleasure, and self-expression. Unlike the New Woman, the flapper tended to associate emancipation with sexual freedom, and she was drawn to the very discourses—sexology and psychoanalysis— that had pathologized the New Woman's desire for equality.[32] These discourses treated sexuality as a distinct domain of personhood and stressed the importance of sexual expression for maintaining psychological well-being. Historians have shown that the companionate model of marriage functioned as a kind of "fantasy bribe" that enticed the flapper into participating in the institutions of heterosexuality.[33] The flapper could in fact satisfy her desire for sexual freedom in marriage. The growing acceptance of contraceptive practices by married women ensured that the flapper would not have to sacrifice her sexual autonomy but could control her fertility even if she married.[34] Moreover, because sexual and emotional intimacy provided the basis of the companionate marriage, she could expect to have a more equal relationship with her husband than an earlier generation of married women had had with theirs. Reinforcing these enticements, the domestic sphere, which provided the cornerstone of the consumer economy of the 1920s, emerged as a site of leisure and pleasure.[35] In this context, the New Woman provided an increasingly undesirable model of womanhood. She came to embody the stereotype of the sexually repressed "old maid." Her critique of patriarchal social and economic arrangements could not compete with the flapper's enfranchisement as a subject of sexual and consumer desire.[36] Indeed, in reforming the institution of marriage so it reflected the modern American woman's needs and desires, social progressives had supposedly rendered that critique outmoded.

Katharine Bement Davis's pioneering survey of the sex lives of 2,200 married and unmarried middle-class, college-educated women, published in 1929, registered this backlash against the New Woman.[37] The survey reflected the influence of Ellis's work on sexual inversion, with Davis likewise assuming a connection between women's romantic friendships and lesbian desire. The section of the survey devoted to women's sexual activity with other women asked, "Have you at any time experienced intense emotional relations with any other girl or woman?"[38] But Davis approached female homosexuality neutrally, as one of many sexual practices in which women might engage, and she described several examples of women who regarded their lesbian relationships as "legitimate" and "healthy" without challenging or contradicting them. Nor did she associate female homosexuality with a desire for social and economic equality. The survey confirmed the impact of the homophobic deployment of the category of the lesbian on a new generation of professional women. Women who pursued careers over marriage and motherhood increasingly risked social and economic ostracism as lesbians. As a result, some of the women who took part in the survey refused to participate in the female homosocial institutions created by the New Woman for fear that in doing so they would render their desire for economic independence suspect. Davis quoted one unmarried professional woman who indirectly acknowledged the impact of the backlash against the New Woman: "The ethics of the homosexual relationships is the most serious problem the business or professional woman has to face today" (263). Another participant in the survey indicated more directly the lesbian panic sometimes experienced by professional women: "In my city some business women are hesitating to take apartments together for fear of the interpretation that may be put upon it" (263–64).

The Cold War construction of the lesbian perpetuated this strategy for containing alternative models of American womanhood. The association between feminism and lesbianism served to discourage women from remaining single and pursuing careers. Indeed, historians have shown that even many women who in the 1950s eventually claimed lesbian identities had difficulty imagining lives that did not include marriage and motherhood.[39] When in *The Grapevine* Stearn titillated readers with stories of wives and mothers who led "secret lives" as lesbians, he failed to examine the pressure of social norms that urged women to marry and bear children. In the 1950s marriage and motherhood emerged as *the* rite of passage into adult womanhood. Women who chose otherwise remained incomplete, not truly female. At the same time, women's educational opportunities expanded significantly in this period, and even white working-class girls increasingly expected to attend college.[40] Moreover, women entered the labor force in greater numbers, had greater access to consumer culture, and experienced greater sexual freedom than their mothers.[41] Simultaneously, however, narrowing gender and sexual norms served to discourage women from capitalizing on these social changes. As Wini Breines has noted, white, middle-class girls in particular did not plan for their futures, even if they went to college, instead waiting until they wed and could receive the guidance of their husbands.[42] The lack of alternative models of womanhood rendered negotiating patriarchal social and economic arrangements especially difficult for lesbians who wanted to avoid marriage and motherhood. As single, career-oriented women, such lesbians did not have access to the institutions that had sustained the New Woman's social and economic independence, but had to create their own, which required financial and other resources, which many did not have.[43] Nor could lesbians enter male-dominated professions without risking exposure as lesbians.[44] Thus they had to choose from a narrow range of less lucrative careers, such as nursing, social work, and teaching, fields traditionally dominated by women, in which their professional aspirations were less likely to arouse their coworkers' suspicions.

Where the discourse of female homosexuality that circulated in the

Cold War era differed from the homophobic deployment of the category of the lesbian earlier in the century was in linking lesbianism directly to questions of national identity. The construction of the lesbian as "un-American," a secretive, duplicitous figure who, like the communist, threatened to subvert the nation, surfaced most fully in the antihomosexual witch hunts conducted by the federal government throughout the 1950s. Although during hearings in 1950 countless medical experts testified that the majority of homosexuals were "well-adjusted" and posed no threat as employees of the government, the Senate issued a report that identified gay and lesbian employees as security risks.[45] Such employees, the report claimed, were emotionally immature, prone to reveal government secrets, and susceptible to blackmail by enemy agents. In 1953 President Dwight Eisenhower issued Executive Order 10450, which barred homosexuals from being employed by the government.[46] The order affirmed the Senate's dubious findings and resulted in a massive government campaign to ferret out homosexual employees. In implementing the order, the civil service encouraged employees to inform on coworkers who aroused their suspicions through, for example, their mode of dress, associates, neighborhood, emotional stability, and even any physical characteristics that seemed "abnormal."[47] When confronted by security officers with questions about their sexuality, many employees simply resigned to avoid facing an investigation that might embarrass them or their families and permanently damage their ability to pursue their careers elsewhere.[48]

This campaign had a particularly devastating impact on female employees.[49] The government provided women access to well-paying jobs with a certain amount of job security, which enabled them to avoid marriage and motherhood if they so desired. Moreover, the neutrality of the civil service insured they could for the most part look forward to advancing in their careers on the basis of merit. The large numbers of women working for the government had long created anxiety among conservatives, who denounced the nation's capital as a "femmocracy," and so-called g-girls, or female employees, provided constant fodder for tabloid journalists.[50] For example, in *Washington Confidential*, a sensationalistic exposé of political and moral corruption in the nation's capital, published in 1951, Jack Lait and Lee Mortimer warned that working for the government perverted women by masculinizing them: "They are a hard, efficient lot, doing men's work, thinking like men and sometimes driven to the place of men—in the proscribed zones of desperate flings at love and sex. Lesbianism is scandalously rampant, frequently an acquired dislocation rather than a pathological aberration."[51] Such a warning attested to the persistence of the sexological understanding of the "artificial" lesbian desire that female homosocial settings supposedly incited in otherwise "normal" women.

To protect their careers, lesbian government workers moderated their behavior to avoid arousing the suspicions of coworkers. They refused to socialize with other lesbians in public, unless men were present, attended social functions with gay male friends as their "dates," and carefully chose their wardrobes and makeup to project a feminine persona.[52] But gender and sexual conformity provided such workers with little or no protection. As a violation of normative femininity, their very desire to succeed in their careers rendered them suspect. Male employees who resented reporting to a female boss or who disliked the evaluation they had received from her could trigger an investigation into her sexuality. The civil service had a "zero tolerance" policy with respect to male and female homosexuality, and even if a female government worker were married, a single lesbian encounter in college provided sufficient grounds for her dismissal.[53] As David K. Johnson has pointed out, the enforcement of this policy worked to solidify the hetero-homosexual binary.[54] According to the rapidly expanding national-security state, a person was either homosexual or heterosexual, regardless of his or her gender presentation.

Despite the emergence of object choice as an overriding principle of social and sexual difference, the older model of lesbianism did not wholly disappear, but continued to bring pressure to bear on the new model.[55] The civil service continued to privilege gender presentation when investigating female employees for lesbianism. For example, in 1958, when two male security officers interviewed Madeline Tress, a Commerce Department economist who was suspected of lesbianism, they noted her "feminine apparel" but also remarked in their report that she was missing two buttons from the front of her dress.[56] For them, the missing buttons—which suggested that she lacked a properly feminine regard for her appearance—confirmed her coworkers' claims that she was "mannish" and suffered from "personality problems."

The older model also continued to shape mass cultural constructions of lesbian identity. For example, in *The Grapevine* Stearn opened a discussion of Hollywood "sex symbols" with the sensationalistic claim: "Some of the most glamorous women in Hollywood—and on Broadway—whose femininity is a household word, are frankly lesbians in their private lives" (98). He then suggested that despite their feminine exteriors, these women secretly wanted to be men. They disguised their aberrant sexuality by marrying men "whose femininity complements their own masculine streak" (100); such men would not seek to subordinate them or control their sexuality. Stearn further challenged the women's authenticity as sex symbols by claiming, "While they look languorous and seductive on screen, in private life they are singularly crisp and businesslike, and can drive a bargain like any man. Thinking like men, but looking like women, they have an advantage that has enabled them to flourish in the jungle that is Hollywood" (98). Stearn thus constructed the women as a kind of intermediate sex, neither male nor female, a construction that recalled the sexological understanding of lesbian identity. Underneath the women's feminine exteriors supposedly lay an inverted gender identity. Thus even as Cold War homophobia validated the new model of sexuality, it continued to incorporate the older model, which associated lesbianism with masculinity. The Cold War discourse of female homosexuality reduced the femme's femininity to a kind of disguise that allowed her to participate in American society while escaping detection. In this way, the discourse neutralized the threat posed by the femme as a woman who made a lesbian object choice but did not appear to reject her femaleness. Despite her gender presentation, the femme supposedly emulated men as much as the butch did.

LESBIANISM AND HOLLYWOOD CINEMA

Cold War Femme focuses on the impact of the Cold War construction of the lesbian on the representation of female sexuality in Hollywood cinema. Hollywood films contributed to the homophobic deployment of the category of the lesbian by constructing narratives of female sexuality that pathologized women's desire for freedom and independence, and thereby reinforced the difficulty that women had imagining alternative modes of happiness and fulfillment. Even movies such as *Pillow Talk* (Michael Gordon, 1959) and *Marnie* (Alfred Hitchcock, 1964), which interrogated the construction of female subjectivity in relation to patriarchal social and economic arrangements, reinstalled marriage and motherhood as the "happy ending" of female sexual development. Such movies were instrumental in decreasing the circulation of alternative constructions of womanhood in postwar American society. At the same time, however, some movies, such as Nicholas Ray's *Johnny Guitar* (1953) and

William Wyler's *The Children's Hour* (1962), contested the Cold War construction of the lesbian, underscoring the devastating social and economic consequences the accusation of lesbianism could have in the 1950s and 1960s. But even as they challenged the narrow model of female identity, such films tended to position viewers as subjects of Cold War sexual epistemology. Even movies made after the 1961 revision of the Production Code, which allowed filmmakers to treat lesbianism with "care, discretion, and restraint," did not always clarify the heroine's desire—an ambiguity that helped reinforce the Cold War fear that the lesbian could escape detection.[57] In examining these tensions and contradictions in its treatment of lesbian desire, I elucidate Hollywood cinema's complicated role in the consolidation of the new system of sexual classification. For even movies that validated the dominant model of womanhood tended to open up the possibility of alternative constructions of female desire.

In part 1, "Screening the Femme," I seek to clarify Hollywood cinema's relation to the reorganization of sexuality by examining in each chapter a different aspect of the Cold War construction of the lesbian. In chapter 1 I investigate Hollywood's strategies for representing the femme through analysis of Joseph Mankiewicz's Academy Award–winning movie, *All about Eve* (1950), in which Ann Baxter plays Eve Harrington, a duplicitous actress who undermines the career of her benefactor, the flamboyant Broadway star Margo Channing (Bette Davis), after gaining her trust. Like the Hollywood sex symbols according to Stearn, Eve uses her femininity to conceal a ruthless ambition, which the film codes as masculine. In other words, *All about Eve* marks Eve as a lesbian by drawing on the older model of sexuality, which associated lesbianism with masculinity. Eve's femininity emerges as a performance that enables her to gain access to Margo's world, which she then proceeds to disrupt by turning the Broadway star's friends against her. In this respect, Mankiewicz's film validated the lesbian panic of the Cold War era. To situate the film in relation to that panic, I trace the shifting construction of the feminine woman who made a lesbian object choice in the discourse of sexology. In so doing I clarify the role of Cold War homophobia in redefining the femme.

In chapter 2 I examine the unintelligibility of the category of the lesbian by discussing Wyler's 1962 screen adaptation of Lillian Hellman's play, *The Children's Hour*, in which Audrey Hepburn and Shirley MacLaine play Karen Wright and Martha Dobie, two teachers falsely accused of lesbianism by one of their students. In emphasizing the lesbian's ability to pass as "normal," Cold War homophobia attributed to her identity an epistemological uncertainty. If the lesbian could pass, how could Americans correctly identify her? Even as Wyler's movie provided a powerful critique of Cold War lesbian panic, it reproduced the conundrum. Wyler had collaborated with Hellman on an earlier adaptation, in 1936—the woman's picture *These Three*—and he remained frustrated at having been forced to censor the play's lesbian theme. Following the 1961 revision of the Production Code, he decided to make a more faithful version, but he worried that Hellman's treatment of lesbianism would no longer resonate with audiences, and he attempted to update it by rendering Karen's feelings for Martha sexually ambiguous. Ironically, in so doing he undercut the movie's critique of the homophobic deployment of the category of the lesbian. The movie ends without clarifying Karen's sexuality, which remains a puzzle the audience must solve. To elucidate the movie's contradictory relationship to the Cold War construction of the lesbian, I examine the two earlier versions of *The Children's Hour*: the play, which originally opened on Broadway in 1934; and *These Three*, which heterosexualized the play's plot. I show that both versions inadvertently reinforced the backlash against female homosocial institutions and practices in the 1930s.

In chapter 3 I explore the persistence of the sexological construction of lesbian identity by analyzing Hitchcock's representation of perverse female desire in *Marnie*, in which Tippi Hedren plays a thief who compulsively robs her employers after she has gained their trust. The movie's interrogation of Marnie's aberrant sexuality intersects with the Cold War construction of the lesbian, with Marnie using her femininity to disguise her problematic relation to the law. But the movie also renders Marnie's lesbianism "artificial" by attributing it to a traumatic childhood experience. Thus her husband, Mark (Sean Connery), can supposedly reclaim her for the institutions of heterosexuality by reorienting her desire. At the same time, however, the movie opens up the possibility of an alternative construction of the heroine's desire by casting doubt on her realignment with the law in the final scene. To situate this treatment of female homosexuality in relation to the Cold War construction of the lesbian, I also look at an earlier film made by Hitchcock, *Rebecca* (1940), which like *Marnie* interrogates the construction of female subjectivity in relation to patriarchal social and economic arrangements. After a whirlwind romance and marriage, the movie's nameless heroine, played by Joan Fontaine, returns with her husband, Maxim de Winter (Laurence Olivier), to his family's estate, which seems haunted by his beautiful and sexually alluring former wife, Rebecca, who supposedly drowned at sea. There the heroine encounters a terrifying version of the female world of love and ritual that reflects a homophobic construction of women's romantic friendships consistent with the backlash, in the 1930s, against female homosociality.

In part 2, "Female Stardom and Cold War Culture," I explore how the circulation of two conflicting models of lesbian desire affected the production of female stars in the Cold War era. In chapter 4 I focus on the remaking of Joan Crawford's screen image such that it came to affirm postwar gender and sexual norms, a process that began with her Academy Award–winning performance in *Mildred Pierce* (Michael Curtiz, 1945), in which she portrays an ambitious, hardworking mother who opens a successful chain of restaurants. From the moment she emerged as a star, in the early 1930s, Crawford had been marketed as a fiercely ambitious actress, a kind of female Horatio Alger who had picked herself up by the bootstraps, and her role as Mildred Pierce exploited this aspect of her screen image. But it also reflected a shift in the construction of normative femininity. Whereas Crawford's ambition had been promoted by MGM as an asset that appealed to Depression-era female audiences, it became problematic in the 1940s and 1950s, and underlay a masculinization of her image, which was reflected in her role as an irresponsible mother in *Mildred Pierce*. Crawford's public image thus existed in a complicated relationship to Cold War gender and sexual norms. By creating a camp effect, Crawford's performance style at once challenged and underwrote the heteronormative construction of womanhood. I develop this argument by examining *Johnny Guitar* (1953), Nicholas Ray's idiosyncratic western, in which Crawford plays Vienna, a gunslinging, cross-dressing saloon keeper persecuted for her gender and sexual nonconformity. By exploiting the campiness of Crawford's persona, the movie reinforced its critique of the incoherence of the Cold War construction of the lesbian.

Bette Davis's screen image underwent a similar transformation in the 1950s. At the height of her stardom, the late 1930s and 1940s, Davis starred in a cycle of enormously popular women's pictures that dislodged marriage and motherhood as the "happy ending" of female sexual development and in so doing provided female audiences with an alternative model of womanhood. In these films, which included *The Old Maid* (Edmund Goulding, 1939), *The Great Lie* (Edmund Goulding, 1941), *Now, Voyager* (Irving Rapper, 1942), and *Old Acquaintance* (Vincent Sherman, 1943), Davis's character more often ended up in an intimate domestic arrangement with a woman than with a man. The narrowing of gender and sexual norms in the Cold War era rendered this aspect of Davis's screen image problematic, and she made a cycle of movies about fading female stars, including *All about Eve*, *The Star* (Stuart Heisler, 1952), and *Whatever Happened to Baby Jane* (Robert Aldrich, 1964), that attempted to remake her screen image such that it validated Cold War gender and sexual norms. These movies punished her by representing her sexually ambiguous performance of femininity as pathological and grotesque, thereby attempting to demonstrate that her appeal as a star had become outmoded. In chapter 5 I elaborate this analysis by discussing *Whatever Happened to Baby Jane*, a horror movie that provided a gothic version of the type of woman's film that had originally established Davis as one of Hollywood's most successful female stars.

Finally, in chapter 6 I turn to the career of Doris Day, one of the most popular female stars of the 1950s and 1960s, showing that Day's wholesome screen image enabled her to appropriate masculinity without undermining her appearance of gender and sexual conformity. Although, starting with *Pillow Talk*, Day increasingly played independent, career-oriented women, her persona, unlike those of Davis and Crawford, resisted construction as lesbian. I begin by examining her performance of masculinity in the musical *Calamity Jane* (David Butler, 1953), in which she plays the title character, a cross-dressing gunfighter, a comic version of Crawford's role in *Johnny Guitar*, released the same year. The role solidified Day's masculinity, which continued to shape her image even after her transformation into a sex symbol in the 1960s. I go on to explore Day's role in *Pillow Talk*, a romantic comedy in which she plays Jan Morrow, a self-assured interior designer who shares a party line with a playboy bachelor, Brad Allen, played by Rock Hudson. In glamorizing her image, the movie marked a departure for Day, who usually played the "girl next door," and she went on to star, in the 1960s, in a series of enormously popular romantic comedies that consolidated her new image. Despite this shift in her image, however, Day's masculinity continued to surface in the type of character she played: a woman who pursues a career and insists on maintaining her sexual autonomy. As a result, her image had a complex relationship to the dominant construction of female sexuality in the Cold War era, at once underwriting and contesting it. Her masculinity constantly threatened to destabilize her image by rendering it sexually ambiguous.

PART I

SCREENING THE FEMME

CHAPTER ONE

REPRESENTING THE FEMME

All about Eve

In the final scene of the Academy Award–winning film *All about Eve* (Joseph L. Mankiewicz, 1950), Eve Harrington (Anne Baxter), the film's manipulative and duplicitous villain, is startled to find a female intruder (Barbara Bates) asleep in an armchair in her living room when she returns home from the Sarah Siddons Award ceremony where she has won an award for her "distinguished achievement in the theater," despite the fact that she has appeared in only one play. Eve picks up the phone to call the police, but puts it down when the intruder introduces herself as Phoebe, the president of the Eve Harrington Fan Club at Erasmus Hall, an all-girls high school in Brooklyn. Phoebe reassures Eve that she sneaked in, while the maid was turning Eve's bed down, "just to look around" and that she is preparing a report on the actress—"how you live, what kind of clothes you wear, what kind of perfume and books, things like that." No longer frightened, Eve sits down on a sofa and languidly lights a cigarette. Because it is the only time in the film that she is shown smoking, her action seems intended to signal a shift in her character. At first she responds impatiently to Phoebe's eager questions about her plans for a career in Hollywood, but when the girl begins to pick up after her, Eve's attitude changes markedly. In a soft, caressing voice, she asks how Phoebe got to Manhattan from Brooklyn. As Phoebe replies that it took her only a little more than an hour on the subway, the film dissolves to a close-up of Eve, who, posed on the sofa seductively, says with a hint of invitation in her voice, "It's after one now. You won't get home till all hours." Returning Eve's gaze, Phoebe replies excitedly, "I don't care if I never get home!"

Starting with Vito Russo in his classic study *The Celluloid Closet*, scholars of images of gays and lesbians in classical Hollywood cinema have used this scene to argue that Eve is coded as a lesbian.[1] Because the Production Code, which regulated the content of Hollywood movies from 1930 to 1968 with the consensus of the major studios, stated that "sex perversion or any inference to it is forbidden," Eve's desire for other women can never be expressed overtly, but can only be hinted at in scenes like this one.[2] For many scholars, Eve is one in a long line of predatory celluloid lesbians in Code-era movies, beginning with Mrs. Danvers (Judith Anderson), the creepy housekeeper who terrorizes the nameless heroine in the woman's picture *Rebecca* (Alfred Hitchcock, 1940), and ending with Jo (Barbara Stanwyck), the jealous and possessive madam of a New Orleans brothel who sexually preys on her girls in Edward Dmytryk's steamy melodrama *Walk on the Wild Side* (1962).[3] Eve does bear some resemblance to these other lesbian villains. A ruthlessly ambitious actress, she manipulates her way into the rarified world of the flamboyant Broadway star Margo Channing (Bette Davis) by passing herself off as one of the star's most devoted fans. She then proceeds to undermine Margo both personally and professionally, going so far as to try to steal her lover and even her identity. Mankiewicz reinforced the movie's lesbian subtext by basing Margo loosely on the Broadway actress Tallulah Bankhead, who was widely rumored to be lesbian and who was involved in a notorious professional rivalry with Davis.[4]

Yet this is only part of the story. Eve's villainy has a political resonance that distinguishes her from the other Code-era lesbian characters to whom she is most often compared. Unlike Mrs. Danvers and Jo, who embody the stereotype of the mannish lesbian, Eve has a feminine gender presentation, which suggests that her character was at least partly inspired by the Cold War construction of the lesbian. Her performance of femininity renders her "unnatural" sexuality invisible, and this is what makes her so threatening as a lesbian. Cold War lesbian panic centered on the feminine woman who made a lesbian object choice. Because her desire for other women could not be attributed to an inverted gender identity, the femme troubled the binary construction of gender and sexual identities. The Cold War discourse of female homosexuality promoted lesbian panic by highlighting the femme's resemblance to the "normal" woman, which supposedly allowed her to spread lesbianism throughout American society while escaping detection. With her ability to pass, the femme could convert impressionable and emotionally vulnerable women to lesbianism more easily than the butch could. She could even marry and continue to participate in what Jess Stearn called the "secret world" of the lesbian without arousing suspicion. The femme was further constructed as un-American; like the communist, she operated in secret, slowly undermining American society from within.

The differences between Eve and other lesbian villains in Hollywood cinema of the 1940s and 1950s suggest that, despite its status as a camp classic, *All about Eve* needs to be understood as a Cold War movie. Since Michael Paul Rogin identified this category of Hollywood film, in 1987, cultural studies scholars have expanded it to include movies that do not deal directly with the Cold War but nevertheless underwrite or legitimate Cold War ideologies, especially those regulating the construction of gender and sexual identities.[5] Eve's queerness, which consists of a combination of femininity and lesbianism that unsettles homophobic stereotypes, indirectly ratified the model of womanhood that became dominant in the Cold War era. Mankiewicz, who wrote as well as directed *All about Eve*, claimed that he conceived of Eve as a lesbian and coached Baxter to play her as such.[6]

Situating the movie's treatment of Eve in relation to the Cold War construction of the lesbian complicates scholarly understanding of Cold War culture. Scholars have tended to approach the 1950s as a particularly homophobic period in American history, when male and female homosexuals faced persecution by the state and functioned, along with communists and fellow travelers, as the "enemy within" in the Cold War discourse of American national identity.[7] As a result, the decade has emerged as the Dark Ages of the lesbian and gay past, a period in which lesbian and gay life is thought to have been pathologically secretive and repressed. The scholarship often stresses that during the antihomosexual witch hunts of the 1950s, more lesbians and gays were expelled from the federal government than suspected communists.[8] Although this view of the 1950s is not unfounded, it glosses over the inconsistencies and contradictions in Cold War gender and sexual ideologies, which when taken more fully into account help elucidate a neglected aspect of Cold War culture, what we might call its queerness. The Cold War construction of the lesbian, in privileging the femme over the butch, inadvertently highlighted the mobility of sex, gender, and sexuality in relation to each other. For if the femme could pass as a "normal" woman, then there was no necessary or causal relationship between femininity and heterosexuality. Moreover, femininity emerged as a role that even the lesbian could master through imitation and repetition. In other words, the Cold War discourse of female homosexuality unintentionally foregrounded the performative aspects of femininity, and in the process demonstrated the lack of congruity between gender identity, sexual practice, and object choice. Underlying *All about Eve*'s representation of the title character is an attempt to resolve this contradiction in the Cold War construction of the lesbian, an attempt that ultimately fails because the movie cannot restabilize the normative alignment of sex, gender, and sexuality that its homophobic treatment of the lesbian throws into crisis.

The film's treatment of Eve's sexuality also provides clues as to how the older system of sexual classification shaped the Cold War construction of the lesbian. To mark Eve as a lesbian, Mankiewicz's movie draws on the visual codes developed by Hollywood to circumvent the prohibition of content involving "sex perversion." These codes reinstalled the association of lesbian desire with an inverted gender identity, thereby suggesting that Eve's performance of femininity disguised an identification with masculinity that surfaces in her ambition and focus on her career. Thus *All about Eve*'s strategy of representing Eve's deviant sexuality indirectly ratified the new system of sexual classification, which privileged object choice over gender identity. One of the effects of its treatment of Eve's performance of femininity was to stabilize the femme's relation to lesbian identity. Although it did not register in her gender presentation, Eve's identification with masculinity aligned her aberrant desire with the Cold War discourse of female homosexuality, which attributed lesbian identity to a pathological rejection of femininity. Eve's identification with masculinity deprives her of the capacity to overcome her lesbianism by reorienting her desire toward men. The movie thus indirectly asserted the femme's difference from the straight woman, showing that the feminine woman who made a lesbian object choice was just as deviant as the masculine woman who did so. At the same time, however, this construction of Eve's identity repressed the femme's difference from the butch. Eve's identification with masculinity suggested that, like the butch, the femme wanted to be a man, even if that desire did not express itself in her gender presentation.

DECOUPLING THE BUTCH AND THE FEMME

In 1950, at about the same time that Mankiewicz began to draft the script for *All about Eve*, the Senate Appropriations Committee held widely publicized hearings on the government employment of homosexuals and "other sex perverts." Roy Blick, the chief officer of the District of Columbia vice squad, created panic when he testified that thousands of federal employees had been arrested on morals charges, many of them across from the White House in Lafayette Square, a notorious gay male cruising venue.[9] Following the hearings, the committee issued a virulently homophobic report asserting that male and female homosexual employees of government agencies were vulnerable to blackmail by foreign espionage agents and thus constituted a threat to national security. The report also claimed that unless such employees already had a police record, and female homosexuals almost never did have one, it would be virtually impossible to ferret them out.[10] Citing medical findings that challenged the association of homosexuality with gender inversion, the report declared, "All male homosexuals do not have feminine mannerisms, nor do all female homosexuals display masculine characteristics in their dress or actions."[11] It elaborated: "Many male homosexuals are very masculine in their physical appearance and general demeanor, and many female homosexuals have every appearance of femininity in their outward behavior."[12] In making these claims, the report indirectly linked homosexuals to the communists and fellow travelers also under investigation by Congress. If Americans could no longer identify male and female homosexuals by their gender identities, then like communists and fellow travelers they could infiltrate government agencies and subvert them from within by converting their coworkers. The report claimed ominously, "One homosexual can pollute a government office."[13]

The fear that male and female homosexuals could participate in American society without arousing suspicion can be traced in part to the Kinsey reports on male and female sexuality, which despite their dry scientific style became instant bestsellers when they were published in 1948 and 1953, respectively.[14] Alfred C. Kinsey, who himself had experimented with homosexuality, hoped that in showing how common homosexual activity was in American society, the reports would persuade medical professionals and criminologists that gays and lesbians deserved sympathy and tolerance, instead of persecution and punishment. Fifty percent of the men Kinsey and his assistants interviewed admitted to being aroused by other men, 37 percent said that they had had at least one homosexual experience since adolescence, and 4 percent claimed that they were attracted exclusively to other men.[15] Few of these men fit the stereotype of the fairy, and Kinsey categorically stated that "inversion and homosexuality are two distinct and not always correlated types of behavior."[16] Moreover, undoubtedly alarming many readers, he also asserted that "persons with homosexual histories are to be found in every age group in every social level, in every conceivable occupation in cities and on farms, and in the most remote areas of the country"—in short, from sea to shining sea.[17] Although Kinsey's report on female sexuality, which was published three years after the release of *All about Eve*, could not have influenced the film's reception, it revealed extensive homosexual activity among women, though not as extensive as among men. Twenty-eight percent of the women interviewed admitted that they responded erotically to other women, 13 percent that they had experienced orgasm with another woman, and fewer than 2 percent that they were attracted exclusively to other women.[18] Medical experts contested the report on male sexuality because it threatened to normalize homosexual activity among men.[19] But for the most part they accepted the report on female sexuality because it seemed to confirm their belief that women's growing social and economic equality had led to a rise in lesbianism in American society.[20]

In underwriting the new system of sexual classification elaborated in the Kinsey reports, the Cold War construction of the lesbian reversed the positions that the butch and the femme had traditionally occupied in homophobic discourse. For this reason, it marked a significant shift in the homophobic deployment of the category of the lesbian in American society. Historically the feminine woman who made a lesbian object choice had gone virtually unnoticed by medical experts. Her aberrant desire became visible only in the presence of the masculine woman who made a lesbian object choice. When sexologists began to name and classify sexual perversions in the late nineteenth century, they subjected the masculine lesbian to more intense scrutiny than the feminine woman who aroused her desire.[21] Although it is important to avoid subsuming the history of the female invert into that of the butch, there are historical continuities between the two that justify seeing the female invert as the butch's historical antecedent.[22] Because Victorian gender ideologies associated femaleness with a biologically determined sexual passivity and receptiveness, a woman had to assume a masculine gender identity to exercise sexual agency.[23] This logic lay behind the sexological claim that a man's "soul" resided in the body of the masculine woman who desired other women. By heterosexualizing her desire, this model naturalized the normative alignment of sex, gender, and sexuality. But at the same time, the female invert threatened patriarchal privilege by showing that men could not claim a monopoly on masculinity. Because it did not line up with her anatomical sex in the socially prescribed way, her gender identity indicated that the relation between maleness and masculinity was not necessarily causal. This threat underlay sexology's tendency to focus on the female invert at the expense of the feminine woman who responded to her sexual advances.[24] In explaining the female invert's perverse desire in terms of her gender identity, sexologists sought to neutralize this threat.

But even as it helped to consolidate patriarchal social arrangements, this model of perverse female desire produced the feminine woman who made a lesbian object choice as a conundrum that sexologists could not solve. Since her gender identity was in alignment with her anatomical sex, they could not account for her desire for other women. In accordance with their biological determinism, they conceived of the feminine lesbian as the passive recipient of the masculine lesbian's sexual advances and in so doing deprived her of sexual agency.[25] Havelock Ellis claimed that the feminine woman's desire for other women was "artificial" and could be prevented from developing into a degenerative condition by segregating her from female homosocial environments, where she might encounter female inverts. He also argued that the "normal" woman who entered into a relationship with a female invert belonged to "the pick of the women whom the average man would pass by."[26] In other words, the feminine woman who made a lesbian object choice could not even get an average man, which supposedly reduced her to submitting to the female invert's advances. Thus sexologists did not consider these women, commonly known as femmes, truly lesbian. They believed that such women would willingly forsake their deviant relationships to be with a heterosexual man. The feminine lesbian did not begin to attract the same homophobic scrutiny as the masculine lesbian until the early twentieth century when object choice began to displace gender identity as the organizing principle of sexuality.[27] This process occurred unevenly and over several decades. Indeed, the Cold War construction of the lesbian played a crucial role in this process by identifying the femme as a threat to American society. The Cold War discourse of female homosexuality minimized the significance that the older system of sexual classification attached to the gender differences among women who made a lesbian object choice. It thereby helped to consolidate the hetero-homosexual binary, which depended on a decline in the importance of gender identities and roles for classifying sexual acts and actors.

This construction of the femme's identity was not confined to sexology and other forms of homophobic discourse; it even permeated butch-femme subcultures of the 1940s and 1950s. Both butches and femmes tended to view the butch as the true lesbian and to believe that the femme's participation in the lesbian subculture was dictated more by circumstance than by a sense of a fundamental difference from "straight" women. Indeed, many butches thought that femmes could not be counted on to defend the subculture when local politicians pressured the police to "clean up" the bars and other places where they socialized, because they would supposedly retreat to "normal" relationships to avoid the stigma of having a butch as a lover. As Elizabeth Lapovsky Kennedy and Madeline D. Davis have shown, this subcultural view of the femme did not begin to change until the late 1950s, when sexual attraction to women began to displace masculinity as the basis of lesbian identity.[28] The Cold War discourse of female homosexuality solidified the femme's identity as a lesbian by privileging her sexual desire over her gender identity. As Stearn supposedly discovered while researching *The Grapevine*, because she could disguise her sexual nonconformity, the femme could infiltrate the institutions of heterosexuality and destabilize them by continuing to participate in the lesbian subculture.

ALL ABOUT THE COLD WAR FEMME

All about Eve's representation of perverse female desire simultaneously reflected and contributed to this new understanding of the feminine woman who made a lesbian object choice. In the opening shots of the flashback that forms the majority of the film, Eve seems more butch than femme. The flashback begins with the camera tracking Karen Richards (Celeste Holm) as she gets out of a taxi and walks down a dark alley toward the back entrance of the theater where Margo Channing has been appearing in the lead role of a play written by Karen's husband, Lloyd. When a voice behind her calls out, "Mrs. Richards," Karen stops and turns toward the camera, which cuts to a close-up of her peering off-screen. The film then dissolves to a long shot of Eve Harrington, who emerges from a doorway dressed in a soiled men's trench coat and hat. The lighting and composition of this shot throw Eve's masculine appearance into relief: brightly lit, she faces the camera, framed by the doorway, which is in shadows. The contrast between the baggy coat and the sexy, low-cut evening gown that showed off her figure at the awards ceremony in the preceding scene could not be more striking. Even her voice marks her as a butch. In contrast to the soft-spoken, almost girlish woman she appears to be in later scenes, Eve here calls out to Karen in a deep, husky voice, one she does not use again until the final scene, where she seduces the youthful Phoebe. This butchness clashes with her resemblance elsewhere in the movie to the lesbian who supposedly threatened American society because her normative gender presentation rendered her sexual nonconformity invisible. This clash occurs because the movie can mark Eve as a lesbian only by drawing on the visual codes developed by Hollywood to circumvent the censorship of its treatment of "sex perversion."[29] But the masculinization of Eve's appearance in this scene serves to identify her femininity elsewhere in the film as a performance, and it is therefore crucial to the film's ideological project. Eve's masculinity works to contain the threat she poses as a feminine woman who makes a lesbian object choice by suggesting that her sexual deviance reflects a rejection of femininity that does not register in her gender presentation, except in this scene.

Eve quickly dispels the impression created by her masculine appearance once she enters Margo's dressing room and adopts the stereotypical feminine demeanor that characterizes her in most of the movie. Bordering on a parody of femininity, Eve's manner reinforces the impression that she is performing a role. She apologizes for intruding, as though she did not feel worthy of being in Margo's presence, and when Karen encourages her to talk about herself, she hesitates as if reluctant to make herself the center of attention. Karen's desire to hear her story provides Eve with an opportunity to demonstrate her skill as an actress, and she cannot pass it up. She concocts a clichéd story of tragic heterosexual romance that seems intended to disguise her lesbianism. As sentimental theme music swells on the soundtrack, she claims that she married a young man in the air force shortly before he was shipped off to the South Pacific and that she took a job in a brewery to support herself while he was gone. On the day she was supposed to meet him in San Francisco, where he was to be on leave, she got a telegram informing her that he had been killed in battle, and so ended her dreams of domestic bliss. Eve makes up this story to mask her ambition to become an actress. She claims to have turned to acting to escape from her drab life as a widow and secretary. But in a later scene in which several of the characters discuss the sacrifices they have made for a life in the theater, she remarks, "I've listened backstage to people applaud. It's like waves of love coming over the footlights and wrapping you up." With this comment, she reveals her "monstrous" desire to be the center of attention, to be an object of adulation like Margo, which in this scene she nevertheless disavows.

The way in which the dressing-room scene is shot heightens the sense that Eve's femininity lacks authenticity, that it is an act designed to deceive Margo and the others, who sit on one side of the dressing room while Eve sits on the other, as though facing an audience. Close-ups of Eve as she tells her hackneyed story are crosscut with close-ups of Margo and the others, who seem spellbound by her performance. Birdie Coonan (Thelma Ritter), Margo's wisecracking assistant, is the only one in the "audience" who is not taken in by the performance, even though she appreciates its power. As Margo wipes tears from her eyes and blows her nose, Birdie comments irreverently on the story's conventionality: "What a story! Everything but the bloodhounds snapping at her rear end." Still, Eve's consummate skill in playing the part of aggrieved war widow enables her to gain entry into Margo's world, for, unlike Birdie, Margo is so moved by Eve's story that she takes Eve home with her and hires her as an assistant.

The film's treatment of Eve's relationship with Margo indirectly ratifies the Cold War construction of the lesbian. Eve threatens to destabilize the institutions of heterosexuality by lesbianizing Margo's domestic arrangements. This threat first manifests itself when she accompanies Margo to the airport to see off Bill Sampson (Gary Merrill), Margo's lover as well as her director, who is going to Hollywood to make his first movie. In this scene, Margo resembles the "normal" woman who supposedly lacks the capacity to resist the masculine lesbian's sexual advances. This scene is as close as the film can come, without violating the Production Code, to implying that Eve's and Margo's relationship transgresses the boundary between homosocial desire and lesbian identity. As Bill and Margo kiss goodbye on the runway, Eve stands behind them with her eyes averted, as though the sight of them kissing made her jealous, or at least uncomfortable. When Bill turns away and begins to walk toward the plane, the camera cuts to a medium shot of Eve approaching Margo from behind with a tender look on her face. She is about to place her hands on Margo's shoulders when Bill turns and shouts from the runway, "Hey, Junior, keep your eye on her, don't let her get lonely, she's a loose lamb in a jungle." The film then dissolves to another medium shot of Eve, who in response to Bill's words looks longingly at Margo. This look makes her reply—"I will"—sound more ominous than reassuring. The final sequence of shots, which shows Eve and Margo walking down the

BUTCH-FEMME CODING IN *ALL ABOUT EVE.*

airport corridor arm-in-arm, looking like a butch-femme couple, under-scores the differences in the two women's gender styles. Eve's masculine-looking trench coat and hat provide a striking contrast with Margo's ele-gantly tailored suit and fur coat. Margo's voice-over as the scene fades out reinforces these visual codes, further indicating that, with Bill gone, the two women now form a couple: "That same night we sent for Eve's things, her few pitiful possessions. She moved into the little guest room on the top floor. The next three weeks were out of a fairy tale, and I was Cinderella in the last act. . . . The honeymoon was on." In positioning Eve as Prince Charming, Margo's voice-over reinforces Eve's association with masculinity.

Margo's nonnormative domestic arrangements indicate her problem-atic relationship to the institutions of heterosexuality even before Eve moves in. She shares her household with Birdie, a former vaudevillian whose hard-boiled manner codes her as a working-class butch. From the beginning, Birdie cannot understand how Margo can be taken in so easily by Eve. When in the opening shots of the flashback Karen invites Eve backstage to introduce her to the star, Margo seems immediately taken with her. Birdie, however, looks Eve up and down skeptically, as if she already sees through her. When the usually rude and sarcastic Margo turns polite and charming, Birdie exclaims, "Oh, brother!" and storms out of the dressing room, vowing not to come back "till you get normal," as though Margo's interest in Eve were unnatural. In this scene, Eve who looks butch but acts femme transgresses the gender norms that govern the lesbian subculture, as does Margo's attraction to her.

Ritter's screen image contributed to Birdie's coded identity as a butch.[30] Like Eve Arden, Ritter perfected the role of tough-talking, wise-cracking sidekick in several Hollywood movies of the 1940s and 1950s in which she played secondary characters whose sexuality was ambiguous or suppressed by the plots. For some viewers, the convergence of Ritter's life on- and offscreen may have reinforced the coding of her identity in *All about Eve*. Though a wife and a mother, Ritter participated in the butch-femme subculture that flourished on Fire Island, New York, during those years, before the resort's transformation into a gay male mecca.[31] Birdie vanishes from the film following the famous scene in which Margo warns her party guests, "Fasten your seat belts, it's going to be a bumpy night." By that point in the film, Margo has begun to realize that Eve has deceived her. In other words, Eve eventually displaces Birdie as the lesbian who threatens to destabilize the institutions of heterosexuality. Because Birdie has served her purpose of rendering Margo's identity sexually ambiguous, the movie can dispense with her and replace her with Eve.

In *All about Eve*, the fear that the lesbian might spread her deviant sexuality throughout American society surfaces in an emphasis on the homoerotic relations of looking that are central to female spectatorship.[32] The Cold War construction of the lesbian seems to have made Mankiewicz particularly anxious about this aspect of Hollywood cinema, which emerges as one of the movie's central themes. The film treats identification with the female star as the first step on the female spectator's path to lesbianism. Eve's desire to be Margo is inextricably bound up with her desire to have her. One of the star's most devoted fans, she has traveled from city to city so as not to miss any of her idol's performances, or so she claims. As Margo's personal assistant, Eve has an opportunity to study the star more closely. Before Birdie vanishes from the movie, she warns Margo that Eve "thinks only about you, like she's studying you, like you was a book, or a play, or a set of blueprints, how you walk, talk, eat, sleep." The alternation in Eve's desire between wanting to be and wanting to have Margo brings her and Margo's honeymoon to an abrupt end. Margo begins to worry that Eve intends to rob her of her identity. In this way, the movie associates female spectatorship with a perverse form of reproduction.

The complex play of identification and desire underlying Eve's obsession with Margo is captured in the scene in which Margo discovers Eve backstage holding up Margo's costume in front of a mirror and bowing repeatedly. The scene opens with Eve in the wings, watching the end of Margo's performance. Close-ups of Eve gazing at the star are crosscut with long shots of Margo bowing to an audience that remains offscreen. The shot–reverse shot sequence positions Eve as a stand-in for the unseen audience, but because she is literally acting the part of the adoring fan, the distinction between female star and female spectator collapses. As Margo exits backstage, she passes by Eve and teases her for crying at the performance, which she has seen countless times: "Not again!" In the following scene Margo's and Eve's positions relative to each other have reversed. Star becomes spectator, and spectator star. Margo emerges from the dressing room in search of Eve, who has volunteered to return the costume to wardrobe, and finds her backstage with it. Standing in roughly the same place Eve stood in the earlier scene, Margo watches as Eve pretends to be her and bows to an imaginary audience represented by her reflection in the mirror. In her fantasy, Eve is simultaneously star and spectator. This scenario reproduces a homophobic construction of lesbian identity by suggesting that Eve's desire reflects a narcissistic fixation with her own image. Although Margo has already become disenchanted with Eve, she smiles indulgently while watching her, as if flattered by the impersonation, which appeals to her own narcissism.

With this reversal of their relationship, it becomes unclear whether Eve has seduced Margo or Margo has seduced Eve. On the one hand, Eve has beguiled Margo with her flattering adulation, so much so that the star does not realize how ambitious her personal assistant is until she has already been betrayed. On the other hand, Margo's magnetic appeal as a star has implanted in Eve a perverse desire to be her. Margo encourages Eve's obsession, until she begins to feel threatened by it. Aware that Mankiewicz had based Margo's character on Tallulah Bankhead, many reviewers assumed that Davis's performance was an impersonation of the flamboyant Broadway actress.[33] Margo's resemblance to Bankhead further queers her character and reinforces the lesbian subtext of her relationship with Eve. Despite her relationship with Bill, Margo recalls an actress known for her gender and sexual nonconformity. Moreover, she enters into intimate domestic relationships with both butches and femmes. As a result, her sexuality cannot be understood in terms of any of the historically available categories.

Margo's physical appearance in this scene contrasts markedly with her appearance in the preceding one, in which we have seen her onstage and in costume. Dressed in an old bathrobe and smeared with cold cream — in short, stripped of all of the accoutrements of femininity that underlie her glamour as a star — she looks dowdy and middle-aged, the antithesis of Margo Channing the Broadway star Eve emulates. Here the movie calls attention to the performative aspects of Margo's femininity, which, like one of her roles, requires a sophisticated wardrobe, makeup, and a glamorous hairstyle, as well as an enormous amount of concealed labor, both her own and Birdie's. In this respect, her femininity is not much different from Eve's. After all, she shares Eve's penchant for performing offstage as well as on, and, like Eve, she tends to perform her femininity to excess. Yet there remain enormous differences between the types of femininity the two perform. Whereas Eve's is the conventional femininity that Cold War nationalism promoted as essential to the nation's security, Margo's is the flamboyant femininity of the diva, which is by definition excessive and theatrical. But neither Margo's nor Eve's style of femininity appears to be authentic or natural. Rather, the movie encourages us to see femininity as an act or role that Margo and Eve perform like any other. Karen calls attention to the performative aspects of Margo's gender presentation in the party scene. When Margo, in a particularly malevolent moment, derides Karen as a "happy little housewife," Karen replies indignantly, "Stop being a star and stop treating your guests as your supporting cast. . . . It's about time [you] realized that what's attractive onstage isn't necessarily attractive off."

The movie's representation of Eve's and Margo's relationship registers the fear that the feminine woman who makes a lesbian object choice will reproduce herself almost endlessly by converting other women to lesbianism. In the movie's closing shots, Phoebe takes Eve's award into the bedroom, puts on the sequined cloak Eve wore to the awards ceremony, and stands in front of the bedroom mirror in long shot, holding up the award. As she begins to bow to her own reflection, the camera cuts to a medium shot, showing her image multiplied almost infinitely in the three-way mirror. By echoing the scene in which Eve pretends to be Margo, this scene suggests that the complex play of desire and identification that began with Margo and Eve continues with Eve and Phoebe. Like Eve, Phoebe stages a fantasy in which she is simultaneously star and spectator. But the difference is that Phoebe emerges as a virtual clone of Eve. When Addison DeWitt (George Sanders) shows up with Eve's award, which she has carelessly left in a taxi, we discover that Phoebe is just as manipulative and duplicitous as her idol. When she answers the door, Phoebe coyly tells Addison that she already knows who he is, and when Eve later asks who was at the door, she lies: "It was just the taxi driver returning your award." Moreover, the multiplication of her image in the mirror suggests that, like Eve, Phoebe has the capacity to spread lesbianism throughout society. Like the lesbian conjured by the Cold War discourse of female homosexuality, the aspiring actress threatens to become legion.

RESTABILIZING HETEROSEXUALITY

All about Eve seeks to resolve the contradictions in the Cold War construction of the lesbian by incorporating Margo into the institutions of heterosexuality. One of the effects of Cold War lesbian panic was to destabilize the category of woman by calling into question its foundation in heterosexuality. *All about Eve* tries to restore the connection between femininity and heterosexuality by normalizing Margo's identity, which entails transforming her femininity from a performance into the "real" thing. The movie increasingly emphasizes the differences between her and her protégé. The more Eve treats her like a "set of blueprints," the more Margo separates herself from her. At the party Margo becomes unusually bitchy to her. Mounting the stairs to her bedroom, she turns to Bill when he asks suggestively if she wants any help getting into bed, and replies sarcastically, "Put me to bed? Take my clothes off, hold my head, tuck me in, turn out the lights, and tiptoe out? Eve would, wouldn't you, Eve?" When an embarrassed Eve replies, "If you'd like," Margo snaps, "I wouldn't like!" All but forcing Eve to declare her lesbianism, this exchange could not be more coercively homophobic. For Eve to maintain her compliant, stereotypically feminine demeanor, she must reveal that she is willing to engage in intimacies with Margo that are more properly reserved for her heterosexual lover, Bill. Margo's reply, "I wouldn't like!," seems intended to assert her difference from her protégé, to make clear that she, Margo, is a "normal" woman. Now that Bill has returned from Hollywood, Margo prefers to have him keep her from getting lonely, and he follows her upstairs to put her to bed.

In stabilizing Margo's relationship to the institutions of heterosexuality, *All about Eve* attempts to contain the newly mobile categories of gender and sexuality that its representation of Eve as a lesbian with the ability to perform femininity has put into circulation. This aspect of the film's ideological project surfaces most fully in the scene in which Margo and Karen are stranded in a car while driving back to New York after spending the weekend in Connecticut. Margo apologizes for treating her and Lloyd (Hugh Marlowe) as her "supporting cast." While sitting in the car, Margo makes a distinction between herself as a star, "something spelled out in light bulbs," and herself as the woman who loves Bill "more than anything else in this world." To teach Margo a lesson, Karen has emptied the car of gas so that the star will not make it back in time for a performance and Eve, her understudy, will have to go on in her place, getting her big break. Unexpectedly, Margo reveals that she deeply regrets the sacrifices she has made for her career. "Funny business, a woman's career," she begins ruefully. "The things you drop on your way up the ladder so you can move faster. You forget you'll need them again when you get back to being a woman." Margo has come to believe that a woman cannot have a career and remain a woman. Indeed, what she did not realize while climbing the ladder of success was that womanhood itself is a career. For a woman, the only career that should matter is being a woman, and if she does not allow being a woman to take precedence over her other careers, then, like Eve, who is totally focused on becoming a star, she is not really a woman. Margo goes on to say that womanhood is "one career all females have in common, whether we like it or not—being a woman—and sooner or later we've got to work at it no matter how many other careers we've had or wanted." And what do women need to work at most? What is being a woman all about? Getting a man, because without a man, a woman is not really a woman. Margo concludes by stating, "In the last analysis nothing's any good unless you can look up just before dinner or turn around in bed and there he is. Without that you're not a woman." In other words, *All about Eve* attempts to rearticulate femininity and heterosexuality, precisely the normative alignment of sex, gender, and sexuality that it has disrupted through its representation of Eve as a lesbian who is all but indistinguishable from a straight woman. If, as Margo insists, being a woman depends on having a man, then, despite her femininity, Eve is not one.

Stabilizing the categories of gender and sexuality the movie has rendered mobile, however, requires more than clarifying Margo's sexual identity. To begin with, Margo's and Bill's relationship can hardly be described as normatively straight. The difference in their ages—Bill is eight years younger—provides a constant source of tension between them, and at forty Margo has no interest in motherhood. Despite the increasing acceptance of women as sexual subjects in the 1950s, motherhood remained the primary purpose of women's sexual activity. Moreover, Bill and Margo have been involved with each other for many years but maintained their independence, and the movie implies that they will continue to work as well as sleep together. In the restaurant scene in which Bill and Margo surprise Karen and Lloyd by announcing that they have decided to get married, Margo never clarifies her career plans. Because of her speech in the car, critics have assumed that she plans to retire from the stage, but all she says in this scene is that she does not want to play the part of Cora in Lloyd's new play because she is too old for it, a remark that leaves the door open for her to play other parts that are more appropriate for her age. Nor does Margo appear quite as committed to making a career out of being a woman as she has claimed. In the scene in which Eve accepts the Sarah Siddons Award, the film dissolves from a close-up of her as she expresses her appreciation of Margo as a "great actress and a great woman" to a close-up of Margo in a characteristic pose, a cigarette raised in her hand, her head turned slightly to one side, a contemptuous look on her face—a pose that indicates that she is more of a star than Eve will ever be. Finally, the film ends with an image not of Bill and Margo living happily ever after in wedded bliss, but of Phoebe in front of the mirror, her reflection multiplied almost infinitely. Translating into visual terms the fear that the lesbian will proliferate in numbers and influence, this image interpellates the spectator into the paranoid subject position underlying Cold War nationalism.

THE FAIRY AND THE FEMME

The contradictions in *All about Eve*'s ideological project are even more apparent in its treatment of Addison DeWitt, the despicable but powerful theater critic whose laudatory review of Eve launches her career. Addison provides a striking example of the mobility of femininity. Among Code-era movies, *All about Eve* is unusual for having a male character who is coded as gay as well as a female character who is coded as lesbian. Addison displays all of the signifers of male homosexuality in classical Hollywood cinema. Like Waldo Lydecker, the killer fairy played by Clifton Webb in Otto Preminger's classic film noir *Laura* (1944), Addison wears elegantly tailored clothes; speaks with an upper-crust accent; has a dry, bitchy wit; and is associated with a feminized profession.[34] After Addison has taken Margo to task in his review for playing roles inappropriate for her age, Bill describes him as a "venomous fishwife," an epithet that summarizes the feminized position Addison occupies in the film's gender and sexual hierarchies. The party scene further encodes his identity as a fairy. When several of the characters are assembled on the stairs discussing life in the theater, Addison alludes to the theater's historical association with gender and sexual nonconformity in ways that identify him as deviant. Upsetting the others, who insist that he is wrong, he declares, "We all have abnormality in common. We're a breed apart from the rest of humanity, we theater folk. We are the original displaced personalities." In claiming that he belongs to a "breed apart," one defined by its "abnormality," he all but declares that he is a homosexual. Even more incriminating, from a homophobic point of view, is his association with Eve. Addison is as ambitious and calculating as she is. As he himself says to her, having caught her in a lie in a hotel room before her opening night in New Haven, "You're an improbable person, Eve, and so am I. We have that in common. Also, a contempt for humanity, an inability to love and be loved, insatiable ambition, and talent. We deserve each other." What he cannot say here, but what all this adds up to, is that what they have most in common is their homosexuality. His claim that they deserve each other because they cannot love or be loved echoes assertions that medical experts routinely made about gays and lesbians in the 1950s, when homosexuality was thought to be a psychopathology rooted in narcissism.

Addison provides a more explicit example than does Eve of the way in which the older system of sexual classification continued to shape the treatment of "sex perversion" in movies of the Cold War era. Addison appears to be a woman trapped in a man's body, and thus his presence in *All about Eve* reinstalls the link between gender and sexual nonconformity that Eve's performance of femininity calls into question. In this respect, the movie's interrogation of perverse desire exemplifies what David M. Halperin has called the "irreducible definitional uncertainty" of the category of the homosexual.[35] Building on Eve Kosofsky Sedgwick's distinction between universalizing and minoritizing definitions of homosexuality, Halperin has argued that earlier traditions or models of gender and sexual nonconformity have not wholly disappeared, but persist alongside and in direct conflict with a "newer homosexual model derived from a more recent, comparatively anomalous system that privileges sexuality over gender."[36] As a consequence, "the homosexual" has no coherent meaning, but rather is a product of a "cumulative process of historical overlay and accretion."[37] The coexistence in *All about Eve* of irreconcilable models of homosexuality provides a concrete example of this process and helps to explain Eve's alteration between butch and femme roles. Even as the movie underwrote the Cold War construction of the lesbian, it solidified the association of male and female homosexuality with gender inversion. Thus it showed how the older model of sexuality continued to exert authority over the newer one underlying Cold War homophobia.

In basing Addison's character on the older model, the movie undercuts its attempts to stabilize the normative alignment of sex, gender, and sexuality. As a fairy, Addison's character highlights the mobility of femininity. His homosexuality indicates that femininity lacks a causal relation not only to heterosexuality, as Eve's lesbianism has shown, but also to femaleness. Yet precisely because he is a fairy, Addison helps to mark as unnatural those performances of femininity that are not grounded in either. One effect of his sadomasochistic relationship with Eve is to pathologize their gender and sexual nonconformity. In the scene in the hotel room, Addison slaps Eve and then strips her emotionally by exposing each one of her lies, beginning with her supposed marriage to a pilot killed in battle, which he sneers was "an insult to dead heroes and the women who love them," and ending with her revelation that she loves Lloyd and that he is leaving Karen for her. By demonstrating that, unlike the other characters, he knows how duplicitous and manipulative she is, Addison gains control over Eve. As if in a trance, she replies in a monotone, "Yes, Addison," when he asks, "Are you listening to me?," and again when he asks, "And you realize, and you agree, how completely you belong to me?" The movie translates his mastery into visual terms by cross-cutting close-ups of Eve sobbing on the bed with medium shots of him looking down at her contemptuously. This treatment of their relationship suggests that despite her gender conformity, Eve is as sexually deviant as Addison. With this scene, her sexuality displaces her gender as the defining characteristic of her identity.

DOING TALLULAH

Perhaps the greatest obstacle *All about Eve* faced in reconciling Cold War gender and sexual ideologies was Davis's campy performance. The reviews in *Time*, *Life*, and *Newsweek* noted Davis's apparently deliberate imitation of Bankhead: her hairdo, facial expressions, husky voice (the result of being hoarse, or so Davis claimed when pressed by reporters to explain why she sounded so different in *All about Eve* from her other movies), and exaggerated mannerisms all resembled those of the Broadway actress, as did her wardrobe, which Edith Head designed after looking at film stills of Bankhead.[38] Bankhead was known for her gender nonconformity as well as her lesbianism. Her weekly radio program, *The Big Show*, which debuted on NBC in 1950, the same year *All about Eve* was released, always ended with Meredith Willson, her musical director, wryly uttering the line, "Thank you, Miss Bankhead, sir!"[39] The resemblance between Davis and Bankhead, a camp icon, gave Davis's performance a camp inflection that it might otherwise have lacked, especially for gay male audiences who adulated both stars.

But even without the resemblance, Davis's performance would have lent itself to camp appropriations. Of all the female stars of Hollywood's golden age, Davis was perhaps the one most often impersonated by drag queens in the 1950s and 1960s, for good reason. Davis was not only one of Hollywood's most flamboyant stars, but also famous for her own exaggerated mannerisms and facial expressions. Impersonating Bankhead only intensified her histrionic acting style. To capture the campiness of Davis's performance in *All about Eve*, some critics have gone so far as to describe Margo as a drag queen impersonating Davis.[40] In promoting a camp mode of reception, Davis's performance style undercut the movie's project of realigning femininity with femaleness and heterosexuality. The camp effect of Davis's performance denaturalized femininity by highlighting its constructedness. Her glamorous gender presentation was literally a copy of a copy, Bankhead's. Her model was a gender-nonconforming woman considered by many to be a lesbian and whose femininity was thought fake, designed to conceal a core masculine identity ("Thank you, Miss Bankhead, sir!"), and so there was nothing authentic or natural about it. For this reason, Margo's stated definition of femininity, which anchored it to both femaleness and heterosexuality, may have struck viewers as contradicted by Margo herself.

All about Eve's campiness by no means counteracts its ratification of the Cold War construction of the lesbian. Certainly it never displaces the homophobia of the movie's representation of Eve. Indeed, the movie's contradictory relation to the Cold War discourse of female homosexuality shows that it is precisely the uneasy relationship between the campy and the homophobic elements of the movie that exemplifies the queerness of Cold War culture. By calling attention to the mobility of femininity in relation to both femaleness and heterosexuality, the film's homophobic treatment of Eve's aberrant desire disrupts the alignment of sex, gender, and sexuality on which the category of woman depended during this era. Although Eve can pass for straight, her core identity remains masculine; her butchness in both the opening and the closing scenes of the movie encourages this construction of her identity. The contradiction in her identity can be traced to the persistence of the stereotype of the mannish lesbian. The Cold War discourse of female homosexuality may have helped to displace this stereotype by accelerating the process whereby sexual desire for women overtook masculinity as the basis of lesbian identity, but the stereotype did not disappear, for the butch continued to be seen as more lesbian than the femme. As a result, the lesbian's masculinity continued to appear natural, whereas her femininity emerged as fake, a disguise meant to conceal her sexual nonconformity. But *All about Eve*'s essentialist construction of its villain's sexual identity cannot contain the mobility of femininity to which her ability to pass as straight calls attention. The film's examples of queer femininity are too compelling, especially the one provided by its star, Davis, whose performance style disrupted its project to underwrite heteronormative institutions and discourses. These examples denaturalize femininity, even as they seek to immobilize it, by reanchoring it to the straight female body. In so doing, they reveal camp's potential to destabilize the normative construction of masculinity and femininity. For this reason, *All about Eve* is not only one of the most homophobic, but also one of the queerest movies of the Cold War era.

CHAPTER TWO

LESBIAN UNINTELLIGIBILITY

The Children's Hour

In 1961, the director William Wyler approached Lillian Hellman about adapting for the screen her hit Broadway play *The Children's Hour* (1934).[1] The play centered on two teachers, Karen Wright and Martha Dobie, whose lives are ruined when one of the pupils, a spoiled, manipulative girl named Mary, accuses them of lesbianism, and they unsuccessfully sue the girl's grandmother for slander. Wyler and Hellman had already collaborated on an earlier adaptation of the controversial play, the film *These Three* (1936), in which Merle Oberon and Miriam Hopkins played the two unjustly accused teachers. But the Hays Office, which administered the recently revised Production Code, had prohibited them from addressing the central issue explored in the play, the permeable boundary between female homosocial desire and lesbian identity.[2] In the final act, an anguished Martha confesses that she loves Karen "the way they said I loved you," before exiting the stage and committing suicide.[3] In accordance with the Production Code, Hellman transformed Martha's unrequited love for Karen into an unrequited love for Karen's fiancé, Joe Cardin, a struggling doctor. In the movie, when Karen (Oberon) punishes Mary (Bonita Granville) for lying, the girl vindictively tells her socially prominent grandmother, Mrs. Tilford (Alma Kruger), that Martha (Hopkins) and Joe (Joel McCrea) have been secretly carrying on an affair. Although *These Three*, which was both a critical and a box-office success, sealed Wyler's reputation as one of Hollywood's best directors, he always regretted that he and Hellman had capitulated to the Hays Office and heterosexualized Martha's illicit desire.[4] Thus it is hardly surprising that when, in 1961, under enormous pressure from the studios, which hoped to reverse the postwar decline in movie attendance by producing more "adult" fare, the Production Code Administration revised the Code so that "homosexuality and other sexual aberrations may now be treated with care, discretion, and restraint," Wyler decided to make a more faithful adaptation of *The Children's Hour*, one that dealt openly and sympathetically with Martha's love for Karen.[5]

Although Hellman encouraged Wyler to pursue the project, she was reluctant to collaborate with him on it. Blacklisted following her testimony, in 1952, before the House Un-American Activities Committee (HUAC), in which she famously declared that she would not "cut [her] conscience to fit this year's fashions" and refused to name names, Hellman remained wary of Hollywood and did not want to undertake a project that might embroil her in a censorship battle with the studios.[6] Instead, she urged Wyler to hire the screenwriter John Michael Hayes, who had written the scripts for several critically acclaimed "adult-themed" movies, including *Peyton Place* (Mark Robson, 1957) and *Butterfield 8* (Daniel Mann, 1960).[7] But Wyler was not at all happy with Hayes's script, which he thought adhered too closely to Hellman's play. Wyler realized that the play's treatment of lesbianism was dated and that the movie would need to appeal to audiences whose views, as the revised Production Code indirectly acknowledged, had shifted considerably since the 1930s. Indeed, as one reviewer complained after the film's release in 1962, Hellman's play had addressed the issue of lesbianism "with a degree of reticence that was a little behind the sophistication of the times" even in 1934, when it opened on Broadway.[8] Wyler managed to persuade Hellman to revise Hayes's script, which she continued to do two weeks into production. But even with Hellman's intervention, Wyler failed to achieve his goals for the movie. Shirley MacLaine, who played Martha, told one of Wyler's biographers that in the end the director "chickened out. He said so himself. He gutted scenes we had in the middle of the picture, which showed Martha was in love with Karen. He got scared. He said he couldn't do it."[9] Wyler's alleged loss of courage may explain the movie's disappointing reception. *The Children's Hour* was one of the few films he made during his forty-year career that got panned by critics and did poorly at the box office.

Wyler's attempts to update Hellman's play so that its treatment of lesbianism would resonate with contemporary audiences ironically resulted in an even more homophobic adaptation than the censored *These Three*. Wyler's movie had had the potential to provide a searing critique of Cold War homophobia.[10] When Hellman returned to Broadway, in 1952, after a long hiatus, to direct a revival of *The Children's Hour*, at least some reviewers commented on the parallels between the moral panic caused by Mary's unfounded accusation and the antilesbian witch hunts of the 1950s. For example, in a review for *Women's Wear Daily*, Thomas Dash emphasized the new production's topicality by noting that "gossip about sexual aberrations, actual and implied, has become more prevalent in our depraved days of 1952 than it ever was in 1934."[11] Wyler's adaptation elaborated these parallels and in so doing indirectly contested the Cold War construction of the lesbian as a threat to the nation's security. The homophobic deployment of the category of the lesbian emerges in the film as a mechanism for gaining women's consent to postwar gender arrangements. Despite their normative gender presentations, Karen (Audrey Hepburn) and Martha have no way to defend themselves against Mary's accusation, and they must abandon their careers and isolate themselves from the community. But the movie's relationship to the Cold War construction of the lesbian was far from clear-cut. For even as it contested the lesbian panic of the 1950s, the movie reproduced the sexual epistemology responsible for that panic.[12] As Julie Erhart has pointed out, the final version of *The Children's Hour* treats lesbianism "less as an identity or set of practices to be explored than a condition to be apprehended."[13] Although several scenes early in the film hint at her desire for Karen, Martha does not even recognize her own lesbianism until Mary's accusation. This belated recognition shifts attention away from the injustice of Karen's and Martha's persecution, focusing it instead on the social anxieties promoted by Cold War culture, anxieties that reflected the increasing dominance of a model of sexuality in which object choice, sexual practice, and gender identity did not line up neatly. Because of this shift in focus, the film ends up ratifying the Cold War construction of the lesbian. Martha's lack of knowledge about her own sexual desire confirmed the epistemological uncertainty that the Cold War discourse of female homosexuality attributed to lesbian identity.

Hellman's need to abide by the Production Code's prohibition of the explicit treatment of "sex perversion" does not fully explain her heterosexualization of its plot when adapting it for the screen in 1936. The play centered on how the emergence of the category of the lesbian affected what the historian Carroll Smith-Rosenberg has called "the female world of love and ritual."[14] The product of an increasingly outmoded social and sexual formation, Martha cannot accept the new definition of her love for Karen. But in representing Martha's sexuality as perverse, Hellman inadvertently validated a homophobic construction of sentimental women's culture that gained currency in the 1920s and 1930s as part of a backlash against the New Woman. Such a representation affirmed the potential of female homosocial institutions, like Karen's and Martha's boarding school, to promote lesbian desire. By contrast, *These Three* reaffirmed the romantic friendships such institutions fostered, thus attempting to reclaim them from the stigma of lesbianism. Hellman's screen adaptation insists on the compatibility of female homosocial bonds and heterosexual desire, but in so doing reinscribes the homophobic construction of female homosocial institutions. Its treatment of Karen's and Martha's relationship seeks indirectly to reassure audiences of the fixity of the boundary between female homosocial desire and lesbian identity. Locating the two earlier versions of *The Children's Hour* in their historical context helps to clarify how Wyler, despite his ideological project, transformed Hellman's play into a Cold War text by reinforcing the indeterminacy of "the lesbian."

CONTESTING LESBIAN PANIC

Hellman based her play on William Roughead's account of a scandalous nineteenth-century lawsuit, known as the Great Drumsheugh Case, involving two Scottish teachers, Marianne Woods and Jane Pirie, who were forced to close their boarding school when one of their pupils, Jane Cumming, accused them of engaging in sexual relations with each other.[15] Woods and Pirie sued for libel Cumming's grandmother, Dame Helen Cumming Gordon, who had repeated the accusation to the parents of the other pupils without first confronting the teachers and allowing them to refute the accusation.

Scholars have rightly criticized Hellman for refusing to address the issues of race raised by Roughead's account of the lawsuit.[16] Cumming was the illegitimate daughter of Dame Gordon's only son and the Indian woman he lived with before his death in Calcutta, and Roughead's representation of the girl's role in the case turns on a racist construction of black female sexuality. He others the girl by attributing to her an impure sexual knowledge that reflects her "mixed blood."[17] Lest his readers dismiss his account as sensationalistic or licentious, Roughead insists that his interest in the lawsuit resides "in the fact that *the charge was false*" (127; original emphasis), even though it was corroborated by another pupil at the school, Janet Munro. But because of her whiteness, Roughead refuses to believe Munro's testimony and claims that she was contaminated by "the foul imaginings of the Indian" (132). Moreover, he relates Cumming's "foul imaginings" to her identity as a "dusky damsel from the East" (117), which supposedly made her more prone to evil than her

Scottish schoolmates. According to him, the girl gained her knowledge of tribadism, the sexual practice she claimed she saw the two teachers engage in regularly, during her childhood in India, where she developed the "fertile and infragrant imagination" (135) that enabled her to concoct her "monstrous fiction" (135) and thus exact retribution on her teachers for disciplining her. Roughead in this way represents lesbianism as foreign and exotic, an "unnatural" sexual practice introduced into British society by racialized others. In making Mary Tilford, the character in *The Children's Hour* based on Cumming, white, Hellman avoided having to address the complicated nexus of race, sexuality, and nation that Roughead's account highlighted.

Hellman claimed that she was drawn to the story of the two unjustly accused teachers because she could treat it "with complete impersonality. I hadn't even been to boarding school."[18] She supposedly wanted to avoid fictionalizing her own experience, which she worried would mark her as a woman writer. But Hellman's choice of material was not as arbitrary or as removed from her own experience as she asserted.[19] Indeed, as a professional woman who inhabited the margins of the institutions of heterosexuality, she was deeply implicated in the material. In the 1920s and 1930s, when Hellman was coming of age intellectually, female homosocial institutions such as women's colleges and settlement houses became the focus of anxieties about lesbianism. Of particular concern was the practice of "chumming," or the romantic friendships such institutions fostered.[20] Social reformers and medical professionals worried that such friendships promoted what the sexologist Havelock Ellis had called "artificial lesbianism" in his widely influential book, *Studies in the Psychology of Sex*, by which he meant a form of lesbianism that did not entail a cross-gender identification and that could be reversed.[21] Such friendships, he claimed, had the potential to sexually corrupt otherwise "normal" and "healthy" women, or women with normative gender identities, by implanting in them an "unnatural" desire for members of their own sex. In his book *Love in the Machine Age: A Psychological Study of the Transition from Patriarchal Mores*, published in 1930, the progressive social critic Floyd Dell directly linked the formation of homosexual identities to homosocial institutions by denouncing the "unwholesome fashionable practice of sex-segregated schools [that] brings young people into a homosexual atmosphere."[22]

Historians have traced this reaction against female homosocial institutions and practices to the transformation of women's roles following the First World War.[23] In addition to winning the right to vote, women began to attend college and enter the workforce in increasing numbers. They also began to live apart from their families before marrying and to seek more freedom to experiment sexually. In this context, the ideology of separate spheres for men and women emerged as incompatible with patriarchal social and economic arrangements. Female homosocial institutions and practices functioned as a sign of women's increasing freedom and independence from men and as such threatened to undermine male dominance at home and in the workplace. In associating these institutions and practices with lesbianism, social reformers and medical professionals encouraged women to channel their desire away from each other and toward marriage and motherhood.[24] The "companionate" model of marriage that emerged in the 1920s attempted to entice women into participating in the institutions of heterosexuality by persuading them that they could fulfill their desire for equality and sexual fulfillment through marriage.[25] The backlash against sentimental women's culture helped to transform the New Woman from a model of female independence and professionalism into an "old maid" whose friendships with other women masked an "unnatural" lesbian desire.[26] For example, in 1929, J. W. Meagher, one of the proponents of companionate marriage, asserted that "the driving force in many agitators and militant women who are always after their rights is often an unsatisfied sex impulse, with a homosexual aim. Married women with a completely satisfied libido rarely take an active interest in militant movements."[27] As a consequence of the backlash, the flapper, whose sexual exploits epitomized women's growing freedom and autonomy, eventually displaced the New Woman as the quintessentially modern woman. Unlike the New Woman, the flapper did not avoid participating in the institutions of heterosexuality but always chose marriage and motherhood over career.

Hellman's play had a complicated relationship to these shifting constructions of modern womanhood. Although its treatment of Martha suggests that she rejects the New Woman as a model, the play contests the homophobic deployment of the category of the lesbian. Mrs. Mortar, Martha's spiteful and meddlesome aunt, who teaches elocution at the school, expresses the homophobic construction of female homosocial institutions and practices most clearly in the play. She provides the first indication that despite Martha's normative gender presentation, her friendship with Karen is rooted in a lesbian desire. A former actress with a histrionic streak, Mrs. Mortar sets a bad example for the students, and

Martha and Karen decide that she should leave the school. When Martha informs her of their decision, Mrs. Mortar spitefully accuses her niece of wanting to get rid of her because she knows that she secretly desires Karen. Mrs. Mortar asserts that she "wasn't born yesterday" (19), indicating her familiarity with the contemporary discourse of female sexuality that enables her to correctly interpret Martha's attachment to Karen, although the female world of the boarding school has enabled Martha to mask her lesbianism. Despite Martha's denials, Mrs. Mortar insists that Martha resents Karen's fiancé, Joe: "And it's unnatural, just as unnatural as it can be. You don't like their being together" (20). Moreover, Mrs. Mortar traces her niece's "unnatural" love for Karen to her childhood, thereby suggesting that it does not represent a momentary transgression or stage she will outgrow, but constitutes an identity. Mrs. Mortar reminds her niece that she has always carried her friendships with other women "too far": "You were always like that even as a child. If you had a little girl friend, you always got mad when she liked anybody else" (20). Further echoing the homophobic construction of women's romantic friendships, Mrs. Mortar implies that her niece should abandon her career and follow a more traditional path, one that ends in marriage and motherhood. She cruelly warns her niece, "Well, you'd better get a beau of your own now—a woman of your age" (20).

Although in attributing the homophobic construction of female homosocial bonds to the petty and vindictive Mrs. Mortar Hellman undermined its authority, she did not wholly reject it. Martha's confession of her desire for Karen in the play's final scene ratifies the backlash against sentimental women's culture by underscoring the permeability of the boundary between female homosocial desire and lesbian identity. At the same time, however, the play showed how the emergence of the category of the lesbian rendered outmoded the female world of romantic friendships. Martha dismisses her aunt's insinuations about her love for Karen as "disconnected unpleasantness" (19). Unlike her aunt, she lacks familiarity with the contemporary discourse of female sexuality. Instead, her knowledge of love and desire reflects her identity as a New Woman. After they lose their lawsuit against Mrs. Tilford, Martha assures Karen that she has loved her "like a friend, the way thousands of women feel about other women" (71). In other words, Martha's participation in female homosocial institutions has enabled her to experience her feelings for Karen as "normal." But Mary's accusation, which signals the emergence of a new system of sexual classification, has transformed the meaning of those feelings. As a result, Martha can no longer experience them without feeling "all dirty" (71). Despite her confession, Martha refuses to accept her new identity. She makes a distinction between herself and women who identify as lesbian. When Karen insists that "other people aren't destroyed" (70) by the label of lesbianism, Martha asserts, "They are the people who believe in it, who want it, who've chosen it" (70). Martha's failure to identify with such people underscores her predicament as a historically constituted subject of desire. The redefinition of her identity has created a "big difference" (72) between her and Karen, which helps to explain her suicide. She cannot face a future dominated by unrequited love. Before killing herself, she remarks, "I can't stay with you anymore, darling" (72).

The play's representation of Mary further complicates its relationship to the backlash against the New Woman. Based on bullying and coercion, Mary's bonds with the other girls turn inside out the schoolgirl practice of chumming. For example, when she decides to run away from school at the end of act 1, she asks Peggy for bus fare, but Peggy has been saving up her allowance to buy a new dress and refuses to give it to her. In a startling display of brutality, Mary forces her to hand over the money by twisting her arm "hard and expertly" (30). Moreover, when Evelyn attempts to intervene by prying Peggy's arm loose, Mary slaps her violently. Mary's power over the other girls is psychological as well as physical, as when she prevents Rosalie from revealing that she has lied about Karen and Martha by threatening to tell her grandmother that Rosalie has stolen another girl's bracelet. Terrified of ending up in reform school, Rosalie reluctantly agrees to take "the worst oath there is" (44) and swears to do whatever Mary asks. Thus when Karen and Martha challenge Mary's story by pointing out that she could not possibly have seen them kissing and fondling each other, she forces Rosalie to tell her grandmother that she was the one who saw them. In other words, Mary has a perverse relation to female homosocial bonding, which renders it virtually unrecognizable. When Karen and Martha discover that it is Mary who has accused them of lesbianism, Karen denounces the girl in terms that pathologize her identity, informing an incredulous Mrs. Tilford, "Your Mary's a strange girl. A dark girl. There's something very awful the matter with her" (51). In this way, the play suggests that Mary, and not Martha, is the one who threatens to contaminate the female world of romantic friendships.

Although Mrs. Mortar bears responsibility for introducing the homophobic construction of female homosocial bonds into the community, Mary is the one who circulates it. Peggy and Evelyn overhear Mrs. Mortar describe Martha's jealousy of Joe as "unnatural," but they do not understand what she means and later ask Mary to explain it. Mary then passes on what the two girls have told her to her grandmother, who as one of Lancet's most prominent citizens has the power to enforce the homophobic construction. At first, Mrs. Tilford chastises Mary for engaging in idle gossip, but Mary embellishes her story by claiming that she has seen the two teachers having sex. Mrs. Tilford believes her because she does not understand how a child could possibly know about "such things" unless she had witnessed them. But Mary has gained her knowledge of lesbianism by reading late at night, when the other girls are asleep, *Mademoiselle de Maupin*, a scandalous French novel whose cross-dressing heroine sleeps with both men and women.[28] (She solidifies her bonds with Peggy and Evelyn by letting them read the novel's "dirty" passages.) Horrified by her granddaughter's story, Mrs. Tilford repeats it to the parents of the other girls without first confronting Karen and Martha and allowing them to refute it. In this way, the play contested the backlash against the New Woman. The homophobic deployment of the category of the lesbian emerges as a mechanism for perpetuating patriarchal social arrangements. As independent professional women, Martha and Karen threaten those arrangements, having transgressed the boundaries of normative femininity by pursuing careers instead of marriage and motherhood. In spreading her granddaughter's malicious lie, Mrs. Tilford insures that they no longer provide the girls in the community with an alternative model of womanhood.

The play's emphasis on the consequences of Mary's lie for Karen and Martha reinforces the critique of the homophobic deployment of the category of the lesbian. Martha's confession of her love for Karen foregrounds the discursive construction of sexuality. The discourse about Martha—the lies, rumors, and gossip that spread through the community—*produces* her lesbian identity, even though she has never engaged in lesbian activity. She remarks bitterly, "There's something in you, and you don't know it and you don't do anything about it. Suddenly a child gets bored and lies—and there you are, seeing it for the first time" (71). The shift in the construction of her identity establishes a hierarchical relationship, between her and Karen, that reflects the consolidation of the hetero-homosexual binary, which the backlash against the New Woman signaled. As Karen's last name indicates, the scandal renders her sexuality "right" by marking her as a "normal" heterosexual woman. But despite this "big difference" between her and Martha, the consequences of the scandal are no less devastating for Karen. When Joe announces that he has resigned from the hospital and taken a position in Vienna, where no one will know about the scandal, she realizes that they would never be happy together and ends their engagement so he can remain in Lancet, where he grew up, and continue working at the hospital: "I'd hate you for what I thought I'd done to you. And I'd hate myself, too. It would grow and grow until we'd be ruined by it" (67–68). Moreover, Mrs. Tilford reveals that she has discovered the truth from Rosalie and her granddaughter and has arranged for a public apology and explanation *after* Martha has acknowledged her lesbianism and committed suicide. Thus Karen can never derive any satisfaction from the vindication of her reputation. She remarks bitterly, "You're old, and the old are callous. Ten, fifteen years left for you. But what of me? It's a whole life for me. A whole God-damned life" (76).

RECLAIMING SENTIMENTAL WOMEN'S CULTURE

Although as one of Hollywood's leading screenwriters, Hellman was an outspoken critic of the Production Code, unlike Wyler she never expressed any regret about heterosexualizing the plot of *The Children's Hour* when adapting it for the screen.[29] She understood the importance of the female world of romantic friendships for Hollywood, which exploited it by creating a genre, the "weepie," or women's picture, designed specifically for female audiences, and by promoting female stars who appealed primarily to women. Thus it is hardly surprising that when drafting the screenplay for *These Three*, Hellman followed the conventions of the women's picture.[30] In so doing, she reaffirmed female homosocial institutions and practices. As a review in *Variety* noted, this shift in Hellman's approach to the material resulted in an adaptation of the play that was "an extraordinary offering, especially for women."[31] But despite its appeal to female audiences, the movie's relationship to the backlash against female homosocial institutions and practices was even more complicated than the play's. In the play, both Karen and Martha are in their late twenties, and they have dreamed of starting their own school since they were roommates in college. Their devotion to the school and to each other renders Mary's accusation more credible because their domestic arrangements resemble the sort of "Boston marriage" that many New Women entered into. By contrast, *These Three* opens with Karen and Martha graduating from college, and although they are roommates, they do not seem especially devoted to each other. Moreover, they decide to start the school spontaneously, while packing their trunks after the graduation ceremony. Neither of them knows where she will go or what she will do for a living. But Karen has inherited her grandmother's farm, and when Martha mentions that she might look for a job as a teacher, Karen impulsively suggests that they turn the farm into a boarding school. These revisions indirectly acknowledged the homophobic construction of female homosocial bonds by seeking to reassure audiences that there was nothing "unnatural" or deviant about the two women. No one can confuse their relationship with a Boston marriage.

These Three also indirectly acknowledged the backlash against female homosocial institutions by emphasizing the compatibility of female homosocial desire and heterosexual romance. Unlike the play, the movie contains several scenes that center on Joe's and Karen's courtship. The couple first meets when Karen and Martha arrive at the farm and discover that it has fallen into disrepair. Joe, who has been collecting honey from a beehive in the attic, is immediately attracted to Karen, and he woos her while helping her and Martha renovate the farm. Meanwhile, Martha falls in love with Joe, but she hides her feelings because she does not want to betray her friendship with Karen. In this way, *These Three* attempted to counter the backlash against women's romantic friendships by stabilizing the boundary between lesbian identity and female homosocial desire. Martha's devotion to Karen does not prevent her from falling in love with a man. But the movie undercuts this project by shifting genres in the sequence of scenes that shows Joe's and Karen's courtship. Temporarily interrupting the women's picture that centers on Karen's and Martha's friendship, this sequence has all the elements of a romantic comedy, including a leading man, Joel McCrae, closely associated with the genre, as well as a heavy dose of slapstick comedy.[32] It opens with Joe swinging Karen over his shoulder and carrying her off kicking and screaming to an amusement park, where he intends to ask her to marry him. But nothing goes as planned. Karen teases him by ignoring him and riding the merry-go-round. When he falls asleep, she wakes him by popping a balloon in his hand, and he walks off in a huff. The sequence ends with him blurting out that he loves her, and her kissing him. One of the effects of this shift in genres is to mark the *in*compatibility of female homosocial bonds and heterosexual desire, which turn out to require two different modes of representation. Romantic comedy emerges as better suited than melodrama for representing Joe's and Karen's relationship.

Despite the lesbian panic encoded in its construction of the friend-ship between Karen and Martha, the movie's treatment of female homo-social institutions and practices differs markedly from that of the play. In the play Mrs. Mortar enforces the norms of female homosocial bond-ing by warning her niece that she has carried her affection for Karen too far; in spitefully warning Martha that her jealousy of Joe is "unnatural," Mrs. Mortar reveals an aspect of her niece's identity that her niece does not yet recognize, but will eventually acknowledge. But in the movie Mrs. Mortar (Catherine Doucet) is the one who violates the female world of romantic friendships, by undermining Martha's bond with Karen. She knows that Martha has fallen in love with Joe but hidden her feelings out of loyalty to her friend, and wanting to punish Martha for asking her to leave the school, Mrs. Mortar uses this information to fabricate a malicious lie: although she knows that Martha would never betray her friendship with Karen by having an affair with Joe, she provokes Martha by claiming falsely that she has seen the doctor leaving Martha's room late at night. Fearful that her aunt will poison her friendship with Karen by spreading gossip about her and Joe, Martha warns her: "There's been no trouble in this house, and I won't let you do your usual job of start-ing any." Their angry encounter ends abruptly when they hear a book drop outside the door and discover that Rosalie (Marcia Mae Jones) and Evelyn (Carmencita Johnson) have been eavesdropping on their conver-sation.

These Three's attempt to recuperate female homosocial bonding sur-faces more fully in its treatment of Mary, which magnifies her violation of the schoolgirl practice of chumming. As in the play, Mary (Bonita Gran-ville) forces Rosalie to take an oath of obedience by threatening to reveal that she has stolen another girl's bracelet. But Mary's power over the girl is more harrowing in the film, wherein Rosalie has a crush not on Karen, but on Martha, and her oath thus forces her to betray a beloved teacher. When Karen and Martha confront Mary about her lying, Rosalie at first denies having told Mary about Martha and Joe, but Mary walks over to the sofa where she is sitting and comments pointedly, "I remember when you said it. It was the day Helen Burton's bracelet was stolen, and nobody knew who did it, and Helen said that if her mother found out, she'd have the thief put in jail." The scene is shot in a way that highlights Rosalie's torment. She must choose between violating her crush on Martha and facing exposure as a thief. Close-ups of Mary leaning over the girl menacingly are crosscut with close-ups of a terrified Rosalie reeling back and crying hysterically. Martha unintentionally adds to the pressure the girl feels by kneeling down beside her and saying reassuringly, "There is nothing to cry about, Rosalie. You must help us by telling the truth. That's all."[33] Rosalie, in close-up, looks frantically back and forth at Mary and Martha before screaming wildly, "Yes, yes, I did say it, I did tell Mary, what Mary said was right!" She then collapses on the sofa. Although she has protected her own secret, she has done so by ruining the reputation of the teacher she loves.

These Three eventually restores the female world of romantic friendships, which Mary's lie has turned inside out. In the closing scenes, Rosalie reaffirms her love for her teacher by confessing all. Although in the play Mrs. Tilford discovers that Mary has coerced Rosalie into corroborating her story, in the movie it is Martha who ferrets out the truth. When Mrs. Mortar mentions the stolen bracelet, which Martha had not known about, Martha goes to Rosalie's home and appeals to the girl's feelings for her. This scene contrasts markedly with the one in Mrs. Tilford's drawing room: whereas Mary stood over Rosalie threateningly while she struggled to make up her mind, Martha sits on the porch looking up tenderly at the girl, who stands in the doorway. When Rosalie begins to back away in fear, Martha reminds her, "We used to be friends." She then pulls the girl gently toward her and remarks, "Someday when you're grown up you'll know what it is to have something mean your whole life to you. That's the way I feel now, and you're the only one who can help me. Please help me." The girl, realizing that she loves Martha more than she fears exposure as a thief, collapses into Martha's arms and confesses. In the following scene, as Rosalie repeats her confession to Mrs. Tilford, Mary bursts into the drawing room and begs her grandmother not to believe Rosalie's story. Rosalie is again terrified, but Martha wraps her arms around her protectively, which gives her the courage to point at Mary and scream, "She made me do it, she made me lie!" Mary no longer has the power to come between them. Martha rewards Rosalie for telling the truth by bestowing a kiss on her. The film underscores the importance of the kiss by dissolving to a close-up of the girl, who looks up adoringly at Martha with tears in her eyes before rushing out of the room. She realizes that Martha has forgiven her for betraying their bond.

These Three further valorizes female homosocial bonding by restoring the friendship between Karen and Martha. In persuading Rosalie to confess her role in the scandal, Martha is motivated not by a desire to clear her name, but by a desire to redeem her friendship with Karen. During the trial, Karen begins to believe that Martha and Joe have had an affair. Although Joe insists that he has never even thought of Martha, Karen refuses to believe him, and she ends their relationship, remarking bitterly, "People can't believe just because other people tell them to believe." When Karen informs her what she has done and why, Martha feels ashamed that she has never confessed her love for Joe. Despite believing that Martha and Joe have had an affair, Karen has stood by them during the trial, which shows that she has been a better friend to Martha than Martha has been to her. Deciding that Karen deserves to know the truth, Martha admits that she has loved Joe from the beginning. Although her intention is to restore Karen's trust, her confession only reinforces Karen's conviction that she has been betrayed, and Karen therefore asks Martha to depart with Mrs. Mortar. Thus in Mrs. Tilford's drawing room, after Rosalie has confessed, Martha asks the humbled matriarch to deliver a message to her former friend: "Tell her to stay with Joe wherever he is. Tell her I said that. She'll know what I mean." Mrs. Tilford offers to pay Martha damages and to publish an apology in the local newspaper, but Martha wants neither, and she walks out of the house triumphantly. When in the following scene Mrs. Tilford repeats Martha's message, Karen realizes that she never should have doubted Martha's loyalty. As Mrs. Tilford explains that Martha said she would understand the message, the camera tracks in on Karen, who, with tears welling up in her eyes, replies, "Yes, I know what she meant." Karen's sentimental display indicates that Martha has succeeded in repairing their friendship.

Martha's demonstration of loyalty to Karen makes possible the movie's heterosexual resolution. Although we never learn what happens to Martha after she leaves Mrs. Tilford's house, *These Three* ends with Karen and Joe reunited in Vienna, where Joe has gone to practice medicine. This resolution seems intended to contest the backlash against women's romantic friendships by reaffirming the compatibility of female homosocial desire and heterosexual love. While it acknowledges the importance of female homosocial bonding, the film also ends in typical Hollywood fashion with the formation of the heterosexual couple—a resolution that seems to require a return to romantic comedy. A light-

MIRIAM HOPKINS AND MERLE OBERON AS JUST FRIENDS IN *THESE THREE*.

hearted musical score, which contrasts markedly with the melodramatic one of the preceding scene, in which Mrs. Tilford relays Martha's message to Karen, signals this return. The final scene opens with the camera tracking Karen as she walks down a street in Vienna searching for Joe. When she reaches his favorite café, she peers into the window, but a waitress blocks him from view. She and Joe eventually recognize each other, and as they kiss in the doorway of the café, the camera pans the other diners who laugh uproariously and nod their heads in approval. In other words, the movie continues to indicate the *in*compatibility of female homosocial desire and heterosexual love at the level of form, thereby undercutting its attempt to reclaim women's romantic friendships. Moreover, the movie's ending suggests that heterosexual love should eventually displace female homosocial desire in women's lives. Although Martha and Karen reaffirm their bond, they never see each other again. Thus even as *These Three* valorized women's romantic friendships, it indirectly ratified the homophobic deployment of the category of the lesbian. The only way that Martha can repair her friendship with Karen is by enabling her to reunite with Joe and then disappearing from her life.

When Hellman directed the Broadway revival of *The Children's Hour* in 1952, she made several revisions that magnified the political resonance of its treatment of a false accusation of lesbianism.[34] Although in the original version the scandal serves to normalize Karen's sexuality, to render it "right," in the revised version the scandal permanently destabilizes her claim to heterosexual normality. Rather than ending her relationship with Joe so that he can remain in Lancet and fulfill his dreams for the hospital, Karen ends it because she realizes that she can never convince him that she is not a lesbian: "I don't believe you could touch my arm without my wondering why you didn't kiss me, and I don't think you could kiss me without my wondering if you really wanted to. And I'd hate myself for all that. And then I'd hate you, too."[35] The performance style of Patricia Neal, the actress who played Martha, only reinforced Karen's sexual ambiguity. Hellman wanted Neal to convey Martha's lesbianism from the outset, and she encouraged the actress to exaggerate her masculine gender presentation. Several critics objected to this reinterpretation of Martha's character. For example, Walter Kerr complained that Neal's performance was "markedly mannish,"[36] and George Freedley protested that Neal played Martha in too "mannish a fashion."[37] Neal's exaggerated masculinity rendered Karen's normative gender presentation sexually ambiguous. Neal was a foot taller than Kim Hunter, the actress who played Karen, and their contrasting gender styles reinforced the lesbian connotations of Karen's and Martha's mode of intimacy. Indeed, critics may have objected to Neal's "mannish" performance because it encoded Karen/Hunter as a femme. The revised version of the play never clarified Karen's feelings for Martha, but left the audience to wonder if their relationship were homosocial or lesbian.

In adapting the play for the screen almost a decade later, Wyler elaborated Hellman's revisions. In his adaptation, Martha's lesbianism cannot be ascribed to her participation in the female world of romantic friendships. Rather, it reflects a distinct identity or form of personhood that exists apart from female homosocial institutions and practices. Wyler followed Hellman's example by indicating Martha's lesbianism from the outset. Despite MacLaine's claim that he "chickened out," the director introduced several scenes that anticipate Martha's confession of her love for Karen at the end. Although these scenes do not masculinize her appearance, they call attention to a difference between her gender style and

Karen's that seems intended to mark Martha as lesbian. For example, in a scene at the beginning of the movie, as they wash dishes in the kitchen, Martha announces that the school has begun to turn a profit and that she thinks they should spend some of it on a new wardrobe for Karen. Unlike the dowdy Martha, who has always been a "skirt and blouse character," Karen has a glamorous appearance and deserves a more elegant wardrobe than her current shabby one: "You're Fifth Avenue, Rue de la Paix. You need to be kept up."[38] Karen dismisses the idea, but Martha persists, commenting dreamily: "I remember how you used to dress in college. The first time I ever saw you running across the quadrangle, your hair flying. I remember thinking, what a pretty girl." When she finishes speaking, the film dissolves to a close-up in which she looks off-camera wistfully while drying a glass, as if lost in her memories of Karen's attractiveness. In a sequence of scenes later in the film, Martha wears a white blouse and jumper that sexualizes these differences in her and Karen's gender styles; the outfit resembles the student uniform and thus suggests that Martha suffers from an arrested sexual development, that unlike the grown-up Karen, who is engaged, she has remained a girl psychologically.

Wyler also followed Hellman's example in refusing to clarify Karen's feelings for Martha. Indeed, from the beginning, the movie suggests that Karen's attachment to Martha has crossed the line between normative female homosocial bonding and lesbianism. In the revised version of the play Joe accepts Karen's commitment to the school and her friendship with Martha, and when Martha expresses her resentment of his engagement to Karen, he reassures her: "She'll still be with you here" (23). But in Wyler's adaptation Joe is as jealous of Martha as she is of him, and he thinks of her as the proverbial "third wheel" of his relationship with Karen. When he offers to take Karen for a ride in his car, she immediately asks Martha to come with them, but he wants to be alone with Karen and objects: "No, I'm too tired for two girls." After Karen explains that she and Martha had decided to go for a walk before he dropped by, he throws up his hands in frustration and exclaims, "Then go!" Nor does the Joe of the movie understand why he and Karen must delay their marriage, or why she wants to continue teaching at the school after they are married. During their drive in the car, Karen nestles against him and, imagining their life after marriage, remarks, "It will be nice to sit in our own room and read a book." Her vision of married life does not strike Joe as particularly sexy, and he replies incredulously, "Read a book?" Then imitating one of her students, he asks sarcastically, "Oh, Miss Wright, is that what you're going to be doing after you're married, reading books?" In this way, the movie renders problematic Karen's relation to the institutions of heterosexuality. Although Karen reminds Joe that she "couldn't leave Martha until the school was on its feet," in prolonging their engagement she refuses to accede to the dominant narrative of female sexual development. She does not want her relationship with Joe to displace her friendship with Martha.

Despite this shift in the construction of Karen's feelings for Martha, the movie (like the revised version of the play) contested Cold War homophobia by showing how the false accusation of lesbianism could destroy women's lives. In the movie, Mrs. Tilford (Fay Bainter) does not wholly believe Mary (Karen Balkin) when she accuses Karen and Martha of lesbianism, and she decides to confront the two teachers with the accusation. But when she arrives at the school, she first encounters Mrs. Mortar (Miriam Hopkins), who is still angry that she has been dismissed from the school. When Mrs. Tilford asks her about the argument she had with her niece, which Mary has falsely claimed to have overheard, Mrs. Mortar replies, "You would think that a healthy woman her age would have a husband, or at least an admirer. But she hasn't, and she never has had. Young men like her, yes, but not for long because she has no interest in them. Only the school and Karen Wright."[39] Although Mrs. Mortar never explicitly states that her niece is a lesbian or implicates Karen in any of her "fixations," Mrs. Tilford interprets her comments as confirmation of Mary's story and in the following scene warns her nephew not to marry Karen. Like Mrs. Mortar, she never explicitly accuses Karen of lesbianism, relying instead on innuendo. She reminds Joe that Karen "doesn't seem to be able to make up her mind" about marrying him. When he counters that she wants to wait until the school succeeds, Mrs. Tilford remarks insinuatingly, "And there was Miss Dobie." Finally, when Joe reveals that he and Karen have already set a date for the wedding, Mrs. Tilford insists that he must not go through with it because there is something "very wrong" with his fiancée. In this way, Mrs. Tilford magnifies the rumors and gossip that begin to circulate after Peggy and Evelyn overhear Martha's argument with her aunt and repeat it to Mary.

Several critics have noted how the lack of explicit references to lesbianism in the film reproduces one of the central tropes of homophobic discourse: lesbianism emerges as the "love that dare not speak its name."[40] But in relying on innuendo and euphemism, the movie highlighted the epistemological uncertainty that Cold War homophobia attributed to lesbianism. Because the accusation is spread through insinuation and rumor, Karen and Martha have no way to defend themselves. In the scene in which they confront Mrs. Tilford, the matriarch offers no proof to support the accusation except her granddaughter's story. When Joe discovers that his aunt has accused the teachers of lesbianism, his reaction indicates that she needs no other proof than Mary's story. At first he is furious with his aunt for spreading false rumors and asks if she is "sick." But when she refuses to back down, he begins to wonder if she has told the truth. The film shows him in close-up looking at Karen and Martha with a perplexed expression on his face before turning his back on them. Although he continues to side with Karen and Martha against his aunt, his doubt suggests that rumor and gossip are enough to label the two teachers lesbians. As women who have transgressed the bounds of normative femininity by choosing careers over marriage and motherhood, Karen and Martha are already suspect in their sexual identity; they do not ever have to have engaged in lesbian activity. Joe begins to believe that Mary's accusation explains why Karen has prolonged their engagement and wants to continue teaching at the school after they marry. In foregrounding Karen's and Martha's vulnerability, the film showed how the lesbian panic of the Cold War era worked to enforce normative femininity.

One scene in particular conveys the difficulty that Karen and Martha have in defending themselves against the rumors circulating about their relationship. In the scene, they implore Mr. Burton (William Mims), the father of one of their students, to tell them why he has decided to remove his daughter from the school. But all he will say is that they should speak to his wife: "It's not the kind of thing I like to talk about." In this scene, arguably the most powerful in the movie, Martha functions as a diegetic substitute for the viewer. When Mr. Burton leaves with his daughter, Karen runs after him demanding to know what he means. Martha remains behind in the foyer watching the two of them through the screen door. She appears in close-up leaning forward with a puzzled expression, as if straining to hear what they are saying, but they remain out of earshot. The film then cuts to a long shot of Karen and Mr. Burton, who turns away from his daughter in the car to prevent her from overhearing him. He speaks with his head down, as if embarrassed. The film dissolves to another close-up of Martha who looks even more puzzled than before. When Mr. Burton finally drives away in his car, Martha walks through the screen door and stares anxiously at Karen who turns to face her but does not speak. This scene highlights the unintelligibility of the Cold

War construction of the lesbian. Because it is shot wholly from Martha's point of view, we do not know what Mr. Burton has told Karen, only that it is something shameful. We do not learn what he has told her until the scene in which she and Martha confront Mrs. Tilford. But even then Karen speaks euphemistically, informing Joe that his aunt has spread the rumor that she and Martha are "lovers." Before this scene we can only infer that Karen and Martha have been accused of lesbianism. In stressing the indeterminacy of the category, the movie shows why the accusation of lesbianism was so powerful. Despite their feminine gender presentations, Karen and Martha have no way to refute the rumors circulating about them. Indeed, the sexual illegibility of their gender presentations only confirms Cold War sexual epistemology by illustrating the difficulty of correctly identifying lesbians.

Despite this representation of Karen's and Martha's persecution, the movie had a contradictory relationship to the Cold War construction of the lesbian. For even as it contested the homophobia of that era, the movie indirectly ratified the sexual epistemology underlying it. Whereas in both versions of the play Mary fabricates her lie from Martha's argument with her aunt, which Peggy and Evelyn overhear, in the movie she spies on the two teachers while they are in Martha's bedroom. In a scene not in either version of the play, an excited Karen runs upstairs to Martha's room, where Martha is ironing, to tell her the news that she and Joe have finally set a date for their wedding. But rather than feeling excited for Karen, Martha reproaches her bitterly. Karen appears in close-up looking affectionately at a graduation picture of her and Martha above Martha's dresser. Her pleasurable expression suggests that, despite her relationship with Joe, her feelings for Martha have not changed since college. But Martha violently interrupts her reverie by slamming her hands down on the ironing board and exclaiming: "I don't understand you. It's been so hard building this place up, and now that we're getting it on its feet you're ready to let it all go to hell!" She knocks the iron onto the floor, then, suddenly ashamed of her outburst, she apologizes. Karen tells her that she has already forgiven her, and as she opens the door to leave, Martha remarks contritely, "Karen, you know, don't you, I only want the best for you." Karen walks back into the room and kisses her tenderly on the cheek before picking up her coat and departing. This scene is punctuated by a series of close-ups of Mary, who, awakened by the noise of the falling iron, stands hiding in the hallway outside Martha's room eavesdropping on the two women. When Karen kisses Martha, the film dissolves to a close-up of the girl, who looks puzzled, as if she were struggling to understand the meaning of the two women's intimacy.

This scene undercuts the film's critique of the Cold War construction of the lesbian by positioning Mary as a stand-in for the spectator. The two women's intimacy emerges as a puzzle to be solved. Like the girl, we begin to wonder how to interpret Karen's and Martha's interactions. Does their intimacy transgress the boundary between female homosocial bonding and lesbianism? The unintelligibility of the two women's relationship surfaces more fully in a sequence of scenes following the trial. At one point Martha comforts a distraught Karen by placing her hand on her arm affectionately. Then, looking down self-consciously, she withdraws her hand before turning away awkwardly and crying. Her reaction suggests that in the wake of the trial the two women's intimacy has taken on a more explicit lesbian connotation, rendering it "vexed." In emphasizing the difficulty of determining the meaning of the two women's relationship, the movie positions the viewer as a subject of Cold War sexual epistemology; the viewer begins to scrutinize Karen's and Martha's interactions for any sign that might confirm or deny their desire for each other. The movie's treatment of Martha's confession of her desire for Karen further ratifies the Cold War construction of the lesbian. In both versions of the play, Martha's acknowledgment of her lesbianism attests to the porous boundary between female homosocial desire and lesbian identity. But in the film it serves a different function. Because of the scenes earlier in the film that hint at her desire for Karen, Martha's coming out underscores the difficulty of apprehending lesbianism as a form of identity. Although it is increasingly obvious to the viewer, Martha does not even recognize her own lesbianism until Mary's accusation forces her to scrutinize her feelings for Karen.

The film's refusal to clarify Karen's feelings for Martha further complicates its relationship to the Cold War construction of the lesbian. In both versions of the play Martha's confession shocks Karen, and she promises to forget it. But in the film, her reaction is more ambiguous and raises the possibility that she might return Martha's love. In contrast to both versions of the play, Mrs. Tilford informs Karen and Martha that Mary has confessed *before* Martha commits suicide, a textual revision that enables Karen to reaffirm her love for Martha. Rather than alleviating Martha's distress, Mrs. Tilford's offer to publish an apology in the local newspaper only compounds it. When Mrs. Tilford implores the two women to let her make amends for the scandal, Martha laughs hysterically before

FRIENDS OR LOVERS? SHIRLEY MACLAINE AND AUDREY
HEPBURN IN *THE CHILDREN'S HOUR*.

running upstairs to her room, for she has already revealed her desire for
Karen and can no longer face her. Eager to comfort Martha, Karen demands that Mrs. Tilford leave them alone and then follows her friend upstairs. Martha appears in medium shot sitting in an armchair and looking
out the window forlornly with a coat pulled over her. Karen announces,
"Martha, I'm going away some place to begin again. Will you come with
me? We can find work now." But Martha does not see how they can go
away together, and she puts Karen off by promising to discuss it later.
Shots of Karen looking at Martha lovingly are crosscut with shots of
Martha with her eyes closed, pretending to sleep so that Karen will leave
her alone. This scene further problematizes Karen's relationship to the
institutions of heterosexuality: not only does Karen's view of married
life contrasts markedly with Joe's—whereas he looks forward to a life of
romantic passion, she looks forward to a life of reading quietly by the
fire—but her reaction to Martha's confession reinforces the indeterminacy of her desire. Mrs. Tilford's news makes Karen think not about reuniting with Joe but about going away with Martha and starting over.

The final scene elaborates this construction of Karen's desire.[41] Although Joe still wants to marry Karen, the movie avoids the heterosexual

resolution of *These Three* and ends instead with Martha's funeral. The scene opens with Karen reading a passage from the Bible as she sits beside Martha's coffin in the cemetery. When she finishes the passage, she stands up and whispers, "Good-bye, Martha. I'll miss you with all my heart!" As she ushers a weeping Mrs. Mortar into a taxi, she looks wistfully in the direction of Martha's coffin, then walks out of the cemetery. The camera tracks her as she walks past Mrs. Tilford and a handful of other mourners. Joe stands apart, watching her from under a tree, but Karen ignores him, looking straight ahead as she walks past him. Shots of him watching her with a sad, forlorn expression are crosscut with shots of her walking out of the cemetery. A hint of a smile appears on her face, which suggests that she is happy to be leaving Joe behind. This scene, which recalls Martha's triumphant exit from Mrs. Tilford's house in *These Three*, seems intended to confirm Karen's claim earlier in the film that "other people aren't destroyed" by the accusation of lesbianism. Despite everything that has happened, Karen looks forward to starting over on her own and in a new town. Although this ending fails to resolve the movie's contradictory relationship to Cold War homophobia, it provides a more compelling representation of female desire than any of the other versions of *The Children's Hour*. Perhaps Karen fails to return Joe's look and continues walking past him because, like Martha, she realizes that she is a lesbian. At the same time, however, this ending indirectly ratified the Cold War discourse of female homosexuality. Because the movie never clarifies her love for Martha, Karen's sexuality remains a puzzle. Thus, even as the ending opens up the possibility of a more progressive narrative of female desire that does not culminate in marriage and motherhood, it confirms the indeterminacy of "the lesbian."

THE PERSISTENCE OF GENDER

Examining all four versions of *The Children's Hour* clarifies how Wyler's 1962 adaptation undercut the potential of Hellman's play to provide a powerful critique of Cold War homophobia. None of the earlier versions succeeded in constructing a coherent discourse of lesbianism. Even as the original version of the play contested the backlash against the New Woman, it validated the homophobic construction of women's romantic friendships. Martha's confession of her desire for Karen suggested that female homosocial institutions and practices promoted lesbianism. By contrast, *These Three* sought to reclaim female homosocial bonds by demonstrating their compatibility with heterosexual romance. But its heterosexualization of the play's plot inscribed lesbian panic and thus indirectly affirmed the homophobic construction of female homosocial desire. Hellman's 1952 revisions compounded these tensions and contradictions. In rendering Karen's and Martha's relationship more ambiguous, the playwright hoped to strengthen the play's political resonance, but in so doing she seemed to affirm Cold War sexual epistemology, for the revised play never clarifies Karen's love for Martha and thus reiterates the unintelligibility of lesbianism. In elaborating this shift in the construction of Karen's and Martha's relationship, Wyler further problematized the text's relationship to the Cold War construction of the lesbian. Karen's transformation from sexually "right" to potential lesbian inadvertently validated Cold War sexual paranoia. Despite her "Fifth Avenue" glamour, even Karen might be a lesbian. But Cold War homophobia never fully succeeded in prying apart object choice, gender identity, and sexual practice, and the older system of sexual classification continued to shape Hollywood cinema's representation of female sexuality. The feminine woman who made a lesbian object choice continued to be seen as less deviant than the masculine woman who did, and thus she could supposedly overcome her lesbianism. In reinscribing the association of lesbianism with female masculinity, Cold War homophobia repressed the femme's difference from the straight woman.

....

CHAPTER THREE

RECUPERATING FEMME FEMININITY

Marnie

The publicity campaign for Alfred Hitchcock's psychological thriller *Marnie* (1964), in which Tippi Hedren plays a compulsive thief who robs her employers after gaining their trust, misled moviegoers by promoting the film as a "suspenseful sex mystery."[1] Capitalizing on the director's reputation as the "master of suspense," posters for the movie assured moviegoers that "only Alfred Hitchcock could have created a woman so mysterious, so fascinating, so dangerous as Marnie." They also titillated moviegoers by proclaiming that despite her lying and cheating, the heroine was "more woman than any man could resist."[2] In positioning Marnie as a sexually manipulative femme fatale, these descriptions implied the movie was a film noir. But Hitchcock's heroine engages in none of the sexually transgressive behavior that located the femme fatale outside the law, as mandated by the Production Code. For despite her beauty and glamour, Marnie has no interest in men. Indeed, during her honeymoon, she informs her husband, Mark, who has blackmailed her into marrying him after he discovers that she has robbed his publishing company, that she cannot bear to be "handled" by men. Thus the movie's "sex mystery" turns out to be the alluring heroine's aversion to heterosexual intimacy, which the hero, Mark, must solve for the movie to achieve narrative closure. Determined to cure what he understands as a form of illness, Mark embarks on an investigation of his wife's hatred of men. He reads abstruse scientific textbooks with titles like *Sexual Aberrations of the Criminal Female* and hires a private detective to investigate her childhood in Baltimore. To heighten the "mystery" of Marnie's sexuality, Hitchcock cast Sean Connery as Mark. Connery's previous film, *From Russia with Love* (Terrence Young, 1963), in which he played the British secret agent and infamous lady-killer James Bond, had established him as Hollywood's newest heartthrob, yet Marnie seemed totally immune to his sex appeal.[3]

Marnie reflects the persistence of a model of lesbian identity that privileged gender identity over object choice. By treating her aversion to heterosexual intimacy as a "mystery," Hitchcock's film attempted to foreclose the possibility of a lesbian reading of Marnie's desire. Instead, it concocts a traumatic childhood experience to explain her perverse sexuality. Mark eventually discovers that when Marnie was a girl, her mother, Bernice (Louise Latham), who supported them by working as a prostitute, was acquitted of murdering one of her johns, a sailor (Bruce Dern). During the trial, Bernice testified that she struck the sailor with a fire poker when he assaulted her. Because the assault permanently disabled her, the jury believed her story. But a flashback in the movie's final scene reveals that it was Marnie who killed the sailor, when he began striking her mother. Marnie's repression of the memory, which Bernice has taken as a "sign of God's forgiveness," supposedly explains her compulsive stealing, which has enabled her to exact retribution for her traumatic experience by punishing her male employers. After she relives the memory, Mark, whose reading has apparently transformed him into an expert on female sexuality, assures her that "when a child, a child of any age, Marnie, can't get love, it takes what it can get, anyway it can get it. It's not hard to understand." Marnie's recovered memory of the murder supposedly cures her, and she decides to turn herself in to the police. She also informs Mark, as they leave her mother's house, that she would rather live with him than go to prison, thereby registering a shift in her feelings about him that seems intended to show that she has overcome her aversion to heterosexual intimacy. This treatment of Marnie's desire reproduces an older discourse of sexuality in which gender identity, object choice, and sexual practice line up neatly. According to this discourse, Marnie's sex appeal ("more woman than any man can resist") renders impossible a lesbian construction of her hatred of men. Mark can reclaim her for the institutions of heterosexuality by enabling her to relive her childhood trauma, which has prevented her from developing "normally."

At the same time, however, that the movie heterosexualizes Marnie's desire, it attributes to her many of the signifiers deployed by Hollywood cinema to encode female characters as lesbian. The movie's treatment of Marnie's desire recalls the psychoanalytic model of female sexuality that informed the *Newsweek* editor Jess Stearn's exposé of the lesbian's "secret world."[4] Marnie resembles the beautiful and glamorous women interviewed by Stearn who supposedly ascribed their lesbianism to a traumatic childhood experience involving rape or incest. Likewise, Mark recalls the men who developed a "sex obsession" with the femme, who saw her lesbianism as a challenge to their virility, and who wanted to "convert" her to heterosexuality by having sex with her.[5] The intensity of Marnie's attachment to Bernice further encodes her as a lesbian. Though a grown woman, Marnie remains fixated on her mother, which suggests that she suffers from an arrested sexual development. She resents her mother's relationship with Jesse (Kimberly Beck), a girl Bernice babysits during the day, and childishly competes with her for Bernice's attention. By bringing furs and flowers when she returns home after robbing her employers, Marnie also acts more like Bernice's lover than her daughter. Moreover, as Lucretia Knapp has pointed out, Marnie's stealing, which enables her to exist outside patriarchal social and economic arrangements, marks her desire as criminal.[6] Finally, the movie's representation of Marnie incorporates elements of the Cold War construction of the lesbian. Marnie's femininity emerges as a performance designed to conceal her identity as an outlaw; her gender presentation enables her to deceive her employers, who never suspect that she is a compulsive thief. The movie's deployment of these signifiers opens up another possible construction of Marnie's desire, one that Mark's recovery of her traumatic childhood experience never fully displaces. For Mark's attempt to explain Marnie's aversion to heterosexual intimacy in terms of repression overlooks the patriarchal social and economic arrangements that both Marnie and her mother struggle to escape.

Before elaborating this alternative construction of Marnie's desire, I want to examine an earlier film of Hitchcock's, *Rebecca* (1940), which like *Marnie* focuses on the construction of female subjectivity in relation to patriarchal social and economic conditions. In *Rebecca*, which was based on Daphne du Maurier's bestselling novel of the same name, Joan Fontaine plays a young and inexperienced bride who is haunted by the memory of her husband's sexually alluring first wife, Rebecca. When Fontaine's character, who remains nameless in both the novel and the movie, arrives at Manderley, the ancestral home of her husband, Maxim (Laurence Olivier), she becomes obsessed with her predecessor, who supposedly drowned while sailing in a storm, and embarks on an investigation of her sexuality. She encounters the dead woman's ghostly presence everywhere in the house. Her stationery and address book remain on the desk in the morning room, and the servants continue to set the dining-room table with her monogrammed dinner napkins, as if she were still their mistress. Moreover, Fontaine believes that Maxim still loves his former wife, which prevents her from assuming her rightful place as Manderley's new mistress. But Fontaine's obsession with the dead woman mirrors that of Mrs. Danvers (Judith Anderson), Manderley's sinister housekeeper, who is coded as a lesbian, and not that of her husband.[7] When divers discover Rebecca's body in her sunken sailboat, Maxim reveals that in fact he detested the woman, though she was widely admired. By contrast, Mrs. Danvers has carefully preserved Rebecca's bedroom as a kind of monument to her love for her. Fontaine's obsession with her predecessor thus locates her outside patriarchal law, which requires her to bring her desire into alignment with that of her husband. But like *Marnie*, *Rebecca* opened up an alternative reading of the heroine's problematic relation to heteronormative institutions and discourses. Despite its affirmation of heterosexual love, *Rebecca* acknowledges the potential of female homosocial bonds to destabilize the patriarchal order, as revealed by the tensions and contradictions in its exploration of perverse female desire. Its treatment of its heroine manifests a similar ambivalence about the patriarchal discourse of female sexuality, for, like *Rebecca*, *Marnie* both affirms and contests the containment of female desire by the institutions of heterosexuality.

LESBIAN PANIC IN *REBECCA*

Scholars often cite *Rebecca* as a classic example of the female gothic, a cycle of enormously popular women's pictures that represented heterosexuality as an institution of terror for the heroine.[8] In these films, the heroine usually discovers after a whirlwind romance and marriage that recalls the story of Cinderella that the man she has married harbors a dark secret and has been plotting to murder her. But there is a crucial difference between *Rebecca* and the other movies in the cycle—the character who persecutes Fontaine is not her husband but another woman, the formidable Mrs. Danvers. Because of her bond with her former mistress, who treated her as her confidante, Mrs. Danvers refuses to accept Fontaine as her new mistress and constantly sabotages her attempts to assume her identity as the new Mrs. de Winter. Reinforcing Fontaine's fear that she lacks the sophistication and elegance that Maxim needs in a wife, Mrs. Danvers constantly reminds her of her inadequacies in relation to normative femininity. As a result of this persecution, Manderley emerges as an uncanny domestic space in which Fontaine can never feel at home as Maxim's wife. In one early scene, when she answers the phone in the morning room, she informs the caller, "Mrs. de Winter has been dead now for over a year," and hangs up before realizing that the caller wanted to speak to her, not to her predecessor. Fontaine eventually asserts her identity as Manderley's mistress by ordering Mrs. Danvers to remove Rebecca's stationery and other belongings from the morning room. But Mrs. Danvers thwarts Fontaine's attempt to redefine their relationship by persuading her to attend Manderley's annual costume ball wearing a replica of a gown depicted in an ancestral portrait. Fontaine thinks that her choice of costume will prove to Maxim that she has finally adapted to her new role as his wife, but the choice only provides further evidence that she lacks the qualities necessary for carrying out her responsibilities as Manderley's mistress. As she discovers too late, Rebecca had worn the same costume to the ball the year before, so when Fontaine appears in it, Maxim assumes that she has chosen it to torment him and, enraged, orders her to take it off. Fontaine continues to occupy a subordinate position in relation to Mrs. Danvers, until the housekeeper sets Manderley on fire, in the film's famous final scene, and dies when the ceiling of her former mistress's bedroom collapses on her.

This variation of the female gothic implicates Hitchcock's movie in the backlash against the female world of romantic friendships, which informed the two earliest versions of *The Children's Hour*.[9] But whereas *These Three* sought to reclaim female homosocial bonds, *Rebecca* stigmatized them by associating them with lesbianism.[10] Fontaine's sexual paranoia is triggered not by her relationship with her husband, but by Mrs. Danvers's attachment to her former mistress.[11] At Manderley, she enters a world where the distinction between female homosocial bonding and lesbian desire has collapsed. The film treats Mrs. Danvers's bond with Rebecca as a perversion of women's romantic friendships, one that both repels and fascinates Fontaine. When producer David O. Selznick submitted the movie's script to the Production Code Administration for approval, Joseph Breen warned him that "it will be essential that there is no suggestion whatever of a perverted relationship between Mrs. Danvers and Rebecca."[12] Breen mentioned in particular the scene where Mrs. Danvers shepherds Fontaine through Rebecca's bedroom and suggestively handles the dead woman's garments, including her diaphanous nightgown, which the housekeeper keeps on the bed in a satin cover that she has embroidered with Rebecca's initials. Although it reinforced the lesbian connotations of the housekeeper's love for her former mistress, the scene remained in the movie, only slightly altered to accommodate Breen's objections.

The film's treatment of Rebecca's unruly sexuality further associates female homosocial bonding with lesbianism. As Rhona Berenstein has argued, in the scene in which Maxim reveals his hatred of Rebecca, he describes his former wife in terms that code her as a lesbian.[13] He thrills Fontaine by divulging that unlike other women Rebecca was "incapable of love or tenderness or decency" and that she shocked him during their honeymoon by confessing "things I'll never tell a living soul." Maxim's refusal to repeat these "things," even to Fontaine, his new wife, reiterates one of the most enduring constructions of lesbianism, that it is the love that dare not speak its name.[14] Moreover, although Selznick removed dialogue indicating that Rebecca "despised all men" because it violated the Production Code by referring to her lesbianism, in the movie Mrs. Danvers insists that "love was a game" to her former mistress and that she "used to sit on her bed and rock with laughter at the lot of you," including her cousin Favell (George Sanders), with whom she was having an affair.[15] In other words, Rebecca revealed her true self only to her loyal housekeeper, in whom she confided her contempt of men.

In coding Rebecca as a lesbian, the film ratified the homophobic construction of female homosocial bonds. Rebecca's sexual nonconformity disrupts patriarchal social relations. Maxim occupies a subordinate position in relation to his wife. Her refusal to conform to heteronormative expectations prevents him from exercising his prerogatives as a husband. Rebecca knows that he will sacrifice "everything" to protect the "family honor," and when on their honeymoon she confesses her illicit past, she makes a bargain with him. If Maxim agrees not to divorce her, she will play the part of the "devoted wife" and convince his family and friends that they are the "luckiest, happiest couple in the country." Afraid of a scandal, Maxim accepts her "dirty bargain," but in so doing cedes control of Manderley to her, which allows her to transform it into a space dominated by perverse female desire. Although Rebecca fulfills her promise to turn the estate into "the most famous showplace in England," she takes a flat in London so she can lead a double life, apart from Maxim. Growing careless, she begins to entertain her lovers in the boathouse at Manderley and to taunt Maxim with her sexual infidelities. But Maxim resists asserting his authority as her husband until she suggests that she is pregnant with another man's baby. Losing his temper, he strikes her, which causes her to fall and hit her head on a piece of ship's tackle. But even as he engages in this display of male dominance, he remains subordinate to his wife, for she has learned that she is dying from cancer and has deliberately provoked him into striking her because she wants him to kill her. Nor does Rebecca's death restore patriarchal law to Manderley. Her bond with Mrs. Danvers insures that despite her death, Rebecca's perverse desire continues to dominate Maxim's world. Thus, despite his marriage to the more compliant Fontaine, who never challenges his authority as her husband, Maxim fails to reclaim Manderley for the institutions of heterosexuality.

Rebecca's disruption of patriarchal social arrangements underlies Maxim's attraction to Fontaine. Although, unlike Rebecca, she lacks the three qualities every man supposedly desires in a wife—"breeding, beauty, and brains"—Fontaine does not challenge his manhood, but allows him to dominate her. When Maxim first meets her in Monte Carlo, where she has traveled as the paid companion of a vulgar and domineering American woman, Mrs. Van Hopper (Florence Bates), he is drawn to her lack of worldliness. Attesting to her modesty, Fontaine is embarrassed by her employer, a social climber who pretends to know Maxim better than she does. Mrs. Van Hopper constantly corrects Fontaine's faults, and when she becomes downcast, the older woman chides her harshly: "Oh, come, don't sulk. After all I am responsible for your behavior." Maxim takes on a similar role in relation to the childlike Fontaine. For example, in one scene, he tells her not to bite her nails, as if he were her father. But Maxim's domination of Fontaine emerges as more acceptable than Mrs. Van Hopper's. Fontaine's relationship with her employer provides another example of the dangers of female homosocial bonding. Mrs. Van Hopper has bought Fontaine's companionship, which allows her undue influence over the young and inexperienced woman. Thus, in marrying her, Maxim rescues Fontaine from a female homosocial bond that threatens to corrupt her. Moreover, their marriage promises to restore Maxim's manhood. Shortly after arriving at Manderley, Fontaine confides in Frank Crawley (Reginald Denny), who manages the estate, that she feels inadequate as Maxim's wife and that she wishes she were more like Rebecca. But he assures her without revealing the truth about her predecessor that she will make a better wife for Maxim than the beautiful and accomplished Rebecca ever did: "You have kindliness, sincerity, and if you forgive me, modesty, which mean more to a husband than all the wit and beauty in the world." Despite the differences between her and Rebecca, however, Fontaine's attempts to remake herself in the dead woman's image suggest that she is not as compliant as Maxim assumes, for those attempts violate the patriarchal injunction that she make her desire conform to his.

In an influential reading of the movie, Tania Modleski argues that Fontaine's relationship with Maxim stages a female Oedipal scenario.[16] According to Modleski, Fontaine must displace the older and more worldly Rebecca as a rival for Maxim's love, and she struggles to transform herself into a suitable object-to-be-looked-at, one that transfixes Maxim. Maxim's and Fontaine's formation as a couple supposedly cannot proceed until Fontaine succeeds in turning Maxim's gaze away from the dead woman who continues to obsess him. Thus Fontaine begins to model herself on her more sophisticated predecessor.[17] Although Maxim's paternal role in relation to Fontaine suggests that her attraction to him reflects an unresolved Oedipal conflict, Modleski's reading dehistoricizes the movie's interrogation of female subjectivity by ignoring its relationship to the backlash against female homosocial bonding. For Fontaine's formation as a subject of desire validates the homophobic construction of the female world of love and ritual that circulated in American society in the 1930s. Fontaine refuses to believe Crawley when he assures her that Maxim does not want a wife more in "tune" with Manderley, and she remains fixated on her predecessor. Before leaving Crawley's office, Fontaine pleads with him, "Tell me what Rebecca was really like," which indicates that his remarks about the dead woman have only compounded Fontaine's obsession with her. Moreover, Maxim's revelation that he detested Rebecca makes clear that he does not view his new wife as an inferior object of desire, but positioning her predecessor as a rival for her husband's love allows Fontaine to explore a form of desire rendered taboo by the homophobic deployment of the category of the lesbian. Her belief that she must displace Rebecca licenses her investigation into the dead woman's transgressive sexuality. In other words, it is Fontaine's attachment to Rebecca, not Maxim's, that hinders their formation as a couple.

The sequence immediately following Fontaine's opening voice-over suggests that Fontaine accomplishes the Oedipal task that Modleski assigns to her the first time Maxim encounters her. The sequence opens with the camera panning the sea as it crashes onto the shore, then moves up the side of a cliff to reveal Maxim standing perilously close to the edge. The film dissolves to a close-up of Maxim who peers intensely at the surf below. He takes a step forward, as if to plunge into the sea, but Fontaine shouts offscreen, "No, stop!" As Maxim turns to look at her, the film cuts to a medium shot of Fontaine who stands nearby on a path watching him anxiously. This sequence establishes Fontaine's ability to restore Maxim's manhood by enabling him to escape Rebecca's power. As several critics have pointed out, the movie repeatedly associates Rebecca's illicit sexuality with the sea. Thus Maxim's fixation with the sea in this sequence suggests that despite her death, Rebecca continues to dominate him. To free himself from her control, he almost plunges to his death. But Fontaine's appearance redirects his gaze. Angered by her intrusion, he barks at Fontaine, "What the devil are you shouting about?" But when he notices her meek and unassuming demeanor, he moderates his tone and tells her to "get on" with her walk. As she leaves, the film dissolves to a close-up of him watching her. He then turns to look at the sea, his expression indicating that he cannot believe that he almost jumped from the precipice. He turns again to look in the direction of the departing Fontaine. In other words, despite her inadequacies as an object-to-be-looked-at, Fontaine has already succeeded in displacing Rebecca as the focus of Maxim's gaze. Fontaine's refusal to acknowledge that she has already accomplished her Oedipal task enables her to disguise her socially proscribed desire as a rivalry with another woman.

Instead of staging a female Oedipal scenario, Fontaine's obsession with her predecessor demonstrates the incompatibility of female homosocial desire and heterosexual romance. Mrs. Danvers constantly channels Fontaine's desire toward Rebecca. She has preserved the morning room exactly as her former mistress left it, and when Fontaine enters the room shortly after arriving at Manderley she finds the dead woman's address book, monogrammed stationery, and correspondence on the writing table. Fontaine's actions in this sequence suggest that she has no desire to displace Rebecca. Mrs. Danvers's preservation of the room shows her determination to prevent Fontaine from assuming control of Manderley as its new mistress. But instead of angering Fontaine, Rebecca's belongings arouse her curiosity, and she begins to examine them for clues to Rebecca's life at Manderley. Mrs. Danvers startles her by appearing suddenly in the doorway and asking her what she would like her to serve for lunch. Instead of asserting her identity as her new mistress, Fontaine cowers in her chair and replies incoherently. When the housekeeper departs, Fontaine recommences her examination of her predecessor's belongings. As she picks up Rebecca's address book, she knocks over an antique porcelain cupid, one of Manderley's "treasures," which falls to the floor and shatters into several pieces. This sequence captures the threat that Fontaine's obsession with Rebecca poses to her relationship with Maxim. The dead woman has begun to displace Maxim as the object of Fontaine's desire. Fontaine's reaction to the broken cupid indicates that she recognizes this threat. She looks around guiltily as she picks up the pieces, which she stuffs into the back of a drawer in the writing table and covers over with some of Rebecca's stationery so that nobody will find them.

Fontaine's illicit desire for Rebecca surfaces more fully in the scene in which she explores Rebecca's bedroom, which, like the morning room, Mrs. Danvers has preserved exactly as the dead woman left it. Fontaine seems ashamed of her desire to visit the bedroom. When she notices a photograph of her husband on Rebecca's dressing table, Fontaine looks startled and turns away, as if it had rebuked her for entering the room. Moreover, when Mrs. Danvers discovers her there, Fontaine claims that she entered the room to shut a window, which the housekeeper knows is a lie. Fontaine's behavior suggests that she experiences her desire to see the room as illicit. In exploring the room, Fontaine engages in a forbidden activity, which makes her feel depraved like Mrs. Danvers. As the housekeeper proudly shows her Rebecca's wardrobe, Fontaine is simultaneously fascinated and repulsed by her attachment to her former mistress. When Mrs. Danvers demonstrates how she used to brush Rebecca's hair as she sat at the dressing table, the camera tracks in on Maxim's photograph. Maxim seems to look out at his new wife reproachfully, as if her participation in the reenactment violated their relationship. Fontaine's encounter with the demented Mrs. Danvers causes her to assert her identity as Maxim's wife. She realizes that her obsession with Rebecca mirrors that of the housekeeper, and she experiences lesbian panic. She returns to the morning room and orders Mrs. Danvers to remove Rebecca's belongings. When the housekeeper protests, "These were Mrs. de Winter's things," Fontaine reminds her, "I am Mrs. de Winter now."[18]

In emphasizing the porous boundary between female homosocial desire and lesbian identity, *Rebecca* ratified the homophobic construction of women's romantic friendships. Mrs. Danvers emerges as the stereotypical predatory lesbian, who has the power to corrupt "normal" women. As several critics have noted, Mrs. Danvers seems to induce in the sexually inexperienced Fontaine a trance-like state in which she compulsively acts out the older woman's obsession with her former mistress.[19] By attributing this power to Mrs. Danvers, the movie limits

JOAN FONTAINE TRAPPED BY THE PREDATORY LESBIAN
JUDITH ANDERSON IN *REBECCA*.

the implications of Fontaine's character in its staging of perverse female desire. Maxim can supposedly reclaim Fontaine for the institutions of heterosexuality because unlike her persecutor she has a normative gender identity. Yet despite Fontaine's panicked assertion of her heterosexuality following the encounter in Rebecca's bedroom, Mrs. Danvers retains her hypnotic power over her. When she realizes that the housekeeper has manipulated her into wearing the same costume as Rebecca to the ball, Fontaine confronts her. But Mrs. Danvers refuses to express remorse for humiliating her: "I watched you go down, just as I watched her a year ago. Even in the same dress, you couldn't compare." When Fontaine collapses onto Rebecca's bed in tears, Mrs. Danvers opens a window, one assumes, to give her fresh air. But as Fontaine leans against the windowsill, she whispers: "Maxim doesn't need you. He's got his memories. He doesn't love you. He wants to be alone with her." With these words, the housekeeper projects her own desire onto Maxim. She then encourages Fontaine to jump from the window: "You have nothing to live for really, have you?" She almost succeeds with her plan, but a distress signal from a boat that has run aground near the estate breaks the spell she has cast over Fontaine, who cries, "Maxim, Maxim!" when she notices him running toward the beach. This sequence seems intended to mark Fontaine's incorporation into the institutions of heterosexuality. Her glimpse of Maxim enables her to escape Mrs. Danvers's power by reminding her of their marriage.

At the same time, however, Fontaine's opening voice-over allows for a more complicated reading of her desire, one that exceeds the movie's ratification of the homophobic construction of female homosocial bonding.[20] *Rebecca* ends with Maxim and Fontaine watching Mrs. Danvers as she dies, consumed by flames. She has set Manderley on fire after learning that the investigation into her former mistress's death has exonerated Maxim. Fontaine explains, "Mrs. Danvers, she's gone mad. She said she would rather destroy Manderley than see us happy here." With the fire, all of the obstacles that have hindered Maxim and Fontaine's formation as a couple have been eliminated. In the final shot, the camera tracks in on Rebecca's bed as it goes up in flames. Thus the couple can now fulfill the promise of their romance by living happily ever after. Yet in her voice-over, which frames the movie, Fontaine recalls how she frequently returns to Manderley in her dreams. In these dreams, she thinks she sees light coming from Manderley's windows as she walks along the drive, but then she realizes that the moon has played a "trick" on her and that the house, destroyed by the fire, remains a "desolate shell." These recurring dreams suggest that the predatory Mrs. Danvers's power over Fontaine does not fully explain her implication in the movie's interrogation of lesbian desire. In setting Manderley on fire, Mrs. Danvers insures that it remains a site of perverse female desire and pleasure. When Favell calls Mrs. Danvers from London to tell her the outcome of the investigation, he remarks bitterly, "Now Maxim and that dear little bride of his will be able to stay on at Manderley and live happily ever after." But the fire prevents Maxim and Fontaine from settling at Manderley and heterosexualizing it. Thus Fontaine's constant return to Manderley in her dreams reflects the inability of her marriage to Maxim to contain her desire. Indeed, despite her love for him, she remains obsessed with her predecessor.

LESBIAN DESIRE IN *MARNIE*

Hitchcock's interrogation of female subjectivity in *Marnie* reflected a significant shift in the representation of perverse female desire in Hollywood cinema.[21] Although like *Rebecca*, *Marnie* emphasizes the potential of female homosocial bonds to destabilize the institutions of heterosexuality by promoting lesbianism, it ascribes the heroine's aversion to hetero-sexual intimacy to an "abnormal" attachment to her mother. As E. Ann Kaplan has shown, after the Second World War treatment of mother-daughter relationships in Hollywood cinema increasingly incorporated a psychoanalytically inflected discourse of female sexuality.[22] This dis-course, which reflected "momist" anxieties about women's dominance of the domestic sphere, attributed lesbianism to an aversion to men, which the lesbian had supposedly inherited from her mother.[23] The movie's rep-resentation of Bernice's influence on her daughter reproduces this dis-course. Bernice resembles the man-hating mothers excoriated by Strecker and Lathbury in their momist diatribe about the nation's moral decline, *Their Mothers' Daughters*.[24] Bernice constantly warns her daughter that "men and a good name don't go together," and thereby insures that Mar-nie develops a pathological relationship to the institutions of hetero-sexuality. But Hitchcock's deployment of a psychoanalytic discourse of mother-daughter relationships in *Marnie* leads to a contradiction in his exploration of perverse female desire. Although Marnie's normative gen-der identity supposedly renders her lack of heterosexual desire a mystery, which Mark solves by investigating her childhood, the intensity of her at-tachment to Bernice licenses a lesbian reading of her identity.[25] As Patri-cia White has shown, mother-daughter relationships in classical Holly-wood cinema often provided a cover for lesbianism by allowing two adult female characters to legitimately express passion for each other.[26] Thus, like *Rebecca*, *Marnie* never wholly succeeds in aligning its heroine's desire with the normative construction of female sexuality. Despite her gender presentation, Marnie's relationship with her mother can be interpreted to mean that she has made a lesbian object choice.

Hitchcock conveys Bernice's responsibility for her daughter's "abnor-mal" development in the opening scenes. Bernice has detached mother-hood from the institutions of heterosexuality by raising Marnie on her own, and Hitchcock treats her creation of a purely female domestic space as a perversion of her maternal role. The movie cuts from a sequence of shots in which Marnie rides her beloved horse, Forio, with a happy, care-free expression to a sequence of shots in which she arrives at her mother's row house in Baltimore shortly after a rainstorm. The abruptness of the cut translates into visual terms the injurious effect her relationship with her mother has on Marnie. In marked contrast to the lush, bright setting of the previous sequence, her mother's street appears dreary and ominous. A Navy destroyer looms up in the harbor in the background. Marnie's excitement about returning home is immediately undercut when instead of her mother, the neighbor girl Jessie answers the door: "Oh, it's you!" Perversely, Bernice withholds maternal love from Marnie while showering it on Jessie. Indeed, Bernice interacts with the girl as if she were her mother, underscoring her lack of a maternal bond with her biological daughter. When Marnie places her head in her mother's lap, Bernice shifts uncomfortably in her chair and remonstrates, "Marnie, mind my leg!" But when Jessie appears with a hairbrush, Bernice allows her to sit on her lap while she lovingly brushes her hair. Marnie appears in close-up looking at them with an icy, resentful stare. As this scene indicates, Bernice has allowed Jessie to displace Marnie. Indeed, Bernice wants to recreate the domestic arrangements of Marnie's childhood, but without Marnie. In the following scene, as she and Marnie make a pecan pie in the kitchen, Bernice reveals that she has decided to ask Jessie and her mother to move in with her. Like Bernice when Marnie was a child, Jessie's mother is a "decent, hardworking woman with a little kid to raise." When Marnie reacts jealously to the news, Bernice coldly reprimands her: "Now, Marnie, you oughten to let yourself act jealous of a little ole kid like that!"

Bernice's perversity as a mother transforms domestic space into a site of terror for her daughter. In her mother's house, Marnie often experiences familiar, everyday objects as strange and terrifying. Marnie's symptoms first surface during her visit to her mother. As she begins to embrace Bernice, she notices some red gladiolas in a vase on top of the television and freezes. The film cuts to a close-up in which she stares blankly in the direction of the flowers while the color red suffuses the screen.[27] Marnie's flashback in the final scene reveals that she unconsciously associates the color red with the murdered sailor. Thus this shot serves to indicate that her return home has triggered a memory of the murder. But her reaction to the flowers also manifests her anger at her mother for perverting their relationship. Unable to acknowledge this anger, she represses it by displacing it onto the flowers, which allows her to refrain from embracing her mother. Marnie's memory of the murder threatens to surface again later in the sequence. While taking a nap, she has a nightmare about her childhood in which she is awakened by some knocking. Her mother then asks her to get out of bed, but she is cold and begins to cry. Marnie awakes to find Bernice standing in the doorway of her room trying to wake her for dinner. She begins to tell her mother about the nightmare, which recurs throughout the movie, but Bernice turns and descends the stairs, casting a shadow on the wall behind her, oblivious to her daughter's agitation. The camera remains fixed on her until she disappears from the screen, and we see nothing but her shadow. Reinforcing the scene's eeriness, the tapping of Bernice's cane on the stairs is the only sound we hear as her image fades from the screen. This series of scenes highlights the pernicious influence that Bernice has had on her daughter's psychological development. Marnie's relationship with her mother has made her "sick," and she misrecognizes her mother's rejection as a sign of her inadequacy as an object of desire.

The film traces Marnie's arrested sexual development to this misrecognition. Marnie has imbibed Bernice's hatred of men and uncritically accepted her desire to detach motherhood from the institutions of heterosexuality. When she gives Bernice a mink stole, she assures her, as she arranges it on her shoulders, "We don't need men, Mama. We can do very well ourselves, you and me." Despite her beauty and glamour, Marnie has no desire to function as an object-to-be-looked-at for men. Before she applies for a job at Mark's publishing company, she dyes her hair a dull reddish brown and dresses conservatively in a taupe skirt and jacket. But despite her prim appearance, Mark is transfixed by her as he walks through the office. The intensity of his stare makes her uncomfortable, and shifting in her seat, she pulls her skirt down over her knees. Her behavior in this scene recalls the description offered by one of her former employers, Sidney Strutt (Martin Gable), who after discovering that she has robbed his company, complains that she always pulled her skirt down over her knees "as though they were a national treasure." But at the same time that she moderates her appearance to discourage men from looking at her, she embellishes it to attract her mother's attention. Her outfit during her visit to Bernice contrasts sharply with the one she wears in the following scene during her interview at the publishing company. Bernice notices that Marnie has lightened her hair and warns her that "too blond hair always looks like a woman is trying to attract a man." But Marnie has devised her glamorous look for her mother and replies dejectedly, "Don't you like it?" In this scene, she wears an emerald green silk skirt and jacket, which sets off her new hair color. But even as she seeks to gain her mother's approval as a model of femininity, she takes on a masculinizing role in relation to her mother. When Marnie gives her the stole, Bernice remarks wistfully, "No man ever gave me anything so good!," which suggests that her daughter has provided for her better than any man ever has.

In emphasizing the perversity of her relationship with her mother, the movie identifies Marnie as a lesbian. Bernice's domestic arrangements have supposedly arrested her daughter's sexual development by preventing her from negotiating the Oedipus complex successfully. Without a father, Marnie cannot transfer her desire from her mother to an object supposedly more appropriate: a man. The scene in which Marnie begins working as a secretary at Mark's publishing company elaborates this construction of her identity. The camera tracks in on Marnie, who sits at her desk typing, and rotates until it faces her. As she types, Marnie stares intensely at Susan (Mariette Hartley), one of the other secretaries at the company, who places some documents in a safe in an adjoining office. The camera then pans up to reveal Mark standing behind a glass partition staring intensely at Marnie, who does not know that he is there. This mirroring sexualizes Marnie's look. Just as Mark desires Marnie, Marnie desires Susan. But unable to accept her "abnormal" desire for the other woman, Marnie represses it by displacing it onto the safe.[28] She stares not at Susan, but at the safe, which she intends to rob. This displacement enables Marnie to conceal her lesbianism from herself. She assumes that she occupies a position outside the law because of her compulsive stealing, not because of an illicit desire for other women. Reinforcing this construction of her sexuality, Marnie constantly changes her look to disguise her identity. She deceives her employers by projecting a "finishing-school persona," which enables her to gain their trust before robbing them. In this respect, the movie's treatment of Marnie's sexuality draws on the Cold War construction of the lesbian. Marnie's gender style camouflages her problematic relation to the law and enables her to pass as a "normal" woman.

Despite her coded identity as a lesbian, the movie eventually reclaims Marnie for the institutions of heterosexuality. Mark's investigation into the "mystery" of her sexuality enables him to reorient her desire by allowing him to act as her analyst. Mark never considers the possibility that Marnie's aversion to men may indicate that she has made a lesbian object choice. Although she insists that she has never fallen in love with a man, Mark refuses to believe her: "There must have been a great many men interested in you." But he has misunderstood her, and indirectly admitting her lesbianism, she corrects him: "I didn't say men weren't interested in me. I said I wasn't interested in them." Mark assumes that because men desire her, Marnie must be "normal." Thus he does not understand her panic when he attempts to have sex with her on their honeymoon, and she reveals that she cannot bear to have men "handle" her. He thinks that she must have experienced a trauma as a child and asks, "Why? What hap-

TIPPI HEDREN TRAPPED BY THE PREDATORY HETEROSEXUAL
SEAN CONNERY IN *MARNIE*.

pened to you?" He also asks if she has discussed her aversion to heterosexual intimacy with a psychiatrist. Convinced that he can normalize her
desire, he sets out to "cure" her. But Marnie does not see her lack of desire
for Mark as a symptom—"Oh, men! You say no thanks to one of them
and, bingo, you're a candidate for the funny farm!"—and she implores
him to leave her alone. But Mark turns out to know more about her sexuality than she does. The movie's climactic scene confirms his belief that
a traumatic childhood experience has caused her sexual "aberration." In
reliving the murder of the sailor, Marnie supposedly transfers her desire
from her mother to Mark and thus overcomes her lesbianism. In this respect, the movie's exploration of perverse female desire reflects the persistence of the older model of sexuality. Marnie's incorporation into the
institutions of heterosexuality in the final scene suggests that her recovery
of her memory of the murder has enabled her to bring her sexual desire
into alignment with her gender identity.

At the same time, however, the construction of Marnie's subjectivity also reflects the consolidation of the new system of sexual classification.[29] Despite her assimilation to patriarchal law, Marnie's recovered memory does not fully explain the perversity of her desire. Reliving the trauma that supposedly arrested her sexual development does not enable her to normalize her relationship with her mother. In the final scene, Bernice reveals that after the murder she refused to give Marnie up for adoption, which makes Marnie realize that she has always loved her: "You must have loved me, Mama, you must have loved me!" But Bernice's revelation does not resolve the perversity of their relationship. When Marnie lays her head on Bernice's lap, Bernice reaches out to touch her hair, but suddenly stops, still unable to show her daughter affection. Instead, she peevishly enjoins her, "Get up, Marnie, you're achin' my leg." Bernice's behavior not only recalls the earlier scene in which she warns Marnie to "mind" her leg when she lovingly places her head in her lap. But her words ("Get up, Marnie") eerily echo Marnie's recurring nightmare, in which her mother attempts to rouse her from bed ("Get up, Marnie, get up!"). Moreover, as several critics have pointed out, the heterosexualization of Marnie's desire in the final scene remains ambiguous. As she and Mark prepare to drive away from her mother's house, Marnie declares, "Oh Mark, I don't want to go to jail. I'd much rather stay with you!" This declaration seems intended to indicate the alignment of Marnie's desire with the law. Marnie not only wants to turn herself into the police, but also wants to return with Mark to his family home, WykWyn. But if Marnie's only alternative to married life is imprisonment, it is hardly surprising that she would choose married life. Reinforcing the ambiguity of this ending, Marnie remains fixated on her mother. As Mark leads her from the house, Marnie continues to look at Bernice, who sits rocking in her chair, lost in her own thoughts. Mark has not succeeded in displacing Bernice as the object of Marnie's desire.

The film's lack of a clear resolution opens up the possibility of an alternative reading of Marnie's sexuality, which, unlike Mark's, avoids pathologizing it. From the beginning, the film emphasizes the patriarchal social and economic arrangements that ground Marnie's construction as a subject of desire. In the opening sequence, the detectives who investigate Marnie's robbery of Strutt's firm ask Strutt if he can describe her. He replies emphatically, "Certainly I can describe her. Five foot five, a hundred and ten pounds, size eight dress, blue eyes, black wavy hair, even features, good teeth." This description suggests that Strutt treated

Marnie as an object-to-be-looked-at. Because of its detail, the description amuses the detectives, who realize how Marnie managed to avoid arousing her employer's suspicion. Mark similarly fetishizes Marnie's looks in this scene. Mark, who is one of Strutt's clients, walks into Strutt's office while the detectives are questioning him. When Strutt reminds him that he pointed Marnie out to him the last time he visited the office, Mark exclaims, "Oh, that one, the brunette with the legs!" Marnie's effect on both men suggests that she has learned how to exploit patriarchal structures. The tendency of her employers to fetishize her looks enables her to manipulate them without ceding control of her sexuality. Strutt confesses to Mark: "I knew she was too good to be true. Always so eager to work overtime, never made a mistake." Despite his misgivings about Marnie, he continued to employ her because she improved "the looks of the place." What this suggests is that Marnie's compulsion to steal stems not wholly from her childhood trauma, as Mark speculates in the final scene ("When a child . . . can't get love, it takes what it can get, anyway it can get it."), but from a desire to renegotiate her subordination as a woman. She not only punishes her employers for objectifying her, but avoids having to participate in the institutions of heterosexuality.[30] Because of her thievery, she has no need for a man to support her, and so enjoys an autonomy and independence most women lack.

The film's emphasis on the patriarchal social and economic arrangements that Marnie must negotiate as a woman suggests that, like Marnie's compulsive stealing, Bernice's sex work represents a form of resistance. In the final scene, as she faces the camera in medium shot, Bernice recalls how she became pregnant with Marnie: "There was this boy—Billy—and I wanted Billy's basketball sweater. I was fifteen. And Billy said if I let him, I could have his sweater. So I let him." This account of her pregnancy represents heterosexuality as a system of exchange that forces women to use their bodies as a form of currency.[31] Although Billy abandons her when she tells him about the pregnancy, Bernice never regrets having entered into an exchange with him: "I still got that ole sweater, and I got you, Marnie!" Bernice's experience of heterosexuality as a set of power relations that requires her to cede control of her body suggests that in working as a prostitute, she seeks to redefine her status as a commodity. Prostitution allows her to renegotiate the terms of her commodification by asserting control over the circulation of her body.[32] Her body continues to function as a form of currency, but it "buys" her freedom from the institutions of heterosexuality. Bernice manages to create a mostly female world in which men's participation is strictly regulated. Despite this achievement, however, Bernice renegotiates her subordination as a woman much less successfully than her daughter does. As a prostitute, Bernice continues to participate in a patriarchal form of exchange. In contrast, by stealing, Marnie removes herself from the patriarchal sexual economy altogether and therefore has no need to use her body as a form of currency.

The movie's construction of heterosexuality validates Marnie's refusal to align her desire with the law, an aspect of the movie that surfaces most fully in its treatment of Marnie's relationship with Mark. Although when she interviews for a job at his publishing company Mark suspects that Marnie is the "brunette with the legs" who has robbed Strutt, he pressures Sam (S. John Launer), his office manager, to hire her anyway. Before taking over his father's publishing company, Mark had been a zoologist who specialized in the study of "instinctual behavior," and he views Marnie as a kind of scientific specimen that promises to yield valuable knowledge of human psychology. After Marnie begins working at the company, he constantly tests her for any sign of her "instinctual behavior" as a compulsive thief. Asking her to type one of his scientific papers, for example, he indirectly conveys his suspicions about her identity; when Marnie asks him if his research includes women's "instinctual behavior," he replies, pointedly, that he studies "the instincts of predators, what you might call the criminal class of the animal world. Lady animals figure very largely as predators." Mark views Marnie as a predator. But in indicating his suspicions about her identity, he reverses the positions they occupy in relation to each other. He becomes the predator, and she the prey. This exchange triggers one of Marnie's traumatic flashbacks. Realizing that Mark suspects her of the robbery and feeling threatened, she panics when a violent thunderstorm shatters one of the office's windows. Cowering like a trapped animal, she begs Mark to "stop the colors" and attempts to flee the office. Perversely Marnie's fear arouses Mark's desire. He follows her to the door and begins to kiss her. The film dissolves to an extreme close-up in which Marnie appears catatonic, indicating that she experiences the kisses as a traumatic violation.

This representation of Mark's desire for Marnie reinforces the film's critique of patriarchal social and economic arrangements. That Mark's desire for Marnie increases when he discovers that she has robbed his company suggests that his sexuality is as perverse as hers. Sadistically, he enjoys having power over her. When he tracks her down and tells her that he loves her, she insists: "You don't love me. I'm just something you've caught. You think I'm some kind of animal you've trapped!" Mark readily assents: "I tracked you, I caught you, and by God, I'm going to keep you!" Moreover, by "trapping" her into marrying him, Mark forces Marnie to participate in the very social and economic arrangements that she has managed to escape by stealing from her employers. She comments bitterly that in marrying her Mark will take "legal possession" of her, turning her, in effect, into a piece of property. But despite her entrapment in the institutions of heterosexuality, she retains control of her body, refusing to have sex with Mark during their honeymoon. In so doing, she avoids participating in the system of heterosexual exchange that underwrites male dominance. But, again perversely, Marnie's aversion to Mark, like her compulsive stealing, only increases his desire for her. Although he initially agrees not to "handle" her while they are on the cruise, he eventually rapes her, in a scene that recalls the scene in which he kisses her while she experiences a traumatic flashback. In the rape scene Mark first tears off Marnie's nightgown. When she screams, "No!," he apologizes and drapes his robe around her shoulders, but as he does so he begins to kiss her. The film dissolves to another extreme close-up in which Marnie appears catatonic, a symbolic echo that links the rape to her childhood trauma. Like the sailor's assault on her mother, the rape constitutes a brutal expression of male dominance. Following the rape, Marnie attempts to drown herself in the ship's swimming pool. Through the act of rape, Mark has overcome her resistance to patriarchal authority and solidified her subordinate position in relation to him as his wife.

But even as the film emphasizes the construction of Marnie's subjectivity in relation to patriarchal authority, it insists on assimilating her desire to the law. In this respect *Marnie* contrasts markedly with the final version of *The Children's Hour*, which refuses to clarify Karen's desire by reuniting her with Joe. One scene in *Marnie* highlights the contradictions in its interrogation of its heroine's desire. In the scene, which occurs on the couple's return to WykWyn after their honeymoon, Mark wakes Marnie from one of her recurring nightmares and urges her to seek therapy. At first Marnie resists Mark's attempts to persuade her that she is "sick," for she understands that entering into therapy would entail accepting her subordination as a woman. When Mark pulls up a chair beside her bed and asks her about the nightmare, she comments sarcastically, "You Freud, me Jane?" She also points out the perversity of his fixation: "You've got a pathological fix on a woman who's not only an admitted criminal but who screams if you come near her! So what about your dreams, daddy dear?" Nevertheless, by the end of the scene, she no longer resists Mark's attempts to "cure" her, but accepts his assessment that she needs help. Mark persuades her to free-associate, but when he suddenly asks her about her association with the color red, which he knows triggers her traumatic flashbacks, she panics. Collapsing into his arms, she sobs, "Help me! Oh, God, please help me!" The significance of this turn in Mark's and Marnie's relationship becomes clear in the following scene. Marnie no longer resists her role as Mark's wife, but plays the part of a "society hostess" at a dinner party the night before WykWyn's annual foxhunt. As they greet their guests, she assures Mark, "I'm not a bit nervous," and when he compliments her on her appearance, she registers her pleasure by smiling. The process of Marnie's incorporation into the institutions of heterosexuality begins *before* Mark forces her to return to her mother's house and relive the sailor's murder.

Despite this shift in the nature of their relationship, however, the movie cannot recuperate its representation of the patriarchal institutions and discourses that regulate the construction of female subjectivity. The movie indirectly acknowledges that the realignment of Marnie's gender and sexuality in the final scene reflects an outmoded system of sexual classification. According to this system, the feminine woman who makes a lesbian object choice is not as deviant as the masculine woman who does, and thus she can be incorporated into the institutions of heterosexuality. Mark's investigation into Marnie's past suggests that instead of a refusal to accede to a patriarchal construction of female desire, her aversion to heterosexual intimacy reflects the nonnormative domestic arrangements of her childhood. In working as a prostitute, Bernice perverted heterosexual relations by detaching them from the institutions of marriage and commercializing them. Thus Marnie should be able to overcome her perverse desire by experiencing "normal" heterosexual relations with Mark. But the movie's treatment of Marnie's struggle to renegotiate her subordination as a woman undercuts this attempt to normalize her sexuality, and the final scene calls into question the film's "happy ending" by suggesting that Marnie's assimilation to the law represents a pragmatic rather than a romantic choice.

Thus, like *Rebecca*, *Marnie* emphasizes the inability of patriarchal institutions and discourses to contain female sexuality. But whereas Fontaine's problematic relation to the law underwrote the homophobic construction of female homosocial bonds that circulated in American society in the 1930s—her desire is supposedly perverted by the female world of love and ritual she encounters at Manderley—Marnie's reflected a new set of anxieties that stemmed from the consolidation of object choice as an overriding principle of social and sexual difference. Marnie's femininity does not necessarily mark her as heterosexual. Although reliving her traumatic childhood experience appears to cure her of her compulsion to steal, it fails to resolve the question of her sexual identity. In this respect, *Marnie* validated the model of sexuality underlying the Cold War construction of the lesbian, even as it tried to assimilate its sexually aberrant heroine to a normative construction of womanhood. Despite Marnie's growing acceptance of her role as a "society hostess," her gender identity remains sexually illegible. Thus although it ends in typical Hollywood fashion, with the formation of the couple, *Marnie* underwrote Cold War sexual epistemology in a manner similar to that of the final version of *The Children's Hour*. Like Karen's, Marnie's sexuality has become unintelligible by the final scene of the movie. Because there is no way to know whether Mark has succeeded in displacing her mother as the object of her desire, Marnie's femininity may still mask a lesbian identity.

PART II

·····································

FEMALE STARDOM AND
COLD WAR CULTURE

....

CHAPTER FOUR

JOAN CRAWFORD'S PADDED SHOULDERS

In 1944, shortly before filming began, Jerry Wald, a producer at Warner Bros., approached Joan Crawford about starring in the screen adaptation of James M. Cain's bestselling novel *Mildred Pierce* (1941).[1] Wald was convinced that Crawford was better suited for the role of Mildred than any other actress being considered by the studio, including Barbara Stanwyck, who had recently won critical acclaim for her performance in another screen adaptation of a Cain novel, *Double Indemnity* (Billy Wilder, 1944). After all, from the beginning of her career as a contract player at MGM, Crawford had been promoted as a kind of female Horatio Alger, a fiercely ambitious, self-made woman who had overcome enormous obstacles, including a Dickensian childhood, to become one of Hollywood's most glamorous stars.[2] For Wald, her image fit perfectly with the rags-to-riches story the movie would tell. A suburban divorcée with two daughters to support, Mildred takes a job as a waitress in a diner and works her way up to become the owner of a chain of popular restaurants. Crawford, a maturing star who had not appeared on-screen since signing with Warner Bros. two years earlier, was convinced that the film as described by Wald was just the vehicle she needed to revive her flagging career. But Michael Curtiz, the director assigned to this woman's picture, had other ideas, and when Wald revealed that he had shown the script to Crawford without the director's permission, Curtiz, well-known for his colorful speech, exploded in rage: "Me direct the temperamental bitch! Not on your goddamn life! She comes over here [from MGM] with her high-hat airs and her goddamn shoulder pads! I won't work with her. She's through, washed up."[3] To persuade the director that she was right for the part, Crawford agreed to do a screen test, a humiliating concession that seemed to confirm Curtiz's judgment that she was "washed up" as a star.

Curtiz's reference to Crawford's padded shoulders, one of the defining components of the look developed for her by MGM, suggests that he may have been less concerned about her status as a Hollywood has-been than about another aspect of her image not considered by Wald. During her heyday at MGM—the mid-1930s, when Adrian, the studio's top designer, designed her costumes—Crawford emerged as what was known in the movie industry as a clotheshorse.[4] One purpose of her pictures, in fact, was to showcase Adrian's designs, whose lavishness captivated Depression-era audiences and kept them coming back to the theater, and Crawford's signature look, in particular the square-shouldered gowns and elegantly tailored suits Adrian designed for her to wear both on- and offscreen, deeply influenced women's fashion of the 1930s.[5] As a consequence, movie critics tended to comment on her vivid screen presence and glamorous wardrobe rather than the quality of her acting. Crawford later confessed to an interviewer, "The role of Mildred was a delight to me, because it rescued me from what was known at MGM as the Joan Crawford formula. I had become so hidden in clothes and sets that nobody could tell whether I had talent or not."[6] Although, as Wald's desire to have her play Mildred attests, there was more to the Crawford formula than lavish sets and alluring costumes, Crawford was right that *Mildred Pierce* transformed her public persona. From the first day of shooting, Curtiz was determined to eliminate the fashion-plate aspect of Crawford's image. When Crawford showed up on the set wearing a dress that, although simple in design, had shoulder pads, he reportedly shouted, "You and your damned Adrian shoulder pads! This stinks!," and he tore it off her.[7] He then ordered the picture's costume designer to buy her dresses from Sears so that she would look less like Joan Crawford, the glamorous star, and more like the ordinary suburban housewife she was playing.

For Curtiz, Crawford's image as a clotheshorse might not only prevent viewers from entering the movie's narrative space by distracting them from the plot; it might also conflict with the movie's treatment of Mildred, which differed significantly from the novel's. Crawford's padded shoulders had helped to consolidate her persona as an ambitious, hardworking star who, as Photoplay put it rather melodramatically in 1935, "had carved a monumental career out of nothing. She had satisfied a consuming inner demand to be somebody."[8] Adrian's designs were intended to create a distinctive look that would prevent Crawford from disappearing into her roles, so that her fans could recognize her from one film to another. Adrian decided to capitalize on rather than hide or soften her broad shoulders, and in 1932, while she was making *Letty Lynton* (Clarence Brown), he began adding shoulder pads to her costumes, which in accentuating her shoulders had the effect of narrowing her already narrow hips.[9] As Robert Allen and Douglas Gomery have pointed out in their analysis of Crawford's MGM persona, this look masculinized her and thus "provided an appropriate visual correlative to the 'independent woman' character she so frequently played."[10]

With its complex gender coding, Adrian's famous "Letty Lynton" dress, worn by Crawford in the love scene of that woman's picture and copied by many of the fashion industry's top designers, captured exceptionally well the tensions in Crawford's persona.[11] Made of white chiffon and featuring ruffled mutton sleeves, the dress embodied, on the one hand, the type of femininity promoted by Hollywood (glamorous, decorative, and sexually alluring). On the other hand, the enormous sleeves—mirrored by a peplum- or apron-like extension of the tightly fitted bodice, which accentuated the star's slender hips—highlighted Crawford's masculine mode of embodiment by making her shoulders appear even broader. Thus, like many of Adrian's designs for the actress, the dress simultaneously called attention to the masculine elements of Crawford's persona, such as her drive and ambition, and held them in check.

For Crawford's look to provide a "visual correlative" in *Mildred Pierce*, it had to have a somewhat different meaning, which may explain Curtiz's outburst on the set. Despite Crawford's claim to the contrary, the picture for which she won her only Academy Award did follow the formula developed by MGM, at least in some crucial respects. Like Crawford's Depression-era characters, Mildred is determined to succeed, and her rise to success mirrors Crawford's own, at least in how it was depicted in fan magazines and studio press releases. Where Curtiz's film departed from the Crawford formula was in its representation of its independent, self-made heroine. Crawford's earlier characters aspired to a higher social class, which they usually achieved through good grooming, elegant manners, and proper dress. Such characters were designed to appeal to the star's working-class fans, whose devotion to her was legendary.[12] Executives at MGM felt that her fans would identify with characters who were undergoing similar economic hardships and who, like them, dreamed of a better, more glamorous life. Although when faced with the choice between romance and career, these characters chose romance and thus ended up safely contained in the domestic sphere, their desire to climb

JOAN CRAWFORD WEARING THE FAMOUS "LETTY LYNTON" DRESS.

the social ladder was always validated. By contrast, Mildred's aspirations emerge as a transgression of her identity as a wife and mother, and in the picture's final scene, she reunites with her first husband, Bert (Bruce Bennett), whom she had divorced because he lacked ambition and thus impeded her attempts to better herself. One of the ways Curtiz's film marks Mildred's rise to success is by having Crawford reassume her trademark look, but rather than signifying an alluring combination of masculine and feminine attributes, as it had in her earlier pictures, Crawford's padded shoulders in this film from 1945 visually register Mildred's gender and sexual nonconformity.

Starting with *Mildred Pierce*, Crawford's persona followed a distinctively queer trajectory. Although her Academy Award–winning performance in Curtiz's movie revived her career—she displaced Bette Davis as Warner Brothers's most popular female star—by the 1950s Crawford's persona had become camp, as Pamela Robertson has shown.[13] Despite the postwar domestication of women, Crawford continued to play the same type of character she had played during the heyday of her career at MGM: ambitious career women who resembled Mildred, but unlike her refused to return to the domestic sphere. Whereas the movies Crawford had made during the Depression represented such women as admirable and worthy of emulation so long as they simultaneously embodied an alluring femininity, the ones she made in the 1950s characterized such women as shrewish and emasculating. In a society that defined womanhood in terms of domesticity and motherhood, such women appeared anachronistic and out of place, two of the defining qualities of camp.[14] As Robertson points out, by 1953, when Crawford starred in the idiosyncratic western *Johnny Guitar* (Nicholas Ray), her masculinity had become so pronounced as to render her a camp object.[15] By departing from the MGM formula and disarticulating the masculine and the feminine aspects of her gender presentation, *Mildred Pierce* played a crucial role in shifting the construction of Crawford's persona. Although Mildred's feminine gender style in the final scenes anticipates her return to the domestic sphere by registering the normalization of her desire, *Mildred Pierce* was the first movie Crawford made that pathologized her masculinity. But despite the misogynistic construction of her masculinity in her postwar movies, Crawford's persona had the potential to destabilize Cold War gender and sexual norms by creating a camp effect.

This potential surfaced most fully in *Johnny Guitar*, in which Crawford played Vienna, a cross-dressing, gunslinging saloonkeeper scapegoated for her gender and sexual nonconformity. Although it was panned when it was first released, critics now consider *Johnny Guitar* one of the filmmaker Nicholas Ray's most important films.[16] Ray laid the groundwork for this critical reassessment following the rediscovery of his films, in the 1970s, by a new generation of critics and fans, and he emerged as an auteur who had provided a searing critique of the stultifying conformity of the Cold War era. Ray claimed that he and screenwriter Philip Yordan intended *Johnny Guitar* as a critique of McCarthyism. Even the casting supposedly reflected their opposition to the anticommunist witch hunts, which deeply divided Hollywood.[17] Sterling Hayden, who played the movie's title character, notoriously avoided the blacklist by naming names when he appeared before the House Un-American Activities Committee. Ray pointed to the parallel between Hayden's regret over his testimony, which led Hollywood's left-wing community to ostracize him, and Johnny's struggle to overcome his past as a trigger-happy gunfighter. Ray also claimed that he and Yordan cast Ward Bond as McIvers, the rancher who organizes the posse that terrorizes Vienna, to reinforce the movie's references to the witch hunts. Bond, who was one of Hollywood's staunchest anticommunists, helped found the Motion Picture Alliance for the Preservation of American Ideals, the right-wing organization which enforced the Hollywood blacklist. Ray told an interviewer, in 1973, that he thought "it was a kind of nice inside joke to cast Ward Bond that way."[18] Ray even went so far as to claim that Crawford faced pressure to name names, although she had no history of supporting left-wing causes and was never targeted by any of the congressional committees that investigated communist infiltration of Hollywood.[19]

Elaborating Ray's claims about the movie's political content, critics have suggested that he and Yordan escaped censorship by encoding their critique of Cold War political repression as a western, which enabled them to make a connection between the witch hunts and the vigilante justice that prevailed in the "wild west."[20] These critics have also interpreted Vienna's persecution by the town allegorically.[21] Because she has aligned herself with the railroad, Vienna threatens the economic interests of the wealthy ranchers who dominate the town, McIvers and Emma Small (Mercedes McCambridge). The railroad will bypass the town, and its coming portends their financial ruin. Whereas Vienna's connection to the railroad locates her on the side of progress and modernization, the ranchers' opposition to it identifies them as reactionaries who have a vested interest in preserving the status quo. For these critics, McIvers and

Emma render Vienna a social outcast by connecting her to the Dancin' Kid (Scott Brady), a silver miner with whom she has had an affair; the town mistakenly blames the Kid and his gang for a series of holdups, and the two ranchers turn the town against Vienna by accusing her of providing the gang with a safe haven in her saloon. As these critics have pointed out, the most explicit reference to the McCarthy witch hunts occurs in the scene in which McIvers and Emma capture the youngest and most vulnerable member of the gang, Turkey (Ben Cooper), and pressure him into implicating Vienna in the holdup of Emma's bank. Deploying tactics that recall those of McCarthy when he interrogated hostile witnesses, McIvers reassures the boy, "The truth, son, that's all we want," while Emma falsely promises him that they will let him go if he will tell them that Vienna is "one of you." A terrified Turkey complies, but the posse hangs him anyway.

Although the movie's references to the McCarthy witch hunts seem indisputable, this auteurist reading does not adequately consider *Johnny Guitar*'s complicated gender and sexual politics. With her masculine gender presentation and psychopathic hatred of Vienna and the Dancin' Kid, Emma resembles the stereotypical 1950s lesbian, and her rivalry with Vienna has an intensity that cannot be reduced to the competing economic forces the two women embody. The movie's lesbian subtext suggests that it provided a more complicated critique of Cold War culture than the criticism has acknowledged. For it contested the Cold War discourse of female homosexuality by attributing to Vienna and Emma two different forms of masculinity. The two women perform masculinity in markedly different ways.[22] Whereas Emma's masculinity emerges as a fixed identity, Vienna's resembles a performance. Unlike Emma, Vienna shifts effortlessly between masculine and feminine gender presentations. When she needs to assert her power as a businesswoman allied with the railroad, she dresses and behaves like a man; when she needs to avoid threatening the town's men, she masks that power by dressing and behaving like a woman. In other words, Emma and Vienna exemplify the two different models of female homosexuality that, despite their incompatibility, the Cold War construction of the lesbian incorporated. Whereas Emma's masculine gender presentation functions as a sign of her lesbianism, Vienna's gender practices lack a fixed or stable relation to her sexual desire. In associating Emma and Vienna with these two different models, *Johnny Guitar* exposed the incoherence of the Cold War discourse of female homosexuality—a critique of Cold War lesbian panic that relied on the camp effect of Crawford's persona. Unlike the other movies the actress made in the 1950s, *Johnny Guitar* not only avoids pathologizing her masculinity, but exploits it to destabilize the dominant construction of American womanhood. All this relied on the postwar transformation of Crawford's image initiated by *Mildred Pierce*.

QUEER MOTHERHOOD IN *MILDRED PIERCE*

Mildred Pierce has been central to feminist analysis of classical Hollywood cinema, partly because of the way in which it rewrote MGM's Crawford formula. For feminist critics in the 1980s, Mildred's struggles to achieve a better life for herself threaten to disrupt the patriarchal order, and her redomestication in the movie's closing shots exemplifies the patriarchal operations of classical Hollywood cinema in general, which tended to position the women both on the screen and in the audience as objects, rather than subjects, of desire.[23] Crucial to this analysis has been the picture's split structure, its division into two different genres and visual styles: the melodrama, or woman's picture, of Mildred's flashbacks, in which, prompted by Inspector Peterson (Moroni Olsen), she narrates her rise as a restaurateur; and the film noir that frames these flashbacks.[24] In an influential feminist analysis of the film, Pam Cook argues that the purpose of the film noir element, with its masculine mode of address, is to contain Mildred's narrative authority.[25] Peterson takes control of the narrative away from Mildred by solving the murder of Mildred's playboy husband, Monte Beragon (Zachary Scott), which opens the movie. In the process, he exposes Mildred's attempts to mislead him (and by implication the spectator for whom he acts as a diegetic substitute) by casting suspicion first on her business partner Wally (Jack Carson), and then on herself, so that her daughter, Veda (Ann Blyth), can go free. Critics have explained this containment of Mildred's authority in terms of the conditions of the movie's production, which differed significantly from those of Crawford's Depression-era fallen-woman pictures. The release of *Mildred Pierce* coincided with the return of American GIs from the Second World War and the need it supposedly created for women to make room for them in the workplace by returning to the domestic sphere. Warner Bros. delayed the picture's release until after the Japanese surrendered in September 1945, because it thought the picture would have more resonance in the postwar context.[26] In another influential reading of the film, Andrea Walsh argues that *Mildred Pierce* helped to underwrite the shift to a postwar economy, which depended on a return to a gendered division of labor.[27] Mildred's success in the business world leads to her masculinization both visually and narratively, and she serves as an example of the bad things that supposedly befall women when they leave the domestic sphere and enter the workforce.

Although one effect of Mildred's masculinization was certainly to underwrite the redomestication of women, this analysis overlooks one of the film's central themes: Mildred's incestuous desire for Veda, the spoiled daughter whose social ambitions Mildred struggles unsuccessfully to fulfill. Mildred violates her role as a mother by encouraging instead of containing the perverse desires that circulate through the nuclear family. In so doing, she disrupts one of the nuclear family's primary functions, which is to ensure the reproduction of normative gender and sexual identities. Because of Mildred's perversity or queerness as a mother, it took Warner Bros., which bought the rights to Cain's novel shortly after it was published, until 1944 to develop a script acceptable to the Hays Office, which administered the Production Code.[28] Obviously, the movie could not treat Mildred's desire for Veda as openly as the novel did, and it circumvented the Production Code's prohibition of the treatment of "sex perversion" by drawing on a model of sexuality that aligned gender identity with object choice and sexual practice. One of the purposes of Mildred's masculinity was to translate her "sex perversion" into visual terms, and in so doing to suggest the incestuous desire that perverts the relationship between mother and daughter in the novel without violating the Production Code.[29] But the movie's deployment of this visual strategy undercut its ideological agenda, which suggests that its relation to the reorganization of the economy was not as seamless or unambiguous as the criticism has claimed. For even as the masculinization of Mildred's gender style suggested that women's proper place was in the domestic sphere, it highlighted the performativity of gender and sexual identities. Mildred alternates between normative and nonnormative gender styles, and thus her masculinity emerges as a performance designed to attract her daughter, Veda.

Warner Bros. did not decide to adapt *Mildred Pierce* for the screen until learning that the Hays Office had approved Raymond Chandler's script for *Double Indemnity*, which suggested that it might also approve a script based on Cain's less sordid but no less controversial novel.[30] But rather than tone down *Mildred Pierce*, which treated such themes as adultery and incest, the studio wanted to make it even more lurid by having

Veda murder Monte after Mildred discovers them kissing passionately at the beach house. Ashamed of betraying his wife, Monte reveals that he would never marry "a rotten little tramp" like Veda, and Veda shoots him multiple times. In revising the plot of Cain's novel, Warner Bros. sought to capitalize on the box-office success of the movie version of the author's earlier novel *Double Indemnity* (1936), which unlike *Mildred Pierce* focused on an adulterous relationship that turns murderous.[31] Monte inadvertently implicates Mildred as his murderer by repeating her name as he dies and in so doing associates her with the femme fatale Phyllis Dietrichson (Barbara Stanwyck), who plots her husband's murder in the earlier film. But as Patricia White has pointed out, *Mildred Pierce*'s blending of film noir and maternal melodrama also allowed for the emergence of the lesbian connotations of Mildred's and Veda's relationship.[32] In structuring the narrative as a murder investigation, Warner Bros. avoided scandalizing viewers by deflecting their attention from Mildred's desire for her daughter and focusing it instead on the solution of Monte's murder. Despite this strategy, however, Mildred's desire for Veda remains one of the movie's central themes. Warner Bros. promoted the movie with the teaser "Mildred Pierce—Don't tell what she did," which encouraged viewers to think that Mildred does something bad.[33] But if Mildred does not murder Monte, what does she do that viewers should avoid repeating?

For many critics, the answer to this question lies in the movie's treatment of Mildred as a working mother, which supposedly reflected growing anxieties in the 1940s about the impact of working mothers on the psychological development of their children.[34] Even before the war was over, these critics point out, child-rearing experts began warning that mothers who worked outside the home failed to adequately supervise their children, who then grew up spoiled and undisciplined.[35] Once the war ended, these warnings reinforced the pressure on women to relinquish their careers and return to the domestic sphere. Women who continued to work, it was argued, risked damaging their children, who required their constant attention. Mildred's relationship with Veda, these critics contend, provides an example of these alleged dangers. Mildred compensates for her absence from the home by spoiling Veda. She lavishes on her expensive clothes and jewelry, as well as a fancy sports car, engaging in a form of consumption that audiences might fantasize about but that the postwar economy could not support, as the rationing of consumer goods continued until the late 1940s. In other words, although she does not murder Monte, Mildred might as well have pulled the trigger herself, since as a working mother who neglects her daughter's upbringing, she turns Veda into a murderous vixen.

While the movie's representation of Mildred as a working mother was certainly intended to encourage women to abandon their careers, lest their children turn out like Veda, this reading overlooks Mildred's perversity as a mother who wants to occupy a paternal as well as a maternal position in relation to her favorite daughter. Mildred's attempts to buy Veda's love precede her rise to success. Indeed, she throws herself into her career so that she can give Veda whatever Veda wants. Mildred's first flashback indicates that even *before* she has opened her first restaurant, she has already disrupted the structures of desire and identification on which the reproduction of normative gender and sexual identities depends. Her quarrel with Bert in the flashback's opening scene, though ostensibly about his affair with Mrs. Biederhof (Lee Patrick), really concerns her relationship with Veda, which he considers unnatural. When Bert discovers that Mildred has spent the money she earns from baking cakes and pies for the neighbors on a new dress for Veda, he reproaches her angrily: "I'm so fed up with the way [Veda] high-hats me that one of these days I'm going to let loose and slap her in the face. . . . There's something wrong Mildred, I don't know what, I'm not smart that way, but I know it's not right to. . . ." But before he can finish admonishing Mildred for caring too much about Veda, Mrs. Biederhof calls, which allows Mildred to gain the upper hand in their quarrel. After he tells the widow not to call him at home and abruptly hangs up on her, Mildred remarks sarcastically, "So the noble Mr. Pierce can't talk right now because he's too busy telling his wife that what's wrong with their married life is the way she treats the children." Bert warns her not to go too far or he may call her "bluff," but she has already decided to call his: "You might as well get this straight now once and for all. Those kids come first in this house before either one of us. I don't know whether that's right or wrong, but it's the way it is." Mildred wants to replace Bert as head of the family, so she uses his sexual infidelity as an excuse to throw him out. He threatens to assert control over Veda by putting her in her place, and with him gone, Mildred will not have to compete with him for possession of her beloved daughter.

Further complicating the film's representation of Mildred as a mother, Veda emerges as something of a vixen in this flashback. Mildred's perversity as a mother has already disrupted the reproduction of normative gender and sexual identities in her favorite daughter. In a scene that recalls one in the novel where a manipulative Veda deflects Mildred's anger by arousing a sexual "tingle" in her, Veda urges Mildred to marry Wally, Bert's sleazy business partner. The night Bert packs up his things and leaves, Veda overhears Wally flirting with Mildred, and when Mildred comes upstairs to kiss goodnight her and her sister Kay (Jo Ann Marlowe), Veda comments excitedly, "You could marry [Wally], if you wanted to. If you married him, maybe we could have a maid like we used to, and a limousine, and maybe a new house. I don't like this house, mother." Mildred explains that she does not love Wally, but Veda persists in urging her to marry him, which shocks her mother, who asks reproachfully, "Veda, does a new house mean so much to you that you would trade me for it?" Veda realizes that she has gone too far, and nestling against her mother affectionately, she reassures her, "I didn't mean it, mother. I don't care what we have so long as we're together. It's just that there are so many things I—we—should have and haven't got." When Mildred promises her, "I'll get you anything, everything you want," Veda kisses her and whispers, "You darling!," as though she were rewarding her. But she changes tone abruptly when Mildred, expressing love, leans down to kiss her. Turning her face away, Veda chides her mother, "No need to get sticky about it."

Remarkably, despite the intensity of Mildred's maternal desire in this scene, the movie avoids showing her in close-up. It also avoids adopting her point of view, even though she is the one narrating the flashback. During the scene, she and Veda lie on Veda's bed facing the camera in medium shot. The camera shifts angle only twice. When Veda mentions all the things they could have if Mildred married Wally, the film dissolves to a close-up of Veda, who turns away from the book she has been reading and looks at her mother pointedly. Although one might expect the camera to cut to a reverse shot of Mildred returning Veda's look, the film instead dissolves back to another medium shot of the two. Except for these shifts, the camera remains stationary throughout the scene, which discourages the audience from identifying with Mildred, despite Veda's ruthless manipulation of her desire. Visual strategies like these undercut Mildred's narrative authority by opening up a distance between her and the viewer. As a consequence, the viewer does not automatically accept Mildred's version of events. Far from being the innocent victim in her flashbacks, Mildred, as a mother who refuses to occupy a normative Oedipalized position in relation to her daughter, must accept responsibility for her daughter's sexual precocity.

In the novel, Veda's monstrousness reflects her identification with her father. Unlike the Veda of the movie who "high-hats" the unemployed Bert, the Veda of the novel adores him and resents her mother for divorcing him. Despite the collapse of his real-estate business, Bert retains his "grand manner and fine ways," which his spoiled daughter emulates.[36] In particular, Veda admires his elegant clothes, signs of his former status as a successful businessman, and "the proud inspection of his tuxedo, his riding breeches, his shiny boots and shoes was a daily ritual that not even a trip to her grandfather's was going to interfere with" (15). Moreover, she disapproves of his affair, because she considers Mrs. Biederhof to be beneath him, contemptuously describing the widow as "distinctly middle-class" (16). By contrast, in the movie Veda resents her father's failure to provide for the family and considers him an embarrassment. Although she also contemptuously describes Mrs. Biederhof as "distinctly middle-class," her low opinion of her father's paramour reflects her disapproval of him. For her, his affair with the widow indicates his lack of ambition. This difference between the novel and the movie serves to intensify the sadomasochistic aspects of Mildred's and Veda's relationship. In the movie, Veda's monstrous treatment of her mother has no motivation, except the perverse pleasure she takes in tormenting her. Another effect of the difference between novel and movie is to compound Mildred's responsibility for her daughter's pathological behavior. In the movie, it is Mildred, not Bert, who has implanted in Veda the desire for a more glamorous life—a desire that eventually turns murderous—by spoiling her. In this respect, the movie "updated" the novel so it reflected growing anxieties about working mothers and their impact on their children's development.

By the final scenes, *Mildred Pierce* is no longer a woman's picture centered on the rise and fall of a divorced mother of two children, but a film noir about a femme fatale's treacherous relationship with her lover. As several critics have pointed out, Inspector Peterson prompts each of Mildred's flashbacks by asking her a question about her motivations as a wife and mother, such as why she divorced Bert, which enables the movie to contain her authority as a narrator. The Inspector controls the movie's linear unfolding from the beginning, and the displacement of the woman's picture in the final scenes translates his narrative authority into visual terms. But the shift in genres also enables the movie to address Mildred's desire for her daughter by positioning Veda as a double-crossing femme fatale. This strategy manifests itself most fully in Mildred's final flashback, in which we see Veda kill Monte at the beach house in a jealous rage. Filmed in the same visual style as the noir-like scenes that open the movie, the flashback solidifies Veda's role as a femme fatale whose unruly sexuality has propelled the narrative from the start.[37] When Veda realizes that her mother has seen her and Monte kissing, she gets up from the bar stool where she has draped herself seductively and faces Mildred defiantly: "He never loved you. It's always been me. I got what I've wanted. Monte's going to divorce you and marry me, and there's nothing you can do about it." Monte realizes that Veda has used him to make Mildred jealous, and after Mildred leaves, he makes clear that he has no intention of marrying Veda, which leads her to shoot him. He partially redeems himself by repeating Mildred's name as he dies, which indicates that he continues to love her and regrets betraying her. The scene's visual style reinforces Veda's role as the movie's femme fatale. Whereas Monte and Mildred wear dark clothes and frequently appear in silhouette, such that they are virtually indistinguishable from the shadowy background, Veda wears a shimmering evening gown with a fluffy skirt and a gold lamé bodice that, in reflecting the light, ensures that the viewer remains transfixed by her image.

Veda's emergence as a femme fatale works to position Mildred as the hard-boiled hero whom she sexually double-crosses. The film marks this shift in relation to Veda in part by recoding the businesswoman's gender identity. In her second flashback, where she recounts her rise to success, Mildred begins wearing masculine-looking clothes, fitted suits with padded shoulders that resemble the ones Adrian designed for Crawford during her days at MGM, but with more severe lines. These suits provide a sharp contrast to the simple, loose-fitting dresses she wears in her first flashback, when she is still struggling to support Veda and Kay and has not yet proved that she can make it in a man's world. This shift in Mildred's gender style exploits the tensions in Crawford's persona. At times, *Mildred Pierce* foregrounds the masculine elements of the star's gender presentation, at others, the feminine ones. Thus, where the movie departed most fully from the Crawford formula was in splitting apart the different elements of her persona, which her MGM films, with the help of Adrian's designs, had managed to bind together.

The link between Mildred's masculinization and her desire for Veda emerges most fully in the scene in which she returns from Mexico, where she has gone to try to forget Veda after they quarrel over an extortion scheme Veda has concocted (Veda has secretly married the wealthy Ted Forrester, but when his family insists on an annulment, she pretends to be

JOAN CRAWFORD DRESSED FOR SUCCESS IN *MILDRED PIERCE.*

pregnant in order to extract a financial settlement). In the scene, Mildred wears a suit jacket that, gathered at the waist, emphasizes her broad shoulders and slender hips, and she has a mannish hairdo as well. As soon as she enters the restaurant, she asks her business manager, Ida, to pour her a drink. Ida remarks that she never used to drink during the day, and Mildred replies, "I never used to drink at all. It's just a little habit I picked up from men." Lighting a cigarette, which she holds mannishly between her thumb and forefinger, she begins talking about Veda as if Veda were her lover, instead of her daughter. Ida, who like Bert disapproves of the manipulative Veda, urges Mildred to forget her, but Mildred declares that she cannot: "I went away to try. I was so mixed up. I didn't know where I was or what I wanted, but now I know. Now I'm sure of one thing at least. I want my daughter back." With this scene, the movie comes as close as it can to conveying Mildred's desire for her daughter without violating the Production Code. Mildred sounds like the typical noir hero who knows that the femme fatale has betrayed him with another man but cannot overcome his desire and thus continues to pursue her.

Mildred seems determined to show that she can approximate the norms of masculinity more closely than either Bert or Monte, her two rivals for possession of Veda, can. Both men suffer from impaired masculinities. Although Bert eventually normalizes his gender identity by finding a job in the aircraft industry, it is Mildred who supports the family, by baking cakes and pies for the neighbors, when the film opens. Nor does Bert seem overly concerned about the family's mounting bills. In the opening shots of Mildred's first flashback, he lies on the couch reading the newspaper in the foreground while Mildred ices a cake in the background. Monte deviates from the norms of masculinity even more. Like Bert, he comes to occupy a feminized position in relation to Mildred, but unlike Bert, he never reclaims his manhood. Shortly after they meet, Mildred asks Monte what he does for a living, and he replies, "I loaf, in a highly decorative and charming manner," thereby calling attention to his gender nonconformity. Born into a prominent Pasadena family ruined by the Depression, he lives off the family's dwindling income from some orange groves, and he must constantly borrow money from Mildred in order to take her and Veda to swanky restaurants and nightclubs. Although he resents his economic dependence on Mildred, which undermines his masculinity, he does not want to jeopardize his class identity by working for a living. At one point, when he and Veda walk in on Mildred and Ida, who are examining the restaurant chain's books, he remarks wistfully, "I wish I could get that interested in work." Ida, who disapproves of his dependence on Mildred, replies sarcastically, "Oh, you were probably frightened by a callus at an early age."

The movie emphasizes Mildred's approximation of the norms of masculinity in the scene in which she gives Veda a sports car for her seventeenth birthday. In this scene, which takes place in Mildred's office, Mildred and Monte represent two different types of masculinity that reflect their class differences. As the scene opens, Mildred sits behind her desk writing in a ledger while listening to Wally complain about Monte's spendthrift habits, which are draining the restaurant chain of money. She wears a dark, fitted, pin-striped jacket and matching pleated skirt that reflect her identity as a middle-class businesswoman who embodies the American work ethic. When Monte enters with Veda, his dapper appearance provides a striking contrast to Mildred's. He wears a light-colored tweed jacket, striped shirt, and bow tie, an outfit that reflects his identity as an upper-class man of leisure. Mildred realizes in this scene that despite her competence in performing masculinity, she cannot compete with Monte for Veda's love. As a woman who must work for a living, she can never achieve his class position and fulfill her daughter's social ambitions. Veda appears transformed. Though only seventeen, she wears a stylish outfit that makes her look grown up. Mildred notices her transformation when Veda takes a cigarette from a silver case in her purse, walks over to Mildred's desk, and ostentatiously lights it with Mildred's lighter. Mildred asks when she began smoking, and Veda points to the cigarette case, replying, "Monte gave this to me for my birthday, and I couldn't hurt him by not using it. I mean that would have been dreadfully recherché, *n'est-ce pas?*" Mildred does not speak French, but rather than ask her daughter to translate, which would call attention to her ignorance, Mildred points to a car parked outside the window: "Here's something for your birthday, too. I hope you like it." When Veda, momentarily dropping her sophisticated pose, squeals with delight and kisses her mother, Monte interrupts her by asking, "Hey, how about me, young lady? After all, I picked it out, you know." Here Mildred and Monte compete over which of them can most impress Veda, yet Mildred realizes that Monte has sparked Veda's desire in a way that she cannot, his initiation of the girl into the adult practice of smoking having made this difference clear. As a result, Mildred begins to feel threatened by Monte, and when Vida rushes out to take her new car for a spin, she forbids Monte to see her daughter anymore, thereby eliminating him as a rival. Recalling the scene where she tells Bert to move out, she informs Monte, "You're interfering with my life and my business. Worst of all, you're interfering with my plans for Veda, and I won't stand for it."

Mildred's relationship with Ida serves to reinforce the lesbian connotations of her masculine gender presentation. Film scholars have shown that one of the functions of secondary female characters in classical Hollywood cinema is to consolidate the heroine's identity as a representative of normative femininity.[38] Such characters tend to occupy a liminal position in relation to the institutions of heterosexuality. Although they serve a variety of functions that uphold the dominance of those institutions, they do not need to perform heterosexual femininity themselves so long as they support the heroine's interpellation into the ideology of heterosexual romance. But the tough-talking, wisecracking Ida serves a more complicated function. Instead of highlighting Mildred's normative gender identity, Mildred's sidekick represents the type of sexually marginal woman she threatens to become if she continues to circulate in the public sphere. Like her, Ida occupies a masculinized position in the movie that reflects her participation in the business world. When Mildred informs Wally that she loves Monte, he declares bitterly that he hates all women. Then, looking at Ida pointedly, he remarks, "Thank goodness you're not one." Also like her boss, Ida tends to wear masculine-looking suits that manifest her gender and sexual nonconformity. Where she differs from Mildred is in resembling the stereotype of the man-hating spinster. At one point when Wally watches her adjust her stockings, she remarks contemptuously, "Leave something on me. I might catch cold." She also constantly mocks the male characters for their inadequacy as men. Thus, like many female sidekicks in classical Hollywood cinema, Ida is coded as a lesbian. As such, she serves as a warning to Mildred about her potential destiny if she continues to violate her socially prescribed role as a woman by refusing to return to the domestic sphere.

Mildred solidifies her masculine position in relation to Monte by using him as a conduit for her desire for Veda. She enters into an exchange with him by asking him to marry her. She realizes that she needs to marry him to enhance her appeal as a mother so that Veda will return home. But when he accepts her proposal, he does so only on condition that she sign over to him a third of her business. Although she does not want to agree to his terms, she realizes that they will both benefit from the arrangement. He will recover his manhood by gaining financial independence, and she will acquire the social cachet she has been lacking, despite her success as a businesswoman. When he attempts to kiss her, she turns her face away and seals their bargain by declaring, "Sold, one Beragon." In other words, Mildred uses Monte the same way that Eve Kosofsky Sedgwick has argued men use women to solidify their bonds with other men.[39] In so doing, she consolidates his feminized position in relation to her. Mildred's triangulation of her desire for Veda through Monte also underscores her disruption of the nuclear family's Oedipal structure. Although Veda has a normative gender identity and makes a heterosexual object choice, she carries on an adulterous affair with her own stepfather, which expresses in displaced form her incestuous relationship with her mother. Thus, if Inspector Peterson cares more about investigating Mildred's past than Monte's murder, as several critics have claimed, it is not because Mildred puts her career before her daughter, but because she exposes the perverse desires that threaten to destabilize the nuclear family and need to be contained. As a mother who attempts to occupy a paternal as well as a maternal position in relation to her daughter, Mildred causes Veda to grow up queer. The girl's sexuality cannot be understood in terms of any of the historically available categories of identity.

Despite her masculinity, Mildred retains her ability to perform heterosexual femininity, and she alternates between normative and nonnormative gender styles even after her rise to success. When we first see Mildred, she exemplifies normative womanhood, as constructed by classical Hollywood cinema. The camera tracks her as she walks down the Santa Monica Pier, contemplating throwing herself into the crashing surf below. With this sequence of shots, the movie pays tribute to Crawford's image as a clotheshorse, only to discard that image in subsequent scenes. Dressed in a luxurious mink coat and matching hat, Mildred looks much more glamorous than she does in any other scene in the film. Indeed, with its padded shoulders and fashionable appearance, her outfit recalls the costumes Adrian designed for her during her career at MGM.

As the movie progresses, Mildred's enactments of heterosexual femininity are increasingly limited to her scenes with Bert. A particularly striking example of this aspect of her gender performance occurs in the scene where Bert takes Mildred to Wally's bar on the pier, where Veda, to spite her mother, has taken a job as a tawdry nightclub dancer. Whereas in the previous scene, in which she talked about her daughter as if she were a sexually treacherous girlfriend, she wore an outfit that emphasized her masculine mode of embodiment, Mildred now wears an elegant black dress and a matching hat with a black tulle veil, a look that seems designed to indicate that she and Bert belong together despite the collapse of their marriage. Bert appears to bring out Mildred's femininity, and they resemble a typical husband and wife who are worried about their daughter. Exploiting the feminine elements of Crawford's persona, this scene lays the groundwork for Mildred's reunion with Bert in the movie's closing shots. Mildred's gender conformity allows Bert to reclaim her for the domestic sphere. But despite this narrative resolution, Mildred's alternation between masculine and feminine gender styles complicated the movie's relation to the postwar domestication of women by disarticulating sex and gender. Her return to the domestic sphere notwithstanding, Mildred has demonstrated that women can approximate the norms of masculinity more fully than men can.

FEMALE MASCULINITY IN *JOHNNY GUITAR*

In associating Crawford with a deviant form of motherhood, *Mildred Pierce* marked a significant shift in the construction of her image, one that manifested the gender and sexual anxieties of the postwar era. Until she appeared in *Mildred Pierce*, the star was best known for the fallen-woman pictures she had made for MGM in the 1930s. In these pictures, she played working-class heroines—factory workers, shopgirls, dancers, stenographers—who achieve upward mobility by entering into illicit relationships with powerful men. These heroines refuse to feel ashamed of their sexual transgressions, and despite their identities as gold diggers or kept women, they usually triumph over the sexual double standard that marks them as "tramps," or fallen women.[40] In this respect, the pictures highlighted the obstacles that prevented women from achieving the American dream through hard work alone, which may indicate the source of their popularity with Depression-era audiences. Departing from this representation of the fallen woman, *Mildred Pierce* attempted to redefine Crawford's association with gender and sexual nonconformity, such that it underwrote rather than challenged the dominant construction of womanhood. The movie punishes Mildred for transgressing the bounds of normative femininity, which it associates with her irresponsibility as a mother. For example, Mildred returns from her weekend tryst with Monte at the beach house to discover that Kay is dying of pneumonia at Mrs. Biederhof's house, where Bert has taken her because he could not locate Mildred. Moreover, Mildred eventually loses her business, as well as her daughter, by entering into a transaction with Monte. The rakish ne'er-do-well double-crosses her not only by having an affair with Veda, but also by selling his share of the business, which leaves her unable to pay her creditors. In other words, Crawford's comeback movie showed that her persona could be mobilized to ratify the gender and sexual norms of a new era, which may explain why it revived her flagging career.

By contrast, *Johnny Guitar* attempts not to update Crawford's persona, but to exploit its association with gender and sexual nonconformity. Unlike Mildred, Vienna uses her sexuality to achieve her ambitions. Her rise from saloon girl to saloon owner has depended on her sexual liaisons with the businessmen who run the railroad company. Moreover, she refuses to apologize for or feel ashamed of her sexual transgressions. When Johnny, her former lover, who has not seen her for five years, realizes how she has acquired the saloon, he becomes jealous and expects her to feel ashamed. He remarks pointedly, "Five years is a long time. There must have been quite a few men in between." But so far as Vienna is concerned, all Johnny should care about is that she got what she wanted, her own saloon, which promises to make them both rich once the railroad is built. She insists, "I'm not ashamed of how I got what I have. The important thing is I got it." As a man, Johnny supposedly cannot understand the obstacles she has had to overcome to achieve economic independence. "What right have you to judge?," she demands, then denounces the sexual double standard by which society punishes women like her for transgressing their prescribed role: "A man can lie, steal, and even kill, but as long as he hangs on to his pride, he's still a man. All a woman has to do is slip once, and she's a tramp." This representation of Vienna's sexual nonconformity helps to clarify the movie's camp effect. The movie provided an anachronistic treatment of the fallen woman, one that Ray and Yordan had not revised to reflect the gender and sexual anxieties of the Cold War era. Instead, it recalled the treatment of the fallen woman in Crawford's Depression-era movies. Like those movies, it called attention to the patriarchal structures that prevented women from achieving upward mobility by hard work alone and that forced them to manipulate men sexually. As a result, its representation of Vienna as a self-made woman who is rewarded instead of punished for her sexual transgressions was virtually illegible except as camp.

Where *Johnny Guitar* resembles *Mildred Pierce* is in exploiting the masculine elements of Crawford's persona. From the beginning, Ray's film emphasizes the gender nonconformity of Vienna/Crawford. In the first scene in which she appears, Vienna stands on a balcony overlooking the saloon, legs apart, giving orders to the men below. She wears cowboy boots, a pair of tight Levis, and a fitted black shirt laced up with a string tie. Shot from below, she appears to tower over the men who work for her. When she disappears from the balcony, the movie tracks Sam (Robert Osterloh) as he walks to the kitchen to get a lantern. In a direct address to the audience, he comments, "I've never seen a woman who was more like a man. She thinks like one, acts like one, and sometimes makes me feel I'm not." The movie contains this violation of the realist conventions of classical Hollywood cinema by relocating his comments in the diegesis. The movie immediately cuts to a reverse shot that reveals that Sam has been addressing Johnny and Old Tom (John Carradine), another one of Vienna's men. As Pamela Robertson has noted, Sam's direct address serves to emphasize his comments.[41] Vienna's performance of masculinity renders his own inadequate, such that he feels emasculated by comparison. But unlike *Mildred Pierce*, *Johnny Guitar* avoided pathologizing Crawford's violation of her prescribed role as a woman. Old Tom immediately undercuts the implication of Sam's comments by turning to Johnny and remarking, "I never believed I'd end my days working for

JOAN CRAWFORD AS ONE OF THE BOYS IN *JOHNNY GUITAR*.

a woman and liking it." Indeed, all of Vienna's men admire her for her manly courage, which enables her to resist the ranchers' attempts to intimidate her into shuttering the saloon.

Johnny Guitar also differs from *Mildred Pierce* in exaggerating Crawford's gender and sexual nonconformity. It went further than the earlier movie in splitting apart the masculine and the feminine elements of the actress's persona. Even in the scene in *Mildred Pierce* in which Mildred wears a mannish pin-stripe suit, she also wears a pair of sexy ankle-strap high heels that in accentuating Crawford's shapely legs seem intended to remind viewers of the heterosexual address of her sex appeal. But in *Johnny Guitar*, Vienna's masculinity extends to her sexual conduct. She reverses patriarchal sexual arrangements by treating men as objects to be used and then thrown away. With Johnny's return, Vienna begins to treat the Dancin' Kid indifferently, which puzzles him. He chides her, "I remember when it was different," but she replies coldly, "You remember, I don't. That's the way it goes." But instead of being a violation of her prescribed role as a woman, Vienna's masculinity emerges as a performance designed to protect her from patriarchal power structures. Because she looks, thinks, and acts like a man, men cannot treat her like a tramp, and she therefore retains her sexual autonomy. Both the Kid and Johnny occupy a subordinate or feminized position in relation to her. Rather than them controlling her, she controls them, and they constantly seek reassurance of her love and fidelity. For example, jealous of her liaisons with other men, Johnny pleads with her: "Tell me something nice. Lie to me. Tell me that you've waited for me all these years." Vienna has been waiting for him, but she does not want him to know it, and she impatiently tells him to stop feeling sorry for himself. She does not admit that she has been waiting for him until she knows that he does not see her as he sees other women who have "slipped." When she breaks down and begins to tell him about the other men she has been involved with, he interrupts her, "You got nothin' to tell me, 'cause it's not real. You and me, that's real." Assured that he now views her sexual past as she does, as something that has no bearing on their relationship, she melts into his arms and kisses him. She can occupy a more stereotypically feminine position in relation to him once she knows that he will not attempt to dominate her.

But Vienna's masculinity does not wholly protect her from patriarchal social and economic arrangements. Because of her gender and sexual nonconformity, she becomes a convenient scapegoat for the town's fears, as she seems to embody the social and economic changes portended by the coming of the railroad. In the scene in which the men of the town, goaded by Emma, descend on the saloon to arrest Vienna for the stagecoach robbery, Vienna challenges their authority by drawing her gun on them. Intimidated by her display of manly courage, the men begin to retreat, but Emma refuses to back down. Turning to face her rival, who stands on the stairs in a posture of defiance with her gun drawn, Emma shouts, "Look at her, staring down on us like she's a somebody. You're nothing but a railroad tramp. You're not fit to live among decent people." Despite her masculinity, Vienna is still a woman and therefore, because of her sexual transgressions and regardless of her success as a businesswoman, does not deserve the town's respect. The men do not yet share Emma's view of Vienna, and Vienna eventually convinces them to depart, but this scene marks an important turning point in the film. By publicly labeling Vienna a tramp, Emma begins to displace her as the most powerful figure in the town.

Emma has more success in turning the men against her rival in the scene in which she skillfully takes control of the posse away from McIvers. In this scene, she manages to persuade the men that Vienna represents a more serious threat to the town than the Kid and his gang, who have robbed the town's bank, and that they should go after her instead. Addressing the men, she repeats what Vienna has told them about the coming of the railroad when they confront her about the stage-coach robbery: "You heard her tell how they're going to run the railroad through here, bringin' in thousands of new people from the East, farmers, dirt farmers, squatters. They'll push us out." Further provoking the men toward action, she refers to Vienna's sexual nonconformity, more subtly than when she shocked them by calling her a "railroad tramp": "You're actin' like she's some fine lady and doin' nothin' makes all of you fine gentlemen. Well, she ain't, and you're not." Emma ends her rousing speech by painting a dire picture of the changes to come: "So you better wake up, or you're gonna find you and your women and your kids squeezed between barbed wire and fence posts." *Johnny Guitar* thus allegorizes the Cold War persecution of lesbians and gays, as well as the McCarthy witch hunts. In representing Vienna as a kind of gender and sexual outlaw, Emma transforms her into a symbol of the "progress" that threatens to render the ranchers' way of life outmoded. They cannot prevent the railroad from dislocating them, but they can register their opposition to the social and economic forces it represents by expelling Vienna.

The movie's critique of Cold War homophobia manifests itself more fully in its emphasis on the differences between Vienna's and Emma's masculinities. Like Mildred, Vienna alternates between masculine and feminine gender presentations, an alternation that the movie signals primarily through her costumes.[42] For example, in the scene in which she reaffirms her love for Johnny, Vienna wears a form-fitting red negligee that highlights her shapely figure. Later, when the posse comes to the saloon to arrest her for the bank robbery, she wears a fluffy white gown with puffed sleeves that, as Pamela Robertson has noted, recalls the famous Letty Lynton dress.[43] The gown seems intended to have a similar effect, the containment of Crawford's masculine mode of embodiment, which elsewhere the movie exploits. But Vienna's performances of femininity are by no means limited to the scenes in which she wears feminine attire. At the end of the movie, after she and Johnny have escaped from the posse and are holed up in the Kid's hiding place, Vienna changes into clothes that belonged to Turkey, who was hanged by the posse the night before. Despite her masculine gender style, she manifests a stereotypical feminine concern with her appearance. After she has changed into the clothes, she looks into a mirror so she can adjust a bright-red silk scarf that she has tied around her neck. She also makes breakfast for Johnny, thereby revealing a domestic side. Thus her alternation between masculinity and femininity does not reinforce a binary construction of gender identity, as some critics have claimed.[44] Instead, it highlights the performative aspects of masculinity and femininity, which emerge as a matter of proper representation. In so doing, it associates Vienna with the new system of sexual classification that privileged object choice over gender identity. The mobility of her gender style prevents her masculinity from functioning as a signifier of lesbianism.

By contrast, the film's representation of Emma seems based on a sexological model of gender and sexuality. Emma lacks her rival's ability to perform femininity, and her masculinity emerges as a fixed identity that reflects her object choice. One way in which the movie circumvented the Production Code was by rendering Emma's sexuality ambiguous. She simultaneously resembles a stereotypical lesbian and a stereotypical spinster. As several critics have pointed out, in the scene in which the Kid takes her in his arms and dances with her, she has a horrified look on her face, which indicates that she is both repulsed by and attracted to him. Vienna later explains to Johnny that Emma dislikes the Kid because he "makes her feel like a woman, and that frightens her." Emma feels ashamed of her desire for the Kid and struggles to repress it. Further linking her to the stereotype of the old maid is that during most of the film, out of respect for her dead brother, Emma wears a fitted black mourning dress which bears a striking resemblance to a nun's habit. Thus, in contrast to Vienna, who even when she wears masculine attire functions as an object to be looked at, Emma fails to fulfill one of the female star's most important functions in classical Hollywood cinema, which is to provide audiences with a surplus of visual pleasure. Emma's sexual repression partly explains her hostility to Vienna. Although she constantly expresses disapproval of Vienna's sexual behavior, she seems to envy her sexual freedom. In the scene in which the men confront Vienna about the stagecoach robbery, Vienna notices the body of Emma's dead brother on one of the tables in the saloon, and she lowers her gun to remark consolingly to Emma, "He was a very fine man." But Emma, who does not want her sympathy, snaps, "How would you know? He was one man who never even looked at you!" Emma's vehemence suggests that she would like to receive the same kind of attention from men as Vienna does.

At the same time, Emma's hostility to Vienna has an intensity that cannot be explained in terms of her envy of the more attractive woman and that opens up her rivalry with Vienna to a lesbian reading. *Time*'s review of the movie described Emma as "a sexological square knot who fondles pistols suggestively and gets unladylike satisfaction from watching a house burn down," which suggests that at least some viewers saw through the film's coded representation of the spinster and associated her masculine gender presentation with the sexological category of sexual inversion.[45] Emma not only projects her own transgressive sexuality onto Vienna, but also resents her for not paying as much attention to her as she does to Johnny and the Kid. In another concession to the Production Code, the film implies that Emma's persecution of Vienna as a "railroad tramp" reflects her jealousy of Vienna's relationship with the Kid. But it never clearly indicates which of the two characters makes Emma jealous. When Emma speculates rather preposterously that the Kid killed her brother so that he could "get" her, Vienna remarks scornfully, "You've got it a little twisted, haven't you, Emma? Now you think you can get him. You want the Kid and you're so ashamed of it you want him dead. And you want me dead, too. Then maybe you can sleep nights." Vienna's comments are themselves "twisted" and leave unclear what exactly keeps Emma awake at night. Does Emma feel ashamed of her desire for the Kid, or because she wants him dead? And since she also wants Vienna dead, does that mean she has a desire for her that also keeps her awake at night? Emma compounds the ambiguity about the nature of her desire when in the same scene she claims that Vienna and the Kid "cast the same shadow" and should both be arrested for the holdup of the stagecoach. Emma views Vienna and the Kid as one and the same person, which only confirms Vienna's suggestion that her desire is "twisted." Ashamed of her desire for Vienna, she projects it onto the Kid. But because Vienna desires him and not Emma, Emma resents him and wants him dead. But she also wants Vienna dead, because she reminds her of a forbidden desire that she struggles unsuccessfully to repress.

This representation of Emma appears to contradict the movie's critique of Cold War homophobia by incorporating the discourse of female homosexuality, which constructed the lesbian as a threat to the nation. Although Emma's inverted gender identity prevents her from passing as straight, she resembles the psychopathic lesbian who because of her lack of self-control supposedly threatened to destabilize the nation. Emma manifests her gender and sexual nonconformity in part by inciting the ranchers to mob violence, thus bearing most of the responsibility for the breakdown of social order: she turns the men against Vienna with her hate-filled speech about the railroad's threat to their way of life; she goads a terrified Turkey into implicating Vienna in the bank robbery by falsely promising to let him go if he does; she cold-bloodedly shoots Marshal Williams (Frank Ferguson) when he attempts to protect Vienna from the lynch mob; she sets Vienna's saloon on fire in a frenzy of revenge that connects her to another famous celluloid lesbian, Mrs. Danvers, who burns down Manderley when she learns that her beloved mistress concealed from her that she was dying from cancer.[46] Finally, when none of the men is willing to hang Vienna, even after she offers them one hundred dollars as a reward, she decides to do it herself. (Johnny intercedes, however, and sets Vienna free.) In other words, Emma contaminates the town with her "twisted" desire in much the same way the government claimed that homosexual employees would "pollute" their coworkers unless they were purged.

How do we reconcile this representation of Emma with the movie's critique of Cold War lesbian panic? For in encoding its villain as a lesbian, the movie seems to suggest that female homosexuals did threaten to destabilize American society. But the construction of Emma's character is complicated by McCambridge's performance, which has an exaggerated quality that makes it difficult to take her character seriously. The review of *Johnny Guitar* in *Catholic World* called attention to this difficulty when it claimed that Crawford's performance was a "masterpiece of restraint when compared to that of Mercedes McCambridge . . . who does most of her acting with her teeth and eyebrows."[47] Because of its camp effect, McCambridge's performance seems intended to parody the homophobic categories of the discourse of national security. Emma's psychopathic behavior is so excessive that it had the potential to expose the Cold War construction of the lesbian as nothing more than a hateful stereotype. Moreover, one effect of the movie's representation of Emma was to associate Cold War homophobia with a pathological fear of same-sex desire. In attributing Emma's persecution of Vienna to her inability to accept her lesbianism, the movie suggested that what threatened to destabilize the nation was not gender and sexual nonconformity, but the campaign against them. Emma's determination to punish Vienna for her gender and sexual transgressions results in the collapse of the rule of law. In the scene in which the posse accuses her of committing the bank robbery, the Marshal admonishes Vienna, "Either you side with them or with us. You can't stay on the fence no longer. Show us the way to [the Kid's] lair and save yourself a lot of grief." Here, the Marshal, goaded by Emma, indirectly warns Vienna that she must assume a normative gender and sexual identity. After all, the fence she straddles is not only the one between the town and the gang, but also the one between masculinity and femininity. As a result, she threatens the binary construction of gender and sexual identities, and the town wants to make an example of her by hanging her.

In allegorizing Cold War lesbian panic, *Johnny Guitar* turned the gender and sexual norms promoted by the contemporary discourse of female homosexuality inside out. Whereas the film's treatment of Emma demonizes the fixity of gender and sexual identities, its treatment of Vienna valorizes their mobility. Although Emma gains control over the men of the town, they never fully accept her authority. Seeming to realize that her rivalry with Vienna is more complicated than she acknowledges, they always wait for McIvers to assent to her orders before following them. By contrast, Vienna's men willingly submit to her authority, which suggests that they do not experience her masculinity as a usurpation of patriarchal privilege. Even the men of the town seem to accept Vienna's authority. That the men refuse to hang Vienna after capturing her, which forces Emma to do it herself, underscores the effect of Vienna's gender mobility on the men, for it is her feminine gender style that prevents them from engaging in more violence. With its luminous glow, her fluffy white dress makes her appear almost holy, so that hanging her would amount to an act of desecration, and the men insist that they cannot hang a woman. This scene clarifies the significance of Vienna's alternation between masculinity and femininity. It allows her to claim patriarchal privilege without alienating the men. By contrast, the fixity of Emma's gender identity prevents her from circumventing her subordination as a woman. The men begin to resent her authority because she has overstepped the bounds of femininity by inciting them to mob violence.

Vienna's masculinity also differs from Emma's in that it increases rather than decreases her sexual desirability. Vienna's lovers gladly accept subordination as one of the conditions necessary for securing her love. This aspect of her relationships with men surfaces most fully in Johnny's love for her. In the scene in which he almost kills Turkey—after the boy attempts to impress Vienna by showing off his skill as a gunfighter—Vienna reprimands Johnny for still being "gun crazy." She has expected her former lover to come back a changed man, one who no longer acts impulsively. Johnny's impetuousness as a gunfighter points to a troubling similarity between him and Emma that he must overcome before he and Vienna can reunite as a couple. Vienna demands to know where Johnny keeps his guns. When he tells her that they are in his saddlebags, she replies, "Suppose you keep them there. I'll tell you when to use them."

Looking down as if ashamed, he replies, "You're the boss." But rather than experiencing Vienna's domination as emasculating, Johnny seems to welcome it. He prefers her masculine gender style to her feminine one, a preference that is underscored when Vienna's dress catches on fire in the mineshaft and Johnny tears it off her, thus rescuing her from a potentially deadly femininity. Then, after they have escaped to the Kid's hideout, Johnny helps Vienna put on Turkey's clothes. Finally, in the film's closing shots, he takes her in his arms and kisses her passionately in front of the waterfall that blocks the way to the Kid's hideout. Vienna is still wearing Turkey's clothes. Thus, although the movie follows the conventions of classical Hollywood cinema by ending with the formation of the couple, it differs in one crucial respect: that Johnny and Vienna have the same gender identity raises the question whether their relationship can be understood as heterosexual and thus queers Cold War gender and sexual norms. Johnny's and Vienna's desire for each other cannot be explained in terms of either the old or the new system of sexual classification.

CONTAINING CAMP

The mostly hostile reviews *Johnny Guitar* received suggest that it succeeded in destabilizing the dominant constructions of gender and sexual identities. Critics objected in particular to the camp effect of Crawford's performance. The review in *Time* noted that the middle-aged star "shapes up well in her Levis," but complained that in the scene where she plays the piano while the posse searches the saloon for the Kid and his gang, she resembled a "cowtown Liberace."[48] The review in the *New York Times*, on the other hand, expressed disapproval of Crawford's masculinity, which it claimed rendered her sex only "technically recognized."[49] The review in *Variety* agreed and urged the actress to "leave saddles and Levis to someone else and stick to the city lights for a background."[50] Critics did not limit their criticism of the movie's campiness to Crawford's performance. The review in *Catholic World* dismissed the movie as "unintentionally hilarious,"[51] and the review in *Spectator* denounced it as a "parody of itself" that provided audiences with a "perverted pleasure."[52] Leo Charney has attributed the hostility of these reviews to the movie's generic excesses.[53] According to him, critics objected to the movie because it did not conform to the conventions of the western, but exaggerated them to the point of parody. As Ray pointed out, *Johnny Guitar* was "the first Hollywood western where women were both the major protagonists and antagonists."[54] But the movie's generic excesses cannot account for the hostility of the reviews, which were themselves excessive. This excessiveness indicates that what bothered reviewers was not so much the movie's debunking of the western as its potential to destabilize Cold War gender and sexual norms. Reviewers seemed anxious that audiences would derive "perverted pleasure" from the movie's campiness, which they tried to contain by attacking it.

Despite the reviews, *Johnny Guitar* was one of Ray's few films that did well at the box office. Although there is no way to know for sure, it may be that the aspect of the movie that most resonated with audiences was its camp effect. Vienna's alternation between masculinity and femininity destabilized categories of identity that oppressed gay and lesbian audiences. Adding to its "perverted" appeal, the movie authorized a set of practices associated with the gay and lesbian subcultures by encouraging a camp mode of reception, which the reviews reflected. Moreover, in exploiting the excesses of Crawford's and McCambridge's performance styles, the movie showed that camp had the potential to counteract Cold War homophobia. These aspects of the movie did not nullify the ambiguity of its representation of Emma, which affirmed even as it undermined the Cold War construction of the lesbian. But unlike William Wyler's *The Children's Hour*, *Johnny Guitar* not only avoided underwriting Cold War sexual epistemology, but also exposed the contradictions in the contemporary discourse of female homosexuality.

CHAPTER FIVE

REMAKING BETTE DAVIS

In 1956 Bette Davis starred in *Storm Center* (Daniel Taradash), one of the few Hollywood films made in the 1950s that openly and unambiguously challenged the McCarthy witch hunts. In the movie, Davis plays Alicia Hull, the revered librarian of the Kenport Free Public Library, who when pressured by the town council to remove from circulation a controversial book called *The Communist Dream* refuses to do so. Hull believes that removing the propagandistic book would amount to censorship, and she urges the council to allow her to keep it on the shelves as testimony to the strength of American democracy. But Paul Duncan (Brian Keith), a member of the council who sees in Hull's principled stance an opportunity to further his political ambitions, convinces the council to fire her by accusing her of belonging to several front organizations for the Communist Party. In so doing, he destroys her reputation and nearly drives her from the town. The director, Daniel Taradash, based *Storm Center* on an incident in Bartlesville, Oklahoma, in which Ruth Brown, a librarian at the public library, was fired by the city council, despite thirty years of exemplary service, for circulating "subversive materials," including *The Nation*, *New Republic*, and *Consumer Reports*.[1] Although, unlike the fictional Hull, Brown did not have any "red affiliations" her opponents could exploit, she angered Bartlesville's white supremacists by participating in a civil rights group, and she was fired shortly after she attempted to eat at the lunch counter of a local drug store with two African American friends.[2] Taradash began working with screenwriter Elick Moll on a fictionalized treatment of the incident shortly after reading about it in the *Saturday Review*, but he could not find a studio willing to make the movie until after public opinion turned against McCarthy and he was censured by the U.S. Senate.[3] Even then he had difficulty persuading an actress to play Hull, because of the film's potentially incendiary theme.[4]

Taradash avoided addressing the cause of Brown's dismissal, her civil rights activism, and instead introduced what he called a "love story" centered on Hull's friendship with Freddie Slater (Kevin Coughlin), a boy with a voracious appetite for books who is traumatized when she is fired. Although with her dowdy dresses and stern demeanor, Hull resembles a stereotypical spinster, Robert Ellerbe (Paul Kelly), the only member of the council who opposes her dismissal, describes her as the type of woman who "should have had twenty kids." Since the death of her husband, a soldier killed during the First World War, Hull has devoted herself to the library and the town's children, who grow up viewing her as a guide and mentor. She is especially attached to the egghead Freddie, whose love of books alienates his father, George (Joe Mantell), a factory worker who makes fun of his wife for playing Chopin on the piano. George resents Hull's friendship with his son, which he thinks has prevented him from developing like a "normal" boy. He buys Freddie a catcher's mitt so they can play baseball in the backyard. But the boy continues to prefer the library, and when George meets with Hull to discuss his concerns about Freddie, he complains that a year later the mitt is still on Freddie's desk, "just as new as the day he got it." In other words, George worries that his son will grow up a sissy if he continues to spend all his free time at the library. Hull does not have much sympathy for George's concerns and urges him to stop wishing his son were like other boys: "Your boy is not just an average boy. He's different. Value that difference. We put far too much stress on conformity in this country. The ballpark isn't the only place a person can be a hero. Some people lead very exciting lives locked in a laboratory, or even a library." George looks around the library skeptically, indicating that she has failed to convince him. Later, when he learns about the accusations against her, he derides the librarian's advice as "pinko talk." Her belief that not all boys need to grow up playing baseball emerges as subversive and un-American.

In making George's fears about Hull's influence over his son's development central to the movie's plot, Taradash indirectly acknowledged the Cold War backlash against Davis's sexually ambiguous screen image. Davis's role as Hull recalled her persona in a cycle of enormously popular women's pictures she had made between 1939 and 1943, the heyday of her career at Warner Brothers.[5] As several scholars have pointed out, this cycle challenged the heteronormative construction of motherhood by constructing a discourse of maternal desire that circumvented the role of the father and displaced the mother.[6] The first movie to articulate the star's persona to this discourse was *The Old Maid* (Edmund Goulding, 1939).[7] Set in Civil War–era Philadelphia, *The Old Maid* centers on the fraught relationship between two cousins, Delia (Miriam Hopkins) and Charlotte (Davis) Lovell, who love the same man, the irresponsible Clem Spender (George Brent). When Delia breaks off her engagement to Clem so she can marry a wealthy banker, Charlotte has an affair with him and becomes pregnant. To conceal her sexual transgression, she opens a nursery for war orphans and passes off her daughter, Tina, as a foundling. After Delia's husband dies, Charlotte and Tina move in with her, and Charlotte transforms herself into a stern, disapproving "old maid" to prevent anyone from suspecting that she is Tina's mother. As a result, Tina grows up preferring the more nurturing Delia, who eventually adopts her so she can marry into a prominent family. An embittered Charlotte believes that Delia has robbed her of Tina's love to punish her for having Clem's baby. The other films in the cycle reversed this scenario so that Davis's character occupies the permissive, maternal position in relation to the child, and her rival the prohibitive, paternal one. But regardless of Davis's position in the scenario, all of the films provided a queer representation of motherhood.[8] Even in *The Great Lie* (Edmund Goulding, 1941), the only movie in the cycle in which Davis plays a wife, her character, Maggie, adopts the illegitimate child of her rival, the concert pianist Sandra (Mary Astor), who became pregnant after having an affair with Maggie's husband, Pete (George Brent), before they were married. The movie never raises the possibility that Maggie might have a child of her own with Pete, even after he returns from the Amazon, where Maggie and Sandra believe he died in a plane crash.

The movies in the cycle also challenged heteronormative institutions and discourses by constructing an alternative narrative of female identity that did not culminate in heterosexual romance. Despite their focus on female rivalry, all of the movies ultimately affirm the Davis character's bonds with other women. In the movies, female homosocial desire invariably displaces heterosexual romance as the focus of the narrative.[9] Even in *The Great Lie*, which unlike the other movies ends with Davis happily married, Pete's unexpected return from the Amazon serves less to ensure that Maggie achieves the "happily ever after" of married life than to sustain the film's focus on her competitive relationship with Sandra, who reneges on her agreement with Maggie and descends on the newly reunited couple to claim the baby as her own. She is convinced that if Pete knows that she is the baby's "real" mother, he will divorce Maggie and marry her. Moreover, all of the films except *The Great Lie* end with Davis's character seeking fulfillment in domestic intimacy with another woman. In *The Old Maid*, Charlotte and Delia walk back into the house after Tina's wedding with their arms wrapped around each other. In *All This and Heaven Too* (Anatole Litvak, 1940), Henriette (Davis) overcomes her scandalous past as a governess by embarking on a career as a teacher at a girls' school. In *Now, Voyager* (Irving Rapper, 1942), the most famous of the motherhood films, Charlotte (Davis) persuades Dr. Jaquith (Claude Rains) to allow her to set up house with Tina (Janis Wilson), the daughter of her married lover, Jerry (Paul Henreid), in exchange for ending their illicit affair. In *Old Acquaintance* (Vincent Sherman, 1943), the last film in the cycle, Kit (Davis) and Millie (Miriam Hopkins) put aside their differences and toast the endurance of their friendship. These endings affirmed the alternative domestic arrangements that the Second World War opened up for women, which may explain their enormous popularity with female audiences.

Davis's role in *The Great Lie* illustrates how the cycle destabilized the star's relation to the institutions of heterosexuality. Following Pete's disappearance in the Amazonian jungle, Maggie persuades Sandra to go away with her and have her baby so she can adopt it. She rents an isolated cabin in the Arizona desert where she and Sandra can set up house without attracting the attention of reporters. While waiting for Sandra to go into labor, her doctor (Farrell MacDonald) waxes patriarchal about the importance of motherhood to a woman's identity. He asks Maggie as she paces anxiously, "So you never had a child of your own? Pity. Just the sort of woman who should have had one. Oh well, you'll have plenty of time. Spells life with capital letters. A woman without a child is like a man without an arm, a right arm." But the film's discourse of maternal desire directly contradicts this view of motherhood. Although Maggie wants to have a child, her desire, by masculinizing her, undermines rather than affirms her identity as a woman. As her pacing in this scene indicates, she has taken on the role of the expectant father during Sandra's pregnancy. She carefully monitors Sandra's diet, takes away her cigarettes when she smokes more than her daily allotment, and limits her drinking to an ounce of brandy before bed. When the high-strung Sandra can no longer bear Maggie's restrictions and threatens to burn down the cabin with a lantern, Maggie grabs the lantern and slaps her. Moreover, in the scene with the doctor, Maggie appears distracted when the doctor addresses her, and she constantly looks in the direction of Sandra's bedroom with an anxious expression on her face. Ironically, the doctor tells her that he misses having the expectant father in the room anxiously waiting to hear him say, "Well, old man, it's all over, and they're doing nicely." Maggie's masculine appearance in this scene translates into visual terms her role as expectant father. She wears a pair of slacks, the sleeves of her blouse are rolled up carelessly, and when the doctor disappears into Sandra's bedroom to deliver the baby, she sits down in a chair and spreads her legs apart like a man.

Davis's role in *The Great Lie* rendered her performance of femininity sexually ambiguous. Maggie's gender presentation shifts in relation to that of her rival, Sandra. Her masculinization in the Arizona desert proves temporary, and in the movie's final scenes she assumes a more normative gender style. By contrast, Sandra turns increasingly masculine. She arrives at Maggie's Maryland plantation wearing an elegant knit dress with an elaborate ruffled collar and a plumed hat with a black veil. But in the scene in which she confronts her rival about the "great lie" she has told Pete, she wears a striped jacket with padded shoulders and a white silk blouse that resembles a man's dress shirt; her hair, cut short and parted on the side, also looks masculine. The film underscores this shift in her gender presentation by shooting her from below, an angle that has the effect of magnifying her size so that she appears to tower over Maggie. Sandra's masculinization seems intended to undermine her claims to the baby. Unlike the more feminine Maggie, who wears a fitted wool dress and a pair of high heels, she does not seem to belong in the domestic sphere, married and the mother of a child. But because it can also be interpreted as a response to the shift in Maggie's gender identity, Sandra's masculinization opens up their relationship to a lesbian construction. Despite their rivalry over Pete and the baby, the two women resemble a butch-femme couple, and the "great lie" could be their refusal to acknowledge their desire for each other. In blurring the distinction between female homosocial desire and lesbian identity, the movie threatened to queer the female spectator's identity. Indeed, as Patricia White has argued, all of the movies in the cycle functioned as a "spinster machine" that had the potential to disengage the female spectator's desire from the institutions of heterosexuality.[10]

The Cold War–era backlash against this aspect of Davis's persona, which George's reaction to Hull's "pinko talk" in *Storm Center* reflected, manifested itself most fully in three later films that Davis made about fading female stars: *All about Eve*, *The Star* (Stuart Heisler, 1952), and *What-*

A BUTCH MARY ASTOR AND A FEMME BETTE DAVIS IN *THE GREAT LIE*.

ever Happened to Baby Jane? (Robert Aldrich, 1961).[11] All three movies punish Davis for providing female audiences with an alternative model of womanhood in the 1940s and seek to remake her image so that it conforms to Cold War gender and sexual norms. In each of the movies, the representation of the fading female star emerges as more negative than in the previous one, a pattern that attests to the difficulty the cycle had in updating Davis's persona for the Cold War era. *All about Eve* reinforced its homophobic treatment of lesbianism by exploiting Davis's sexually ambiguous persona and reworking many of the themes underlying Davis's appeal as a star earlier in her career. In the first part of the movie, Margo's domestic life centers on another woman, Bertie, whose masculinity complements her femininity, and she seems in no hurry to marry Bill. Moreover, Margo's rivalry with Eve displaces her relationship with Bill as the focus of the narrative until Margo decides, near the end of the movie, that she wants to be a woman more than a star. But unlike the movies in the motherhood cycle, *All about Eve* underwrites a homophobic construction of female homosocial desire. Margo's desire for intimacy with other women makes her vulnerable to the manipulations of the predatory lesbian, Eve. Perhaps the most striking difference between *All about Eve* and the earlier movies is that it reinstalls marriage as the goal of female sexual development and in so doing attempts to stabilize Davis's relation to the institutions of heterosexuality.

The Star also attempted to remake Davis's image to conform to Cold War gender and sexual norms. In the movie, Davis's character, Margaret Elliot, clings to the belief that all she needs to revive her career is another good part. But she has not appeared on-screen for three years and has lost the "fresh, dewy quality" her agent, Harry Stone (Warner Anderson), tells her all female stars require. *The Star* reprises one of the central themes of *All About Eve*: the lack of fulfillment women supposedly experience when they choose a career over marriage and motherhood.[12] When Margaret is arrested for drunk driving, Jim Johannson (Sterling Hayden), one of her former leading men, bails her out and begins to romance her. But determined to revive her career, Margaret rejects him. Bitterly reproaching Margaret, Jim expresses the film's view of ambitious career women like its star, Bette Davis: "I once thought you were a woman. But I was wrong. You're nothing but a career." Margaret's conflict between her desire to stay on top and her identity as a woman has a poignancy that Margo's struggle lacks. Unlike Margo, Margaret has a daughter, Gretchen (Natalie Wood), for whom she cannot provide a home, because she is bankrupt. *The Star* adopts the same strategy for containing Davis's persona as *All about Eve* does. When Margaret fails a screen test for a part in a film aptly titled *The Fatal Winter*, she realizes that she has lost her appeal as a star and returns, with Gretchen, to Jim. In this way, *The Star* suggested that the new era required a different kind of female star from Davis, one whose persona underwrote a heteronormative construction of femininity.

The Cold War backlash against Davis culminated in *Whatever Happened to Baby Jane?* Although like the other two fading-star films it reworked the themes explored in Davis's motherhood cycle, Aldrich's movie adopted a new strategy for containing her image, by transforming the type of woman's picture the star made during the heyday of her career into a horror movie. In so doing, it indirectly acknowledged the incompatibility of her persona with the institutions of heterosexuality. In the film, Davis plays Baby Jane Hudson, a former child vaudeville star, who lives with and tends to her paraplegic sister, Blanche (Joan Crawford), in a decaying Hollywood mansion. The movie's representation of the two sisters' toxic domestic life seems intended to counter the treatment of female homosocial desire in the motherhood cycle. Before being paralyzed in a car accident almost thirty years earlier, Blanche had been a famous movie star, and she and Jane have been locked in a bitter rivalry over their former careers ever since. Unlike the glamorous Blanche, who sizzled on-screen, Jane lacked sex appeal, and her movie career never took off. As a result, she returns to the gender style that had originally made her a bigger star than her sister: the gender style of her childhood. She begins wearing girlish dresses decorated with bows and ruffles that recall the costumes for her vaudeville act. Her rivalry with Blanche intensifies when a television station broadcasts some of Blanche's old movies, and Blanche begins receiving fan mail. Determined to revive her vaudeville act, Jane orders replicas of her childhood costumes and hires a composer, the creepy Edwin Flagg (Victor Buono), who seems fixated on his mother, to arrange her music. In other words, Aldrich's film attempted to contain Davis's persona by associating it with an outmoded stardom that supposedly no longer appealed to audiences. This construction of the star's persona implied that the type of woman's picture that Davis made in the late 1930s and 1940s no longer resonated with female audiences, because their experience and expectations had been transformed by the Cold War. An assessment of *Old Acquaintance*, which re-paired Davis with Miriam Hopkins, who played her rival in *The Old Maid*, sets the stage for elucidating how *Whatever Happened to Baby Jane?* revised the discourse of female homosocial desire in Davis's motherhood cycle such that it validated Cold War gender and sexual anxieties.

WHAT'S LEFT OF THE ICING

Old Acquaintance counters the discourse of spinsterhood in *The Old Maid* by recasting the rivalry between Charlotte and Delia. Like the earlier film, *Old Acquaintance* traces the ups and downs in a fraught relationship between two women, Millie Watson Drake and Kit Marlowe, over roughly two decades, from 1924 to the Second World War. The parallels between the two movies are striking. Like Delia and Charlotte, Millie and Kit love the same man, in this case Millie's husband, Preston (John Loder), an architect whose career stalls just as his wife's takes off. But, as in *The Old Maid*, the two women's rivalry displaces their relationship with the man as the focus of the narrative. Like Delia and Charlotte, Millie and Kit compete for the love of a child, Millie's spoiled daughter, Deirdre (Dolores Moran). Compounding their rivalry is the fact that they are both successful writers, but whereas Millie grinds out her novels "like sausage," as the reporter Belle Carter (Anne Revere) derogatorily puts it, Kit struggles over hers, which, despite their critical acclaim, fail to sell. But the differences between the two women's pictures are even more striking. Unlike Clem, who despite his affair with Charlotte continues to love Delia, Preston falls in love with Kit and eventually leaves Millie. But when he proposes to Kit, she rejects him, although she loves him; unlike Charlotte, who does not hesitate to deceive Delia, Kit refuses to betray her friendship with Millie. Kit makes a similar sacrifice for Deirdre later in the film, when she discovers that she has fallen in love with the older woman's only other suitor, Rudd (Gig Young). Kit breaks off her relationship with the man so he and Deirdre can marry. In revising the representation of Davis's character in *The Old Maid*, *Old Acquaintance* reclaimed the figure of the spinster. Although Kit also ends up an "old maid," unlike Charlotte, she chooses spinsterhood. Her sacrifices enable her to continue to organize her life around her career and her friendship with Millie.

Old Acquaintance opens with Kit returning to her hometown as the acclaimed author of a novel entitled *Bury My Soul*, which has provoked "considerable discussion in New York literary circles" and established her reputation as an authority on the "modern woman," the subject of her lecture at the town hall. She has not seen her girlhood friend Millie since moving to New York to become a writer, and Millie eagerly prepares for her arrival, bragging to a reporter how "all through school and afterward . . . we were absolutely inseparable." Millie's gender style suggests that she embodies a form of womanhood that is anything but modern. When she arrives at the train station to greet Kit, she wears a jumper with a pleated skirt, a frilly blouse with puffed sleeves, and a hat decorated with lace flowers, an ensemble that reflects her identity as a housewife and mother-to-be. By contrast, Kit wears a mannish suit and tie that seem intended to express her identity as a modern woman. Despite these gender differences, however, neither woman is wholly satisfied with the choices she has made. Kit envies Millie's married life and remarks wistfully when the two women are alone preparing for bed that it must be nice having a husband "to see to things." Likewise, Millie had experienced a "pang of envy" while reading about Kit's success in the local newspaper, and she has written a romance novel entitled *Married in June*, which she hopes Kit will show her editor. But despite her literary ambitions, Millie has no desire to lead the kind of life Kit does. She asks Kit what she intends to do about her life "outside of books," insinuating that a career cannot compensate for the lack of a husband and proclaiming that a woman can have "a career and a life," that unlike her childhood friend, she would never

A BUTCH BETTE DAVIS AND A FEMME MIRIAM HOPKINS
IN *OLD ACQUAINTANCE.*

settle for one without the other. But Kit does not regret that she has pri-
oritized her career. As a modern woman, she does not share Millie's belief
that a fulfilling life requires marriage and motherhood.

Despite her traditional view of womanhood, Millie becomes wholly
absorbed in her career once she discovers how much money she can make
from writing romance novels. Indeed, she shows a masculine drive to
succeed that conflicts with her feminine gender presentation. Unlike Kit,
Millie has no interest in achieving critical acclaim, but instead writes for
the "broad public." She wants a more luxurious life than Preston can provide on his salary as an architect. In the scene in which Millie reveals
that she has written a novel, Kit asks Millie what she will do with all the
money she will make if her books catch on with the public, and she replies dreamily, "I'd have a secretary, two cars, and when my baby comes,
I'd have an English nanny for it, and later a French governess, that is if
it's a girl." In other words, she dreams of a life in which she can escape
the responsibilities of motherhood by relegating her child's upbringing
to servants. Preston does not share his wife's dreams, and her success
causes a reversal in their roles as husband and wife, which makes him feel

emasculated. Millie's absorption in her career leads her to neglect him and Deirdre, and he interrupts his career to fill the void that her neglect creates in their daughter's life. Aware of Preston's growing frustration with their marriage, Kit urges Millie to show him more consideration, but, missing the point, Millie replies incredulously, "I've given him everything, a house, grounds, servants. I make him a definite department in my life, as I do my child." Preston's frustration culminates in the scene in which Millie shows off an expensive pair of diamond earrings she has bought herself. He remarks bitterly that he wishes he could have bought them for her, and when she asks if he would prefer her to give up her career, he shouts, "No, we can stay just the way we are, and you can buy me a nice uniform, and on the cap and collar you can put MWD, the property of Mildred Watson Drake, in diamonds!"

In disguising her masculinity, Millie bears a striking resemblance to the type of woman described by the psychoanalyst Joan Riviere in her article "Womanliness as Masquerade" (1929), which examined why some women engaged in exaggeratedly feminine behavior after a display of masculine knowledge or ambition.[13] According to Riviere, such women sought the approval of their male colleagues by adopting an excessively feminine gender presentation that conflicted with their professional accomplishments. They supposedly hoped to avoid retribution in case the men discovered their gender nonconformity. Riviere attributed the women's compulsive behavior to an unconscious fear of reprisal by their fathers for overstepping the bounds of femininity. Riviere's analysis captures the conflict between Millie's feminine gender style and her masculine ambitions by suggesting that the bestselling author engages in excessively feminine behavior to deflect attention from her lack of conformity to her socially prescribed role as a woman. Millie has an exploitative relation to women's culture that her seemingly conventional married life enables her to conceal from her readers. In emphasizing heterosexual romance and with titles like *Married in June*, *Lingering Love*, and *Too Much for Love*, her novels promote a heteronormative construction of womanhood that her own life calls into question. Not surprisingly, when Preston leaves her, she worries more about the impact a divorce will have on her image as the ideal wife and mother than about the loss of his love. Collapsing into Kit's arms, she sobs, "How can I face people, how can I tell them that he's left me? Everybody envied me so. They thought I had everything and I did, a husband, and a home, and a baby, and a career." Moreover, the more success she has as a writer, the more excessively feminine her gender style becomes. For example, in New York, after her rise to success, she wears a low-cut, sequined gown and several pieces of expensive-looking jewelry. She has filled her apartment with ornate furniture, gilt mirrors, and crystal vases with flower bouquets, all of which seem intended to reassure her visitors of her femininity.

Like the other films in Davis's motherhood cycle, *Old Acquaintance* queers the dominant representation of maternal desire. Despite her masculinity, which she does not attempt to conceal but expresses openly in her gender style, Kit occupies a maternal position in relation to Deirdre that eventually displaces Millie as the girl's mother. The film's complicated maternal scenario recalls that in *The Great Lie*, where Sandra and Maggie circumvent Pete's role as the father by having Sandra's baby together. When Kit takes Deirdre (Francine Rufo) on a shopping spree and buys her an expensive fur coat, Preston chides her for the extravagance. But Kit considers Deirdre partly her own child, and she explains to Belle Carter, a reporter who is waiting to interview Millie, that she was "at the hospital when [Deirdre] was born. As a matter of fact, she gave me her first smile, but her mother said it was gas." In this account of Deirdre's birth, Preston, her father, is conspicuously absent. Moreover, although she never adopts the girl, Kit's connection to Deirdre trumps Millie's biological one. Despite her lack of maternal desire, Millie resents Kit's role in her daughter's life, which exposes her shortcomings as a mother. When Kit tells her that she has bought Deirdre a new coat, Millie rebukes her for spoiling her daughter: "It's about time you had one of your own." But like Maggie in *The Great Lie*, Kit does not want to have a child of her own. Her relationship with Deirdre enables her to fulfill her maternal desire without participating in the institutions of heterosexuality. As a result, she retains her independence, and unlike Millie, she has no need to disguise her masculinity or her focus on her career with a masquerade of womanliness.

Kit's desire to retain her independence also surfaces in her relationships with men. Both times she turns down suitors in the film, she does so to preserve her friendships with other women, which suggests that homosocial desire has displaced heterosexual romance as the focus of her life. Although she recognizes Millie's shortcomings, Kit remains grateful for her friendship during childhood. When Preston asks her to explain her attachment to Millie, she replies that she and Millie "remember the same things" and that after her aunt died, Millie's home was "the only real home I had. Her mother and father couldn't have been nicer to me if I'd been their own daughter." Despite this explanation, Preston refuses to believe that Kit would choose her friendship with Millie over her love for him. He attempts to persuade her to marry him by claiming that their love represents their "only chance" for happiness. But Kit does not believe in romantic love and replies matter-of-factly that "there is no such thing as an 'only chance.'" In her view, the fact that he was married to her childhood friend means that their love "wasn't meant to be." Kit's relationship with Rudd faces similar obstacles. She is ten years older than he, and she hesitates to marry him because she worries that he will fall out of love with her as she ages. While she struggles to make up her mind, Rudd and Deirdre fall in love with each other, which conveniently renders marrying him out of the question. In other words, Kit tends to fall in love with men she has no prospect of marrying. She indirectly acknowledges this tendency when she and Preston meet again in New York, and he asks if she intends to marry Rudd. She explains that she loves him but that there is a "catch," the difference in their ages: "You might know there would be something. Leave it to me." In this way, the film suggests that Kit prefers to remain a spinster. If she married, her relationship with her husband would displace her bonds with Millie and Deirdre as the center of her life.

By contrast, Millie has a deeply ambivalent relation to female homo-social desire. Unlike Kit, she tends to instrumentalize their friendship. She thinks of it in the sentimental terms of women's culture, which suggests that she values it as material for her novels. In the opening scene, she runs out of words to describe their childhood bond until the reporter Charlie (Roscoe Karns), underscoring her triteness, repeats a word she has already used: "inseparable." Moreover, Charlie realizes that she intends to exploit the famous author's visit to her hometown to draw attention to herself. When Charlie asks for a photograph of Kit for the newspaper, Millie claims that the only one she has is of the two of them, and she quickly shuts the table drawer to prevent him from finding a photograph of Kit alone. Millie also seems to value Kit only when she has no one else to turn to. When Preston leaves her, she resolves to make a new life without him and appeals to her friend: "I know I can with you to help me." But afraid that Kit will also eventually abandon her, Millie pleads, "Nothing will ever happen to us, will it? Nothing will ever come between us?" Kit assures her that they will probably end up "two deaf old ladies sharing the same ear trumpet." Millie continues to sob, which suggests that she does not find the prospect of ending up with Kit appealing, and

Kit tries to comfort her by repeating what Millie's mother always told them while they were growing up and got "down in the dumps": "Cheer up, Millie, cheer up, there's always what's left of the icing." The camera tracks in on Kit, who looks tearfully offscreen as she tenderly embraces Millie. Millie is unaware of the sacrifice Kit made for their friendship in the previous scene, where she rejects Preston's love; Kit repeats the words of Millie's mother to console not only her distraught friend, but herself as well.

The film's ending seems to confirm Kit's prediction that she and Millie will end up two deaf old ladies together. In the final scene, after uniting Deirdre and Rudd, Kit returns to her apartment, where she finds Millie waiting to apologize for having caused their falling out. Millie has been writing a new novel based on the "ups and downs" of their friendship, and when Kit tells her the news that Rudd is going to marry Deirdre, she exclaims, "Oh my goodness, this changes everything!" As a romance novelist, she cannot imagine a happy ending that does not include the prospect of marriage, and she does not want to end the novel with the two friends single and commiserating with each other: "The public doesn't expect a sad ending from me, two women left all alone like this." But Kit does not share Millie's belief that they have ended up "all alone," or that such an ending would be sad. As a writer who embodies modern womanhood, she can imagine a happy ending in which two women end up, as she and Millie have, not married but successful and enjoying an intimate domestic relationship with each other. When Millie tells her that she has been thinking of calling the novel *Auld Lang Syne*, Kit suggests that she call it *Old Acquaintance* instead, a title that foregrounds the two women's enduring friendship. With this ending, the film provided female audiences with an alternative narrative of womanhood, one that reclaimed the figure of the old maid. The final scene affirms what Millie's mother always told the women while they were growing up; despite their disappointments, they still have "what's left of the icing"—their careers and their friendship, which might turn out to be all they have ever wanted of the cake. The scene ends with a crane shot of the two women seated cozily on the couch in front of the fire, sipping champagne, indicating that they live happily ever after, despite the lack of men in their lives.

The film's potential to disengage the female viewer's desire from the institutions of heterosexuality is exemplified in the penultimate scene, in which Kit sacrifices her own happiness so that Deirdre can marry Rudd. What is remarkable about the scene is that it echoes the famous ending of the maternal melodrama *Stella Dallas* (King Vidor, 1937), in which Stella (Barbara Stanwyck) stands outside in the pouring rain, tearfully peering through the living-room window of her former husband's home at the wedding of her daughter, Laurel (Anne Shirley); Stella has renounced her claims to Laurel so she can marry the man she loves.[14] In the scene in *Old Acquaintance*, Kit and Deirdre arrive in a taxi in the pouring rain at a nightclub where Rudd is waiting with her father, Preston. Having convinced Deirdre that she has not betrayed her by falling in love with her former lover, Kit peers through the taxi window as Deidre passes through the glass doors of the nightclub and greets Rudd, who takes her by the hand and leads her to her father. When Kit turns again toward the camera, tears stream down her face, mirrored by the raindrops on the taxi window in the background. This echo of the final scene of *Stella Dallas* suggests that Kit's sacrifice has been maternal rather than romantic; she mourns the loss of Deirdre, who has been like a daughter to her, more than the loss of Rudd. But unlike *Stella Dallas*, *Old Acquaintance* does not end with this scene of maternal sacrifice and the formation of the heterosexual couple it enables. Instead, it ends with the scene of female homosocial bonding between Kit and Millie. The romance between Deidre and Rudd makes possible the film's final scene, in which Kit and Millie toast the endurance of their friendship, which is enabled because Kit remains single. In other words, in the film female homosocial desire ultimately displaces heterosexual romance as the telos of woman's identity.

At the same time, the film avoided directly challenging the heteronormative construction of womanhood. The film maintains its focus on Kit and Millie, except in a sequence of scenes that traces the budding romance between Deidre and Rudd. This sequence implies that Deidre will end up a happily married woman, a destiny that Kit has twice rejected to preserve her own autonomy. Moreover, the film affirms the importance of maternal desire in women, even as it queers that desire by associating it with female masculinity. Indeed, Kit's bond with Deirdre seems intended to reassure viewers that, despite her masculine ambitions, the modern career woman is even more maternal than the traditional, domesticated one. Unlike Millie, Kit never allows her own needs and desires to interfere with her responsibilities to Deirdre. Underlying the film's treatment of Millie is a critique of her career focus, which leads her to neglect her maternal responsibilities. The film's complicated relation to heteronormative discourses and institutions may explain its enormous appeal to female audiences. The film allowed female audiences to participate simultaneously in multiple and contradictory discourses of female identity. In its representation of Kit, it provided an alternative understanding of spinsterhood, suggesting that women's happiness did not depend on marriage and motherhood. It also removed Kit's and Millie's relationship from the sentimental domain of women's culture by attributing to them contrasting gender styles. Like Maggie and Sandra in *The Great Lie*, Kit and Millie resemble a butch-femme couple, which allowed viewers to interpret the film's final scene as a depiction of lesbian romance rather than female homosocial bonding.[15] But at the same time *Old Acquaintance* offers viewers the pleasure of participating vicariously in an unfolding heterosexual romance, temporarily interrupting the narrative of Kit and Millie's relationship with scenes of Deirdre and Rudd falling in love.

THE BACKLASH

The filming of *Old Acquaintance* reportedly did not go smoothly. Davis and Hopkins had disliked each other intensely since working together on *The Old Maid*, and they constantly bickered on the set.[16] Davis accused Hopkins of upstaging her in their scenes together, and Hopkins complained that the director, Vincent Sherman, was favoring Davis by giving her more close-ups. The two women's squabbling led a frustrated Sherman to declare, "Sometimes I feel I'm not directing this picture, I'm refereeing it."[17] But Warner Bros. hoped to repeat the box-office success of *The Old Maid*, and it exploited the rivalry between the two stars to generate publicity for the new movie. In so doing, it constructed a discourse of female homosocial bonds more misogynistic than the sentimental one in the film. Even before production on the movie began, *Time* reported gleefully that the two women had already begun quarrelling: "Davis contended that favoritism was being shown Hopkins since her dressing room was slightly closer to the set than hers."[18] In her autobiography, *The Lonely Life*, Davis reinforced this misogynistic narrative by exaggerating the tensions between her and Hopkins on the set of *Old Acquaintance*. According to her, their feuding reached a climax the day they shot the film's most famous scene. In the scene, which recalls the one in *The Great Lie* where Maggie slaps a hysterical Sandra to prevent her from burning down the cabin, Millie accuses Kit of ruining her life by stealing Preston, and Kit, tired of her friend's histrionics, literally attempts to shake some sense into her, before pushing her onto a sofa. Davis exaggerated the violence of the physical confrontation between the two women by incorrectly describing it as a slap, and although the studio had closed the set to prevent the media from revealing too much about the film, she claimed that when they shot the scene, "the rafters above the stage were full of excited spectators. It was rather like a prizefight ring below."[19]

The circulation of a counternarrative of female homosocial bonding in relation to *Old Acquaintance* associated the film with the shrewish, emasculating persona of Davis's so-called bitch roles, which the film's treatment of Kit as a self-sacrificing surrogate mother for Deirdre marginalized. Davis usually had to fight to play such roles, starting with the vixen Mildred Rogers in *Of Human Bondage* (John Cromwell, 1934), which most critics consider her "breakthrough" role. Warner Bros. worried that such roles would alienate her fans, because they were unsympathetic and harsh, and even after the box-office success of *Of Human Bondage*, which the star made for rival studio RKO, the studio continued to cast her as the female lead in the formulaic crime thrillers it churned out in the early 1930s.[20] As a sales executive put it, the studio thought of Davis as a "female Jimmy Cagney." But after Warner Bros. successfully sued Davis in a British court for breaking her contract and signing with an independent film company, it decided to conciliate her by acquiring properties that would exploit the shrewish aspects of her persona.[21] Jack Warner later admitted that these movies consolidated her appeal as a star by transforming her from a "bland and not beautiful little girl" into "a great artist."[22] Although Davis's roles in these movies contrasted sharply with her ones in the motherhood cycle, they reinforced the sexual ambiguity of her persona. Starting with *Jezebel* (William Wyler, 1938) and ending with *Beyond the Forest* (King Vidor, 1949), the last film she made for Warner Bros., they highlighted the incompatibility of Davis's persona with the institutions of heterosexuality. In several of the films, including *The Letter* (William Wyler, 1940), *The Little Foxes* (William Wyler, 1941), *In This Our Life* (John Huston, 1942), *Deception* (Irving Rapper, 1946), and *Beyond the Forest*, she played women who expressed their dissatisfaction with married life by committing adultery or murder, or sometimes both.[23] Instead of alienating female audiences, as the studio feared, these movies increased her popularity as a star, perhaps because she alternated them with women's pictures like *The Great Lie* and *Old Acquaintance*.[24]

Although all three of Davis's fallen-star pictures of the 1950s drew on her shrewish persona, *Whatever Happened to Baby Jane?* went further in articulating that persona with the set of themes explored in her motherhood cycle. Its treatment of the relationship between Jane and Blanche privileged the misogynistic construction of female homosocial desire that circulated in relation to Davis's stardom. In a reversal of the motherhood cycle, Davis plays a vindictive character who terrorizes her crippled sister, Blanche, by imitating her and tampering with her food. Jane's cruelty to Blanche culminates in a scene that seems intended to parody the physical confrontations that Davis's characters had with their rivals in *The Great Lie* and *Old Acquaintance*. Jane returns from picking up her costumes and finds Blanche on the telephone pleading with Dr. Shelby (Robert Cornthwaite) to rescue her from Jane. After violently attacking Blanche, Jane locks her in her bedroom, bound and gagged, so she cannot escape. Moreover, Aldrich's movie transformed the rivalry over a child central to the women's pictures into a rivalry over Jane's former career as a child star. The rivalry begins when Jane and Blanche are girls, emerging from their father's obvious and adoring preference for "Baby Jane Hudson," the family's meal ticket. It turns murderous once the sisters grow up, and Blanche's stardom eclipses Jane's. After attending a Hollywood party at which a drunken Jane entertains the other guests by imitating her sister, Blanche unsuccessfully tries to kill her by running her over, but instead crashes the car into a gate. Left paralyzed, Blanche vindictively blames the accident on Jane, who was too drunk to remember. Ironically, the accident binds the two sisters even more closely together, as Blanche is left in Jane's care, which sets the stage for the film's gruesome climax. When Blanche's loyal housekeeper, Elvira (Maidie Norman), discovers Blanche imprisoned in her bedroom, Jane kills her to prevent her from going to the police. The sisters' domestic life emerges as a nightmarish version of the sentimental female homosocial world depicted in the motherhood cycle.

The first time we see Davis in the film is as a young contract player in some clips from two films she made early in her career, *Parachute Jumper* (Alfred Green, 1933) and *Ex-Lady* (Robert Florey, 1933). The year is 1934, and the clips are supposedly the rushes from Jane's latest picture, *The Longest Night*. They are meant to show that Jane has failed to make the transition from vaudeville to motion pictures because of her lack of sex appeal. Two producers, Marty McDonald (Wesley Addy) and Bert Freed (Ben Golden), who are watching the rushes in a studio screening room, complain about her unexciting persona. When the rushes are over, Marty asks Bert what he thinks, and Bert replies disgustedly, "What's thinking got to do with it?" The studio's contract with Blanche, now a major star, has a clause that requires the studio to make a picture with Jane every time it makes one with her, and in the next scene, as the two men walk across the studio lot, Bert begs Marty to talk to Blanche about letting the studio out of the clause. By including these clips, Aldrich's movie attempted to rewrite Davis's career, glossing over her most memorable roles and focusing instead on the ones that highlighted her lack of sex appeal. Davis made *Parachute Jumper* and *Ex-Lady* when she was still the "bland and not beautiful" contract player Warner Bros. thought of as the female equivalent of James Cagney. But even after she emerged as a major star of women's pictures, Davis was not considered sexy or glamorous, and she tended to receive unfavorable reviews when she appeared on-screen as supposedly beautiful and alluring women.[25] Critics were especially scathing of her role in *In This Our Life*, in which she played the carnal Stanley Timberlake, who betrays her fiancé and seduces the husband of her sister, Roy, played by Olivia de Havilland. Bosley Crowther's review in the *New York Times*, which summed up the critical consensus, complains that Davis "is forever squirming and pacing and grabbing the back of her neck. It is likewise very hard to see her as the sort of sultry dame that men can't resist."[26]

By contrast, the first time we see Joan Crawford in the film is as a young star in a series of scenes taken from *Sadie McKee* (Clarence Brown, 1934), a woman's picture she made during the heyday of her career at MGM. In *Whatever Happened to Baby Jane?*, they are supposedly scenes from an old Blanche Hudson picture that a local television station is showing, and they serve to emphasize the differences between Blanche and Jane as movie stars. All of the scenes highlight Blanche's sex appeal. In the first one, she leans over the leading man and kisses him passionately. In the second, she performs as a scantily clad dancer at a speakeasy and has to fend off the attentions of a libidinous customer. In the third, she visits her sick lover in a hospital and kisses him tenderly. Jane's and Blanche's next-door neighbor, Mrs. Bates (Anna Lee), and her daughter, Liza (Barbara Merrill), are watching the old movie on their television. In contrast to the two producers who watch Jane's rushes, the two women are totally absorbed in Blanche's performance and resent it when the television station interrupts it for a dog food commercial. Although Liza seems more interested in the gossip about their famous neighbors, Mrs. Bates represents the ideal viewer of the woman's picture. During the commercial, she tells Liza to turn down the volume, so she can recount to her the first time she saw the picture, on a date with her husband before they were married. In this way, *Whatever Happened to Baby Jane?* privileged Crawford's persona over Davis's. Whereas it underscored Davis's inadequacy as an object-to-be-looked-at, it represented Crawford as the embodiment of Hollywood glamour and sophistication. Moreover, glossing over Crawford's masculine gender style, which increasingly dominated her screen image in the period in which she made *Whatever Happened to Baby Jane?*, the scenes from *Sadie McKee* associated the star with a heteronormative construction of female desire. Thus, in watching the picture again, Mrs. Bates thinks of her own romance with her husband.

The film reinforces this representation of the differences between the two stars in a sequence of scenes that provide our first glimpse of the mature Davis and Crawford. The sequence reverses the order in which we see the two stars at the beginning of their careers. The film dissolves from a medium shot of Mrs. Bates transfixed by Blanche's image to a close-up of a television showing a scene from *Sadie McKee*. The camera tracks back to reveal Blanche/Crawford in a wheelchair, watching her old picture with a glowing expression on her face—like her neighbor, she has been transfixed by the image of her former self. Though older, she does not appear significantly different from the glamorous star we glimpse on the small screen, as well as in a portrait that hangs over her bed in the background of the shot. She wears an elegant ruffled dressing gown with a floral print and has a sophisticated hairdo. Indeed, she shows few signs of her reclusive life as an invalid. As she lights a cigarette, she remarks with obvious satisfaction, "It's still a good picture."

The film then cuts to a close-up of Jane that seems designed to affront the viewer and to underscore the sharp contrast between the two sisters. We see Jane hunched over the kitchen table working on her horoscope. Bearing little resemblance to the actress we saw in the rushes from *The Longest Night*, she instead resembles a grotesque version of her former self as a child star. She is heavily made up, and her hair falls around her shoulders in ringlets, as it had when she was a child. She also wears a lace negligee decorated with silk flowers that recalls her childhood costumes. Reinforcing the disturbing effect of her appearance is the fact that her girlish attire and curls clash with her gender presentation, which is decidedly masculine. She slugs back a drink, yawns coarsely, and shuffles out of the kitchen. As her appearance attests, Jane, too, remains transfixed by the image of her former self. Moreover, the house is full of memorabilia from her vaudeville career, including a "genuine" Baby Jane doll marketed as a tie-in for her act. But unlike her sister's attachment to her former self,

Jane's emerges as pathological. In a scene that seems designed to caricature the discourse of maternal desire in Davis's motherhood cycle, Jane caresses the doll and performs her old act for it as if it were a real child.

The film's representation of Jane associated Davis's persona with an outmoded form of stardom. As Jane grows up, she loses her appeal as a star, which is tied to a mass cultural form, vaudeville, displaced by Hollywood cinema. But Jane never accepts the failure of her movie career, and her rivalry with her sister extends to their gender styles. Jane is determined to show that she can be as glamorous and alluring as her more famous sister. But her attempts to sexualize her femininity only confirm her association with an outmoded form of mass culture. When she dresses up and goes out in public, Jane looks tawdry, and succeeds only in making a spectacle of her femininity's lack of appeal. For example, in the scene where she pays for a classified advertisement (she is seeking a composer), she wears a tight-fitting dress with a see-through bodice, a pair of ankle-strap shoes, an old fox fur she has pulled out of her closet, and a black velvet beret with a zircon clip in the shape of a butterfly.[27] She has also drawn a beauty mark on her face in the shape of a heart. This scene echoes the one in which Bert and Marty complain about Jane's lack of sex appeal while watching the rushes for *The Longest Night*. There are two men behind the counter who, like the two producers, act as stand-ins for the male viewer constructed by classical Hollywood cinema. As Jane pays for the advertisement, she looks around the office, as though expecting to be recognized as a former star, but the two men's reaction underscores the failure of her performance of Hollywood glamour: bewildered by her appearance, they stare at her incredulously. When one of the men asks for her name so he can write her a receipt, Jane looks at him expectantly and announces, "Maybe you remember me. I'm Baby Jane Hudson." But neither of the men recognizes her, and after she leaves, the one seated at a desk shakes his head and asks, "Who the hell was Baby Jane Hudson?" In other words, Jane fails to make the transition from vaudeville to motion pictures because she embodies an obsolete form of femininity.

Aldrich's film further privileges Crawford's persona by associating it with a normative construction of female homosocial desire. In Crawford's women's pictures of the 1930s, female homosocial bonds never threatened to eclipse heterosexual love, as they did in Davis's, and *Whatever Happened to Baby Jane?* emphasizes Crawford's enormous popularity with female audiences. Unlike Jane, Blanche continues to have appeal as a star, and the television broadcast of her old movies confirms her as-

BETTE DAVIS AS THE SEXUALLY GROTESQUE JANE HUDSON
IN *WHATEVER HAPPENED TO BABY JANE?*

sessment of their quality by reviving her popularity with female viewers. After watching Blanche's picture with her daughter, Mrs. Bates brings her a bouquet of flowers from her garden as a tribute, and Blanche begins receiving fan mail again. In one letter marked personal, a female viewer informs her that when she saw the former star in one of her old pictures, it was "like meeting an old friend." Moreover, overlooking the complexity of Crawford's image, the movie associates Blanche's stardom with a form of female homosocial desire that is wholly compatible with the institutions of heterosexuality. Seeing Blanche again on television reminds Mrs. Bates of dating her husband before they were married, and the author of the letter marked personal watches Blanche's movie with her husband, who shares her appreciation of the former star. This treatment of Crawford's image, which exaggerated its compatibility with a heteronormative model of female homosocial bonding, helps to explain the horror movie's construction of Davis's career. Although Davis's motherhood cycle constructed a discourse of female identity that affirmed the alternative domestic arrangements the Second World War opened up for women, *Whatever Happened to Baby Jane?* represses Davis's popularity with female audiences and instead connects her image to a purely misogynistic understanding of female homosocial desire. The film's emphasis on Jane's jealousy of the more glamorous Blanche—Elvira has retrieved Blanche's fan mail from the trash where a jealous and vindictive Jane has thrown it without showing it to her sister—foregrounds Davis's association with bitter female rivalry, both on- and offscreen.[28]

THE COMEBACK

In associating Davis's sexually ambiguous persona with a form of stardom that supposedly no longer appealed to female audiences, *Whatever Happened to Baby Jane?* avoided the contradictions of Davis's two earlier fallen-star movies. For example, *The Star* anticipated Aldrich's film by linking Davis's gender style to an outmoded stardom, but it attempted to remake her persona for the Cold War era by domesticating it. In *The Star*, Davis's character, Margaret, realizes that she has lost her star appeal when she watches her screen test for the role of the older sister in *The Fatal Winter*. Before the screen test, hoping to show the studio that she can play the younger sister despite the differences in their ages, she slips into the dressing room of the picture's star, Barbara Lawrence, redoing her hair and makeup so she will look younger. She also unbuttons the top of her dress and ties a scarf around her waist to show off her shapely figure. When she arrives on the set, Keith Barkley (David Alpert), the director, pulls her aside and tells her that she looks too young for the part, not realizing that is precisely the effect she wants to create. This scene also highlights the impact that the naturalistic performance style associated with Method acting had on postwar Hollywood filmmaking. Barkley has had a career as a director on Broadway, and *The Fatal Winter* is his first Hollywood picture. The male lead has also come to Hollywood from Broadway, and his mumbled delivery of his lines resembles the acting style of Marlon Brando and Montgomery Clift. By contrast, Margaret embodies studio-era female stardom: she has no desire to appear authentic in the part, but is more concerned about how she will look on-screen, at one point even interrupting the screen test to ask the cameraman to readjust the key light to show off her glamorous beauty. Margaret does not understand that she cannot rely on the acting style that has made her a star. The stage directions describe her character as "sullen," but Margaret flirts inappropriately with the male lead. When Barkley tries to correct her performance, she insists that if her character wants to "win her point," she must use her "sex." After she finishes the screen test, Barkley remarks, "Your fans would love it," which she takes as a sign of his approval. But Barkley has no interest in promoting her stardom, and when she watches the test the next day, she realizes how unsuitable her performance was. Collapsing on the floor of the studio screening room, she repeats her own words hysterically: "Disregard stage directions. Disregard everything!"

Despite the humiliating realization that she has lost her appeal as a star, Margaret still clings to hope for a comeback. Yet, later that evening, she attends a cocktail party with a lot of Hollywood "brass" at her agent Harry's home and suffers several more humiliations. She overhears one of the guests congratulating an older actress who landed the part of the older sister; the actress says excitedly, "Now I can get that tired old diamond clip out of hock," indicating the penurious future that awaits Margaret if she does not relinquish her career. Barbara Lawrence (Barbara Lawrence), the rising star of *The Fatal Winter*, arrives at the party, after the premiere of her latest picture, and the guests immediately swarm around her to find out how it went. Finally, struck by Margaret's dejected look, a director, Richard Stanley (Paul Frees), approaches her about starring in his new picture, *The Falling Star*. He explains that the picture is about a female star who refuses to accept that she is no longer on top. The character is one of those female stars "who play it twenty four hours a day, thinking of themselves, what they look like, what kind of impression they're making, demanding, driving, ambitious." Margaret discerns that he could be describing her and asks how he intends to build sympathy for the character. But she has misunderstood the point of the picture, which is to promote a heteronormative model of womanhood. Stanley replies, "Not sympathy, Miss Elliot, but pity, profound pity, worthy of the gods. This is a great tragedy. Why, my character has denied her birthright, the privilege and glory of just being a woman." Margaret realizes that, like the character Stanley describes, she has denied her birthright by neglecting her daughter, Gretchen, and rejecting the proposal of her suitor, Jim. Abruptly leaving the party, she drives to the home of her former husband, John, where she picks up Gretchen, and then takes her to Jim's. In the movie's closing shot, Margaret and Gretchen rush into Jim's open arms, indicating that the three of them live happily ever after as a family.

In affirming the importance of marriage and motherhood for women, this ending attempted to bring Davis's image into alignment with the new set of gender and sexual norms that emerged in the Cold War era. But in so doing it glossed over the incompatibility of her persona with the institutions of heterosexuality. The movie acknowledged this incompatibility in an earlier scene, wherein Margaret, who is bankrupt, overcomes her pride and goes to John's home, intending to borrow money for her rent. But John, who since their divorce has become a movie star, is on location in Arizona shooting a western, and Margaret instead encounters his wife, Peggy (Barbara Woodell). This scene foregrounds Davis's association with a misogynistic construction of female homosocial desire. Margaret still resents Peggy for breaking up her marriage to John, and she begins arguing with her almost immediately: "You threw yourself at him. You batted those eyes and told him what a great big wonderful man he was, told him how bad I was for him, that I was too busy with my career, that what he needed was a real wife. Pure soap opera, and he fell for it!" Instead of denying it, Peggy insists that it was true. As Margaret's husband, John had resembled a stereotypical housewife and supposedly resented "being Mr. Elliot, living in Miss Elliot's house, entertaining Miss Elliot's guests. Why, he wasn't even Miss Elliot's husband, he was her lover by appointment, when she wasn't too tired or too afraid to muss her hair." Unlike Margaret, Peggy has accepted her subordination as John's wife, and as Margaret opens the door to leave, she boasts, "I've made him happy because I've let him be Mr. Morgan." This scene renders the film's ending implausible. Given her hostility to Peggy, it seems unlikely that

Maggie would suddenly abandon her career to claim her "birthright" and become a housewife like her.

Moreover, Davis's own career contradicted the narrative of female stardom constructed by the movie. Margaret's domestication in the movie's final scene seems intended to show that the new era required a different kind of star from Davis, one whose persona did not threaten to destabilize the institutions of heterosexuality by providing female audiences with an alternative model of womanhood. But Davis's triumph in playing a Hollywood has-been undercut this aim by showing that she had not lost her appeal as a star—the movie was a critical as well as a box-office success. *Time* described it as "a marathon one-woman show and, all in all, proof that Bette Davis—with her strident voice, nervous stride, mobile hands and popping eyes—is still her own best imitator." The movie acknowledged this contradiction indirectly with its title. With its focus on a fallen star, the movie bears a strong resemblance to the one in which Stanley hopes to cast Margaret. It has a similar plot as well as a similar ideological project with respect to women's roles. In describing *Falling Star* to Maggie, Stanley makes no attempt to conceal this project. He explains that although the character is a movie star, she could be "the head of a department store, or the publisher of a newspaper, a politician—anything that generates drive." In other words, Stanley intends his new picture to underwrite the postwar domestication of women. But despite the two films' similar ideological goals, the title of the picture Davis starred in differs pointedly from the title of Stanley's project and highlights the dissimilarity between Davis and the character she played. For, unlike Margaret, Davis remained a star and could not be contained in the domestic sphere.

Although, unlike *The Star*, *Whatever Happened to Baby Jane?* did not attempt to depict Davis's persona as compatible with heteronormative institutions and discourses, it similarly undercut its own attempts to contain her appeal as a star. Davis's role as Baby Jane highlighted aspects of her performance style that had troubled movie critics since her emergence as a star. Regardless of the role she was playing, Davis tended to rely on a distinctive set of mannerisms, which eventually became her trademark: a clipped manner of speaking, a constant darting of her eyes, a nervous clasping of her hands, and an agitated smoking of cigarettes.[29] She also tended to rely on what critic Bosley Crowther derogatorily called "ostentatious tricks"—in particular, elaborate makeup and costumes— and she was known for her willingness to look unattractive, even grotesque, on-screen, if the part required it.[30] For example, in *Mr. Skeffing-ton* (Vincent Sherman, 1944), in which she played a vain, selfish woman who loses her beauty after a protracted illness, Davis spoke in a falsetto throughout the film and wore a grotesque rubber mask in the final half to indicate the ravaging of Fanny's face by disease.[31] This performance style worked best when Davis played high-strung or repressed heroines, like those in *Jezebel* and *Now, Voyager*. But it was not always appropriate, and thus frustrated many of the directors with whom she collaborated. William Wyler, who directed the actress in *Jezebel*, *The Letter*, and *The Little Foxes*, generally considered her three strongest films, thought that her mannerisms expressed not the psychology of her characters, but her own anxieties about acting, and during the filming of *Jezebel* he famously threatened to tie a weight around her neck if she did not stop nervously bobbing her head.[32] He was especially frustrated by her performance as Regina Giddens in *The Little Foxes*, complaining that she relied on "gestures and accentuated speech and tricks that are just plain bad."[33]

Davis's "tricks" lent themselves to a camp mode of reception, especially in the postwar period when a naturalistic performance style increasingly dominated Hollywood filmmaking. This shift rendered Davis's method of acting obsolete, which is one of the necessary conditions for the camp appropriation of cultural objects. The mostly unfavorable reviews that *Whatever Happened to Baby Jane?* received make clear that Davis's performance created a camp effect.[34] Bosley Crowther's reaction in the *New York Times* was typical. Although he avoided the term *camp*, he complained that the "unique conjunction of two one-time top-ranking stars in a story about two aging sisters who were once theatrical celebrities themselves does not afford opportunity to do more than wear grotesque costumes, makeup to look like witches and chew the scenery."[35] Ironically, in attacking Davis for overacting, Crowther and other critics participated indirectly in the film's project to contain her persona by representing it as outdated. But despite its hostile critical reception, *Whatever Happened to Baby Jane?* was enormously popular with audiences, largely because of Davis's campy performance, and Davis received an Academy Award nomination for Best Actress, as she had for her two earlier fallen-star pictures. In other words, the camp classic failed to contain the actress's persona even as it succeeded in rendering it obsolete. Davis's success in playing Baby Jane Hudson, which has become one of her most famous roles, proved that despite her outmoded performance style, she retained her appeal as a star.

DORIS DAY'S QUEER NORMATIVITY

When the producer Ross Hunter approached Doris Day about starring in *Pillow Talk* (Michael Gordon, 1959), a sophisticated romantic comedy about a glamorous New York career girl who shares a party line with a sexy playboy bachelor, he realized that the film would be a departure for Day. After all, Day was best known for the wholesome tomboy characters she had played in a series of musical comedies in the early 1950s. But Hunter was convinced of Day's potential as a sex symbol. He told Jean Louis, the designer assigned to the project, "We've got to change this gal. She is gorgeous. She is stunning. She is something special and the audience doesn't know about it yet."[1] Hunter also thought that Day needed to transform her image if she was going to remain a top star. He later recalled that Day "had been the girl next door for too long, with her freckles and blousy dresses, nondescript hairdo, down-to-earth personality."[2] Day liked the script for *Pillow Talk*, because "the humor came from situation and characterization rather than from jokes," as she later explained, but she doubted that audiences would find her believable as the sophisticated interior decorator Jan Morrow, who must literally fight men off.[3] When Hunter persisted in claiming that she was right for the part, she scolded him, "Oh, Ross, cut it out. I'm just the old-fashioned, peanut-butter girl next door, and you know it."[4] Hunter finally overcame her doubts by reassuring her that audiences would continue to see her as wholesome and pure: "Now, listen, if you allow me to get Jean Louis to do your clothes . . . and get some wonderful makeup on you, and chic you up and get a great hairdo that lifts you, why, every secretary and every housewife will say, 'Look at that—look what Doris has done to herself. Maybe I can do the same thing.'"[5] Hunter was right that *Pillow Talk* would transform Day's career. The enormously successful film was the first in a long line of sophisticated romantic comedies in which a chicer Day starred, and it catapulted her to the top of the Quigley Poll, the annual survey of film exhibitors and distributors that determined the top box-office draws, where she remained until 1965.[6]

Despite its success, however, *Pillow Talk* did not wholly redefine Day as a sex symbol. Her image as a tomboy was firmly established and existed in tension with her glamorous makeover in the film. There are two scenes in *Please Don't Eat the Daisies* (Charles Walters, 1960), the first film that Day made following *Pillow Talk*, that call attention to this tension.[7] In the film, Day plays Kate MacKay, a harried housewife who struggles to balance the competing needs of her husband, Larry (David Niven), a theater critic whose success begins to cloud his judgment, and those of their four unruly sons, David (Charles Herbert), Gabriel (Stanley Livingston), George (Flip Mark), and Adam (Baby Gellert). The most explicit reference to *Pillow Talk*'s transformation of Day's image occurs near the end of the film. Larry has been staying in a hotel in New York so that he can work on his book while Kate renovates their house in the country, a dilapidated Victorian mansion that they buy on the spur of the moment when the lease on their apartment expires. Larry finishes his book sooner than expected and decides to surprise Kate and the boys by returning to the house. But Kate is at the school with the boys, and having forgotten his key, Larry must slip through a window. He becomes exasperated when he cannot locate Kate and the boys anywhere in town. Just before he has to catch the train back to the city, so that he can attend the opening of a new play, Kate and the boys return to the house with their sheepdog, Hobo, in tow. Larry demands to know where they have been, but before Kate can answer, he storms out of the house, slamming the door behind him. Kate, who does not realize how long he has been waiting, throws open the door and shouts angrily, "I was having a rendezvous with Rock Hudson, me, David, Gabriel, Adam, and Hobo—all of us!"

This scene attempts to resolve the tensions in Day's image, which *Pillow Talk* had exacerbated by glamorizing her. For the most part, *Please Don't Eat the Daisies* follows the example of the earlier film in foregrounding the chicer elements of Day's persona. Although as a housewife and mother Kate could not be more different from the single, career-oriented Jan, she has a similar look, especially in the first part of the film, when she and Larry live in New York and dine at fashionable restaurants and attend cocktail parties thrown by Broadway stars. In these scenes, Kate wears fashionable clothes and jewelry, and has the same sophisticated hairdo as Jan. But once she and Larry move to Hooten and Kate renovates the house, the film begins to foreground the masculine aspects of Day's persona. We now see Kate wearing blue jeans and button-down shirts and engaging in masculine activities like mixing paint and sawing furniture. Thus, part of the scene's humor lies in the absurdity of the idea that Kate, a tomboyish mother of four, would be off having an assignation with Rock Hudson, one of Hollywood's sexiest leading men. At the same time, however, the scene discourages audiences from thinking of Day's masculinity as a defining characteristic of her persona by reminding them of her role as Jan. Kate may not have had a rendezvous with Hudson, but Day did in *Pillow Talk*, in which Hudson played Brad Allen, a playboy who attempts to seduce Jan by pretending to be a Texas oilman named Rex Stetson. Thus the idea that Kate/Day might be having an affair with the Hollywood heartthrob is not so farfetched, after all.

A less explicit reference to the tensions in Day's image occurs in an earlier scene. Shortly after Kate and Larry move into the new house, they are visited by neighbors who introduce themselves as the "welcome to Hooten committee." After handing Kate a bunch of daisies, they announce that they are also members of the local drama club, the Hooten Holler Players, and that they have come to ask Larry to find them a new play for their upcoming annual benefit. The scene would be unremarkable if one of the neighbors, Dr. Sprouk (Geraldine Wall, in an uncredited role), were not coded as a lesbian. She is wearing a western-style leather jacket, a white button-down shirt, a dark-brown string tie, and a pair of loose-fitting khaki pants. She also has a ducktail haircut, which, as Madeline Davis and Elizabeth Kennedy have shown, was the hairstyle most commonly worn by butches in the 1950s.[8] Dr. Sprouk's masculine gender style confuses George, who tugs at her coat while she is introducing herself to his mother and father and innocently asks, "Excuse me, are you a lady or a man?" Embarrassed by her son's impoliteness, Kate exclaims, "George!" But Dr. Sprouk, who seems used to the question, pats the boy on the head fondly and replies, "I'm a veterinarian, sonny, it's somewhere in between." Unlike the other neighbors, Dr. McQuarry (John Harding) and Mrs. Hunter (Mary Patton), who reappear in a later scene, Dr. Sprouk is never seen again in the film. She prescribes some sedatives for Hobo, who has not adjusted to life in the country, but her primary function is to provide a spectacle of gender and sexual nonconformity that interrupts the film's narrative flow. The composition of the shots in which she appears seems designed to transfix the viewers: she occupies the center of the screen, framed by the other characters, who stand on either side of her.

How do we explain this gratuitously homophobic representation of a masculine woman? The representation is especially puzzling because Dr. Sprouk's outfit, which makes her look like a cowboy who has been transplanted to the New York suburbs, bears a striking resemblance to the buckskin costume that Day wears in *Calamity Jane* (David Butler, 1953) when she sings the Academy Award–winning song, "Secret Love." That musical, in which Day played the legendary cross-dresser Jane Canary, solidified the masculine elements of Day's image. Reinforcing the link between the two, Day herself had a ducktail haircut in the mid-1950s, which at least some of her fans interpreted as a sign that she was a lesbian. Jackie Stacey's survey of women filmgoers in Britain in the 1940s and 1950s indicates that at least some butches modeled their gender presentation on Day's.[9] Shirley Thompson, one of the women surveyed by Stacey, commented, "Doris Day is the greatest and in the 50s had a haircut called the 'Butch cut,' which I had to be like her."[10] Thus, one of Hunter's goals in glamorizing Day's look may have been to stabilize her persona by rendering it more unambiguously heterosexual. As Thompson's identification with the star indicates, Day's masculine gender presentation lent itself to a lesbian construction, even though the roles she played were marked as heterosexual. The scene with Dr. Sprouk seems intended to consolidate the transformation of Day's image in *Pillow Talk*. It acknowledges that in the past some viewers may have interpreted Day's masculinity as a sign that she was a lesbian, but it also marks the distance that Day had supposedly traveled since *Calamity Jane* by emphasizing the differences between her and Dr. Sprouk. Indeed, the contrast between the two as they stand next to each other could not be greater. Although she appears a bit disheveled from the move, Kate/Day wears a frilly blouse and a pair of tapered slacks that show off her shapely figure. By contrast, Dr. Sprouk embodies the homophobic stereotype of the mannish lesbian. The film encourages viewers to believe that *Pillow Talk* had resolved the ambiguity of Day's gender and sexual identities. Viewers could no longer confuse her with an "in between" woman like Dr. Sprouk. Significantly, it is only after the scene with the veterinarian that the film begins to emphasize Day's tomboyish image, as if it were now safe for it to do so.

Despite the tensions and contradictions in her image, Day has come to epitomize some of the most repressive aspects of postwar American society, in particular its gender and sexual normativity. In their dossier on Day for the British Film Institute, which is one of the few critical assessments of Day's career, Jane Clarke and Diana Simmonds note that, especially for the generation of filmgoers who came of age during the political and social upheavals of the 1960s, Day serves as "*the* model of 50s and early 60s maidenhood before marriage and heterosexual monogamy afterwards; 2.4 children and a two car household, in short the cornerstone of the nuclear family."[11] But Day's construction as normative covers over the potentially unsettling gender and sexual ambiguity of her persona, which films like *Please Don't Eat the Daisies* struggled to resolve. Indeed, the complexity of Day's persona suggests that Cold War gender and sexual norms were much less stable and coherent than scholars have assumed. Because of the masculine elements of her image, Day's films had a more complicated relationship to the domestic ideology underlying Cold War culture than critics have acknowledged, simultaneously ratifying and challenging the normative construction of American womanhood. Although there is no way to know for sure, it may be that the tensions and contradictions in Day's image accounted for her enormous popularity throughout the Cold War era. Louis Pasternak, who produced the musical *Love Me or Leave Me* (Charles Vidor, 1954), told an interviewer, who was surprised by Day's powerful performance in the movie as the troubled torch singer Ruth Etting: "Sure, Doris is a wonderful, wholesome girl, but she *is* complex and she *does* have uncertainties about herself. . . . If she were as uncomplicated as her publicity would lead you to believe, she wouldn't be the tremendous box office draw that she is."[12] As Pasternak suggests here, Day's wholesome, "uncomplicated" image helped to mute or contain the complexity of her appeal as a star so that she appeared normative. Thus audiences could derive pleasure from her movies without calling into question their own gender and sexual identities.

The construction of Day's masculinity as tomboyism limited her transformation into a sex symbol. As Mandy Merk argues in her contribution to the British Film Institute's dossier on Day, tomboyism is usually understood temporally rather than psychologically, as a stage of development that many girls pass through on their way to heterosexual womanhood. Merk explains that tomboyism is a socially acceptable form of female masculinity that is seen as "pre-sexual, adolescent, rather than determinedly celibate or homosexual."[13] Girls supposedly find tomboyism compelling because it offers them "the phantasy of being other/

more powerful than [they] are" and not because they have a deep identification with masculinity that might reveal a truth about their identities.[14] This understanding has only a limited application to Day, who performed a more complicated version of masculinity, one that was never wholly contained by its construction as tomboyism. Day's masculinity remained a recurring element of her image until the end of her film career.[15] Thus it could never be understood in purely temporal terms, as a stage that she would eventually grow out of. Nor could it be seen as "pre-sexual," as a gender identity that did not yet have a sexual meaning. Only one of the masculine characters that Day played, Marjorie in the musical *On Moonlight Bay* (Roy Del Ruth, 1951), was an adolescent girl; all the others were adult women. It was the combination of masculinity and womanhood in so many of Day's characters that opened up her persona to a lesbian construction.

Critics reacted ambivalently to Day's masculinity throughout her career. They did not object to it so long as it was counterbalanced by the other elements of her image and could be explained away as tomboyism. For example, they reacted favorably to *It Happened to Jane* (Richard Quine, 1959), the film that Day made right before *Pillow Talk*, in which she played Jane Osgood, a widow with two small children who takes on a powerful railroad company when it bankrupts her lobster business. The character was the most masculine one that Day had played since *Calamity Jane*, which suggests that the choice of her character's name may not have been purely coincidental.[16] The critic for *Variety* did not even comment on this aspect of the film, instead reassuring filmgoers that "Miss Day, a beguiling figure of outraged womanhood, doesn't lose her essential femininity in the glory of the cause. She is pugnacious but perceptibly female."[17] But even as it attempted to stabilize the meaning of Day's masculinity by rendering it consistent with the other elements of her image, the review acknowledged that it was open to other, less normalizing interpretations. The emphasis on Jane Osgood's gender and sexual normativity, her "essential femininity," seems like a kind of wish fulfillment. By contrast, critics were scathing when Day's movies failed to synthesize the different elements of her image. For example, they panned *Caprice* (Frank Tashlin, 1967), one of Day's last movies, in which she played an undercover agent for a cosmetics company. Day's glamorous look in the film supposedly failed to neutralize her masculinity, so that she appeared to be engaging in a form of drag. The critic for *Today* noted contemptuously that "thanks to a variety of wigs, soft lenses and mod costumes, [Day] looks like an aging transvestite."[18] And the critic for the *New York Times* complained that Day's "nutty clothes and acrobatics cannot conceal the fact that she is no longer a boy."[19]

The containment of Day's masculinity points to an important difference between her and Joan Crawford. Crawford's masculinity came to dominate her image in the 1950s, so that she emerged as a camp object. Because Day's masculinity could be understood as tomboyism, however, it never appeared pathological or castrating like Crawford's; nor did it lend itself readily to a camp appropriation. This may explain why Day's image hovered on the threshold of the lesbian without ever fully crossing it. Although some butches may have modeled their gender presentation on hers, Day was never fully legible as a lesbian. Her wholesomeness was an indelible part of her image and discouraged audiences from understanding her masculinity in sexual terms. Moreover, all of Day's characters exhibited signifiers of heterosexual femininity. They were either happily married wives and mothers, or single career girls, or widowed mothers who almost always ended up married to Hollywood's sexiest leading men.[20] In other words, there was an irreducible taxonomic uncertainty about Day's gender and sexual identities that rendered her persona queer rather than unambiguously lesbian. Just as she was never fully legible as a butch, she was never fully legible as a heterosexual, which explains why *Please Don't Eat the Daisies* had so much difficulty stabilizing her image. The normalization of Day's masculinity contained her transformation into a sex symbol. Because tomboyism is understood as presexual, Day was never fully accessible as a heterosexual object of desire, even in her later films.

QUEERING TOMBOYISM: *CALAMITY JANE*

Calamity Jane was the only one of Day's films that was written especially for her. In 1950, when MGM announced its plans to film the Broadway musical *Annie Get Your Gun*, Day approached Warner Bros. about loaning her out so that she could play the lead. But Warner Bros. was not about to allow Day, who was one of its most popular stars, to work for a rival studio. Partly to appease Day, Warner Bros. developed *Calamity Jane* as a star vehicle for her.[21] The studio also wanted to capitalize on the commercial success of *Annie Get Your Gun* (George Sidney, 1950), and it hired Howard Keel, who costarred with Betty Hutton in the film, to play opposite Day as Wild Bill Hickok. Critics tended to agree that *Calamity*

Jane was, as the review in *Photoplay* put it, "shamelessly reminiscent" of the MGM musical, but the role of Calamity was significantly different from that of Annie and was ultimately better suited to Day's tomboyish image, as Warner Bros. seems to have realized.[22] Unlike Annie, the cross-dressing Calamity, who wears buckskins and a Union Army cap during most of the musical, constantly transgresses the boundaries between genders. She brags about her exploits with her gun and competes with the men over who is braver. She is even mistaken for a man when she leaves Deadwood City, where she is the only woman, and travels to Chicago to bring back the famous actress Adelaide Adams (Gail Robbins) so that she can perform at the Golden Garter, Deadwood City's saloon. Thus the role of Calamity seems have been tailor-made for Day.

Day's role as Marjorie Winfield in *On Moonlight Bay* and its sequel, *By the Light of the Silvery Moon* (David Butler, 1953), had already established the gender and sexual ambiguity of her persona. Based loosely on Booth Tarkington's Penrod stories, the two films were Warner Bros.' answer to MGM's enormously popular musical *Meet Me in Saint Louis* (Vincente Minnelli, 1944), starring Judy Garland.[23] Marjorie is the tomboyish daughter of a small-town midwestern banker, George Winfield (Leon Ames). When *On Moonlight Bay* opens, George has just moved the family to a wealthier neighborhood closer to his bank. Although George feels at home in the new house, which reflects better his position as vice-president of the local bank, the other family members miss their old neighborhood. When Mrs. Winfield (Rosemary DeCamp) complains that the new house is too large for the furniture, George reveals that he has moved the family because "I'd like my daughter to become a wife, not a second baseman." Marjorie enters with the movers, carrying an armchair on her back. Turning to his wife, George says exasperatedly, "There, see what I mean?," and he orders Marjorie to put down the chair, "Good gracious, don't you already have enough muscles?" When she complies, it becomes clear why her father is worried that she may never marry. Marjorie is wearing a baseball uniform and cap that make her look like a boy. Her father explains, "I thought if we moved here, you might meet some nice refined young man, maybe get married." But Marjorie, who does not share her father's aspirations, cuts him off, "Oh, Papa, you're so old-fashioned!" She then runs outside to join the neighborhood boys in a game of baseball. But Marjorie soon outgrows her masculinity, when she meets and falls in love with Bill Sherman (Gordon MacRae), the handsome boy who lives across the street and attends the state university. The

DORIS DAY AS A TOMBOY IN *ON MOONLIGHT BAY*.

film marks Marjorie's transition to heterosexual womanhood in the scene in which she and Bill kiss for the first time. As Bill takes her in his arms, the film cuts to a close-up of Marjorie's hand, which reaches around to the table behind her and knocks her baseball cap onto the floor. We never again see Marjorie in her baseball uniform, which she exchanges for frilly blouses and skirts.

But *By the Light of the Silvery Moon* complicates this representation of Marjorie's masculinity. It opens with the Winfield family's maid, Stella (Mary Wickes), standing in the front yard of the house in medium shot and introducing each member of the family in a direct address to the camera. When she reminds the audience that the Winfields have two children, a boy and a girl, the film dissolves to a medium shot of a Model T parked in the driveway. As Stella says in a voice-off, "That's the girl," Marjorie slides out from under the car and stands up wiping her hands with a cloth. She is wearing overalls and is covered with grease. When her brother, Wesley (Billy Gray), informs her that Bill, who at the end of *On Moonlight Bay* went off to war, is returning home, she runs into the house exclaiming, "Isn't it wonderful?" But her father comments dryly, "It might be more wonderful if he were coming home to a charming feminine young lady instead of a grease monkey." This opening contradicts the earlier film's representation of Marjorie's masculinity as a form of tomboyism by indicating that she has not outgrown it, despite her initiation into adult heterosexuality. Indeed, she continues to engage in masculine behavior even after Bill returns and they become engaged. When their car breaks down on their way home from a dance, Marjorie makes Bill feel incompetent by sliding under the car, tinkering with the engine, and restarting it.[24] In representing Marjorie in this way, the film indirectly acknowledged the complexity of Day's masculinity. Although that masculinity did not conflict with her clean, wholesome image, it could never be fully assimilated to the category of the tomboy.

Despite the importance of the role of Marjorie in defining Day's image, critics have tended to normalize her performance of masculinity in *Calamity Jane*, arguing that the film disavows rather than affirms Calamity's nonnormative gender and sexual aspirations.[25] Calamity supposedly demonstrates acceptance of her proper role as a woman by moving from a homosocial identification with Hickok to a heterosexual desire for him. Although these critics acknowledge the ambiguity of the film's narrative resolution, they locate that ambiguity in Calamity's performance of masculinity earlier in the film, which renders her initiation into feminine subordination in the final scene unbelievable. Thus they reduce Calamity's masculinity to a form of tomboyism that she eventually outgrows. But this argument fails to consider the way in which *Calamity Jane* both exploited and amplified Day's masculinity. *On Moonlight Bay* and *By the Light of the Silvery Moon* demonstrated that Day's films could highlight her masculinity without jeopardizing the other elements of her image, which were already deeply entrenched. Indeed, the role of Marjorie consolidated Day's image as the girl next door, even as it rendered her gender and sexual identities ambiguous. Because Marjorie's masculinity does not prevent her from performing normative femininity, *Calamity Jane* could go even further than the earlier two films in masculinizing Day's persona without destabilizing it. In contrast to Marjorie, Calamity never normalizes her gender presentation. She does not resist initiation into femininity so much as fail at it, and she continues to cross-dress, even after she recognizes her "secret love" for Hickok. Thus her masculinity emerges as a fixed identity. But it does not unambiguously signify lesbianism. The film ultimately validates Calamity's homosocial identification with Hickok, albeit queerly, by having her marry him. As a result, Calamity cannot be classified according to any of the historically available categories of gender and sexuality.

From the beginning, the film represents Calamity's masculinity as deficient. In the opening scene, Millie (Paul Harvey), the owner of the Golden Garter, announces, "Drinks are on the house!" The men crowd around the bar, blocking Calamity, who fires her gun to disperse them. When they step aside to let her through, Calamity strides up to the bar, but rather than a whiskey, she orders a sarsaparilla. Then, as she leans against the bar, she slips and falls, provoking the men's laughter. Further undercutting her masculinity, Hickok constantly reminds her that she is a woman and that she should dress and act like one. When Calamity overhears some of the men talking excitedly about Adelaide Adams, who functions in the film as an icon of heterosexual femininity, Calamity asks Hickok what makes the actress so special. Waxing lyrical, Hickok compares Adelaide to Circe, Aphrodite, and Helen of Troy. He then looks Calamity up and down and adds more prosaically, "She's charming, a lovely figure, everything that a woman ought to be," the implication being that Calamity is not. In a later scene, he challenges Calamity's account of her heroic rescue of Lieutenant Danny Gilmartin (Philip Carey) when he is taken hostage by the Sioux. Hickok has a skeptical look on his face, which indicates that he thinks that, to impress the men, Calamity has exaggerated the number of Sioux she killed. When Calamity notices the look, she asks him if he believes her. He replies sarcastically, "Oh, sure, only with you killing them redskins off so fast, I wonder why the government even bothers sending the army." As he walks away, Calamity shoots her gun at him and asks if he is calling her a liar. As he turns back toward her, he shoots her gun out of her hand, showing that he is a faster draw, then says derisively, "Oh why don't you ever fix your hair." Finally, as Calamity is leaving for Chicago to bring Adelaide back, Hickok cajoles her, "When you get to Chicago, notice the women, how they act, and what they wear. Get yourself some female clothes and fixings, you know, dresses, ribbons, perfume, things like that." She might never rival Adelaide in terms of sex appeal, but he suspects that if she ever "dolled up a bit . . . [she'd] be a passable pretty gal."

Although these taunts imply that Calamity has transgressed her proper role as a woman, the film does not represent her masculinity as a simulacrum, as an imitation of the real thing. Calamity performs feats of courage that far surpass any of Hickok's in the film, and he competes with her as much as she competes with him. Indeed, his taunts about her appearance seem intended to undermine her masculinity specifically so that it does not detract from his own. When he and Calamity sing the duet "I Could Do without You," he indirectly acknowledges that she threatens his masculinity. Lyrics like "in the ointment you're the fly" and "you're the tack in my shoe" indicate that he sees her as a rival and needs to minimize her. Further complicating their relationship, Calamity identifies with Hickok as if he were an older brother. She looks up to him and models her masculinity on his. She brags about his exploits as much as she does her own. In the opening scene, in which she sings "Whip Crack Away!," she jumps up on the table where he is playing poker with his back to the camera and introduces him to the audience as "The Man the sheriff watches / On his gun there are more than 27 notches." When he stands up and turns toward the camera, he towers over her menacingly, making clear his superiority to her, which she willingly acknowledges: "On the draw there is no one faster / And you're flirting with disaster / When Bill Hickok's reputation you malign." Because of her identification with Hickok, Calamity resembles a boy more than a tomboy. Calamity's masculinity emerges as immature, as not yet fully developed; hence the film's emphasis on its deficiency. All of Calamity's faults—her boasting, her tall tales about her clashes with the Sioux, her competition with the men over who is braver—can be taken as signs of immaturity. She behaves like a boy who does not realize that he is not yet grown up. Thus her masculinity cannot be reduced to a way of resisting initiation into feminine subordination.

The film does not identify Calamity's masculinity as nonnormative until she leaves Deadwood City, where she is the only woman, and travels to Chicago. Although her infatuation with Danny marks her as heterosexual, Calamity discovers in Chicago that her gender presentation is sexually ambiguous, which throws her into crisis. The men and women who pass her on the street as she walks from the train station to the theater where Adelaide is performing gape at her as if they do not know whether she is a man or a woman. One of the passersby, a woman who bumps into Calamity when she stops to gawk at another woman who is wearing a bustle and swinging her hips exaggeratedly, even seems to find her sexually attractive. She winks at Calamity and waves coyly as if inviting her for an assignation. Calamity is too busy marveling at all of the city's unfamiliar sights and sounds to notice the gender and sexual trouble that she is causing, and after giving the woman a puzzled look, she moves on. But when she arrives at the theater, she can no longer ignore the social signification of her gender presentation. Adelaide, who has already left for Paris, has bequeathed her costumes to her maid, Katie

Brown (Allyn McLerie), and when Calamity enters the dressing room, she is trying one of them on. Although Katie is not as voluptuous or talented as her former employer, Calamity mistakes her for the star and exclaims, "Gosh Almighty, you're the prettiest thing I ever seen. I never knew a woman could look like that." She reaches over to touch Katie's costume, but Katie, who thinks that Calamity is a man, slaps her and tells her to leave the dressing room before she screams. At first Calamity laughs, but then she realizes that Katie's confusion is not so funny. She examines herself in the mirror, as if for the first time, and realizes how her gender style must look to others: "I reckon I do look a mite strange to a lady like you. Guess I ain't much to look at." But she soon overcomes her shame by reminding herself that she has skills that other women lack, "There ain't a woman in the world I can't outride or outshoot. Everybody can't have a figure like Adelaide Adams."

Calamity experiences a more serious crisis over her gender identity after she and Katie return to Deadwood, and she persuades Katie to move out of the Golden Garter into her cabin so that she can protect her from the men of the town. But the cabin is barely habitable, and Katie cannot conceal her disappointment. Calamity has never noticed the dirt and grime before, and Katie's reaction makes her ashamed of her masculinity. Even though she is a woman, Calamity does not know how to keep house. In other words, the scene painfully repeats Calamity's experience in Chicago, when she realizes for the first time how "strange" she looks to others. But this time she does not overcome her shame as easily. She begins to think that she lacks more than a voluptuous figure, and that her feminine deficiencies encompass her whole identity. When Katie politely tells her that the cabin is not so bad and that they can clean it up, Calamity contradicts her: "It's not fit for a dog, let alone a lady. . . . I didn't know it, just like I didn't know how far from being a lady I was until I saw you in that dressing room in Chicago." She punctuates this admission by slamming a chair angrily into a table. Picking up Katie's bags, she begins to leave, but Katie stops her and reassures her that all the cabin needs is "a woman's touch." She takes a quick turn around the cabin, brushes some dust off a table, and begins singing, "A woman's touch / The magic of Aladdin's lamp couldn't do so much." Handing Calamity a broom, she motions her to sweep the floor. By the end of the scene, after Katie and Calamity have performed the duet "A Woman's Touch," the two have transformed the cabin into a "shining castle built for two." As Katie teaches her how to keep house, Calamity's appearance undergoes a

DORIS DAY AND ALLYN MCLERIE CODED AS A
BUTCH-FEMME COUPLE IN *CALAMITY JANE*.

transformation. When the scene opens, she is wearing buckskins, a ban-
dana, and an army cap, but as it progresses she takes on a more noticeably
feminine appearance. Halfway through the scene, we see her in a plaid
flannel shirt and pair of pants that show off her figure. By the end of the
scene, she has on a dress that is similar in style to the one that Katie is
wearing. Thus part of the magic of Katie's touch has been to domesticate
Calamity so that her gender presentation no longer appears sexually ambiguous.

Critics usually cite this scene as evidence that the musical treats Calamity's masculinity as a form of tomboyism.[26] In teaching Calamity how
to keep house, Katie supposedly reconciles her to her proper role as a
woman. By the end of the scene, the argument goes, Calamity has overcome her resistance to feminine subordination and is now prepared to
marry Hickok. But this reading overlooks the sexual ambiguity of the
two women's relationship. Calamity's crisis in Chicago encompasses
more than her gender identity. As Eric Savoy has noted, because of her
manly appearance, Calamity's gawking at other women has homoerotic
overtones.[27] Moreover, Katie experiences Calamity's looking and touch-

Doris Day's Queer Normativity   167

ing in the dressing-room scene as sexually threatening, although admittedly she thinks that Calamity is a man. The sexual ambiguity of their relationship surfaces more fully in the cabin scene. As they renovate the cabin, they resemble a butch-femme couple setting up house together. Their gender styles remain dichotomized throughout most of the scene, and they follow a gendered division of labor. In a parody of heterosexual domesticity, the feminine Katie cooks and cleans while the masculine Calamity saws and hammers.

Finally, it becomes clear in the scene in which Hickok and Danny visit the cabin that Katie has exacerbated rather than resolved Calamity's gender trouble. Calamity fails to master femininity, and her masculinity emerges as a fixed identity. Both Hickok and Danny want to ask Katie to the upcoming ball, but she insists that one of them must take Calamity or she will not go. They have not yet seen Calamity, who is visiting a sick neighbor, and both of them refuse to take her. Katie scolds them, "Oh I know what you're thinking, both of you. She just isn't lady enough to make social appearances with such distinguished gentlemen. Calamity's fine on top of a stage coach or behind an ox team." Hickok replies defensively, "Well, she isn't beautiful!" Katie looks out the window and sees that Calamity is on her way back to the cabin. She thinks that they will change their minds when they finally see her, and she repeats, "Calamity's not beautiful, huh? You boys have a big surprise in store for you." Hickok and Danny draw straws to determine which of them will take Calamity. When Hickok loses, Katie tells him to keep his eye on the door, convinced that he will no longer feel disappointed when he sees Calamity. But unknown to her, Calamity has fallen into the creek while crossing it, and her dress and face are covered with mud. When she walks through the door, she looks like a freak of femininity in her mud-caked, form-fitting yellow dress. Hickok and Danny roar with laughter while Katie exclaims "Calamity!," indirectly acknowledging that her attempts to feminize the other woman have had a calamitous result.

Calamity does not abandon her attempts to master femininity until the scene of the ball, in which she discovers that Danny loves Katie. As the scene opens, Calamity wears a man's overcoat and wool scarf on her head, looking like the same old Calamity. But when she and Hickok arrive at the ballroom and she removes her coat, she appears transformed. She is wearing a glamorous, low-cut evening gown, and her hair is tied up with ribbons and flowers. At first, Hickok does not recognize her, but when he realizes who she is, he can hardly believe his eyes: Calamity does rival Adelaide in terms of sex appeal. The men begin to compete with each other over who will dance with her, and she becomes the belle of the ball. But Calamity again reveals that she has failed to master femininity. When she discovers Danny and Katie kissing in the garden, she feels betrayed and prepares to leave the ball. But as she is putting on her coat, she sees them drinking punch on the other side of the room. She picks up a gun and shoots the glass out of Katie's hand, shocking the other guests with her manly behavior. She and Hickok then return to the cabin, where she packs up Katie's things. She takes off her evening gown and tells Hickok, "Throw that in with the rest of her man traps!" Calamity no longer has any desire to normalize her gender identity. Because she feels that Katie has betrayed her, she associates femininity with artifice and deception. When she appears at the Golden Garter in the following scene, she has reassumed her masculine appearance. She interrupts Katie's performance and warns her that she had better be on the stagecoach leaving town the next day, as if they were two gunfighters headed for a showdown. In this way, the film emphasizes the fixity of her gender identity.

Ironically, Calamity's failure to master femininity establishes a parallel between her and Katie. Although in comparison to Calamity Katie is a model of femininity, she too struggles to normalize her gender identity. In Chicago, before Adelaide leaves for Paris, Katie attempts to persuade her to give her a part in her show. She tells the star that she has always dreamed of appearing onstage, but Adelaide does not take her seriously. Although Katie's voice is "fine for choirs and weddings," she doubts that "it would carry beyond the footlights." When Katie persists with the idea, Adelaide looks her up and down condescendingly and says, "Well, it isn't just your voice. Your other equipment is hardly adequate." After Adelaide leaves, Katie examines her figure in the mirror and then tries on one of Adelaide's costumes to see how it fits. She does not want to believe that she is less sexy than the star. In other words, Adelaide has the same effect on Katie that Katie has on Calamity when in the same scene she mistakes her for a man. Adelaide makes Calamity feel ashamed of her gender identity, and Calamity begins to want to be more like Katie. When Calamity enters the dressing room and mistakes Katie for the star, Katie does not correct her. She feels vindicated by the mistake, which suggests that she does have sex appeal after all. But Katie's attempt to pass as Adelaide ends disastrously when she first appears onstage at the Golden Garter and fails to project her voice beyond the footlights, just as the star had predicted. As her performance begins to flounder, the men become rowdy, and she is forced to admit that she has lied about her identity. The men almost riot, but Calamity intervenes and persuades them to allow her to continue performing.[28] Although Katie is no Adelaide, the men come to accept her as she is. This parallel between Katie and Calamity helps to clarify Calamity's failure to master femininity. In the film, gender identities are fixed and immutable. In imitating Katie's femininity, Calamity engages in a form of passing, which is why she ultimately fails at it. She cannot repress her masculinity but must learn to accept it. In other words, the film validates rather than repudiates Calamity's nonnormative gender aspirations.

The emergence of Calamity's masculinity as a fixed identity renders ambiguous the musical's narrative resolution. Although in the film's closing shots Calamity and Hickok look like a typical bride and groom about to embark on their honeymoon, there is nothing typical about their marriage, and this solidifies their homosocial affiliation. In the scene in which Calamity warns Katie to leave Deadwood, Hickok affirms Calamity's masculinity by intervening in the confrontation between the two women. Katie refuses to feel intimidated by Calamity and asks one of the men in the audience to lend her his gun. She wants to show that she is as good a shot as Calamity, who she tells to hold up her glass so that she can shoot it out of her hand. As Katie shoots, the film cuts from a medium shot of Calamity holding up a broken glass to a medium shot of Hickok, who is seated in a chair with his gun drawn and smoking, which indicates that he is the one who has shot the glass. One of the men shouts, "By golly Katie's done it!," and the audience rushes the stage to congratulate her. Calamity experiences Katie's triumph as a kind of castration. She tearfully watches the men crowd around Katie, then walks out of the saloon with her head down, as if disgraced. Although in intervening in the confrontation Hickok has hoped to humiliate her, he has not wanted to undermine Calamity's masculinity. In the following scene, he admits to Calamity that he shot the glass out of her hand, because she "needed a lesson." In showing her jealousy, Calamity has acted like a woman and lost the respect of the men. He scolds her, "You're a fake, Calam. You dress, talk, ride, and shoot like a man but think like a woman, a green-eyed, snarlin', spittin' female!" He then asks if she really thought that she could prevent Katie from loving Danny, and without waiting for an answer, he says derisively, "That's female thinkin'!" In other words, Hickok wants Calamity to reclaim her masculinity. Calamity needs to stop thinking like a woman and begin thinking like a man so that she never again makes a "blasted fool" of herself in front of the men. Significantly, in the process of reaffirming Calamity's masculinity, Hickok and she discover that they love each other. Hickok realizes that he wants Calamity to reassert rather than renounce her masculinity, and Calamity realizes that he accepts her as she is.

Calamity Jane's validation of Hickok's and Calamity's homosocial affiliation surfaces more fully in the next scene, in which Calamity, dressed like a man, sings the song "Secret Love" while riding into town. The lyrics indicate that she never loved Danny but has always loved Hickok. Calamity's buckskin costume in this scene, which is much more stylish than the one she wears earlier in the film, seems intended to show that she is no longer ashamed of her masculinity and wants to show it off. But it also makes her love for Hickok seem oddly homoerotic: she could be easily mistaken for a man singing about his love for another man. Adding to the scene's homoerotic overtones, the song is full of images of love as open book and open door, as Eric Savoy has pointed out.[29] Such images equate her discovery of her love for Hickok with coming out of the closet, especially since the discovery is simultaneous with her affirmation of her own masculinity. The sequence of scenes that follows only reinforces these homoerotic overtones. When Calamity arrives in town, the men look glum and barely acknowledge her. At the Golden Garter, a crowd has gathered to watch Millie take down the signs announcing Katie's performances. Calamity learns from one of the men that Katie has heeded her warning and left on the stagecoach. Calamity instructs Millie to put the signs back up and gallops off to bring Katie back. As she rides out of town, she passes Hickok, who is wearing an identical buckskin costume, except that it is dark brown. They stop and kiss, but they look more like brothers than an engaged couple. When Calamity finally catches up with the stagecoach, she tells Katie excitedly that she and Hickok are getting married. Katie stammers that she thought that Calamity loved Danny, but Calamity replies, "Oh, that was female thinkin', and nothin' will get you into more trouble!," implying that in loving Hickok she engages in male thinking. Thus the film's ending validates rather than represses Calamity's homosocial identification with Hickok. In marrying Hickok, Calamity does not accede to heterosexual femininity but affirms her masculinity. Because she and Hickok share the same gender identity, their relationship, like that of Vienna and Johnny in *Johnny Guitar*, resists classification as heterosexual.

This narrative resolution helps to explain why *Calamity Jane* was so important in shaping Day's image. Because Hollywood cinema continued to link gender and sexual nonconformity, the film opened up Day's persona to a lesbian construction by validating Calamity's masculinity.[30] Although several scenes provided audiences with a glimpse of a more glamorous Day, lest they forget why she was one of Hollywood's most popular stars, the film solidified the masculine elements of her image by emphasizing the fixity of Calamity's gender identity. Day tended to gloss over the tensions and contradictions in her image, but she understood the way in which they contained her emergence as a sex symbol later in her career. When an interviewer asked her why she thought that *Pillow Talk* had revived her career, she replied, "I had become a new kind of sex symbol—the woman men wanted to go to bed with, but not until they married her. Sexy but pure."[31] This answer acknowledged how her wholesomeness continued to shape her image, even after *Pillow Talk* glamorized her, so that she appeared sexy and pure simultaneously. But it did not acknowledge how her masculinity also limited the remaking of her image. Because of her wholesomeness, Day's masculinity, even when it was amplified in films like *Calamity Jane*, could be normalized as tomboyish.[32] But it existed in tension with the more glamorous aspects of her persona. These three elements—Day's masculinity, her wholesomeness, and her glamour—worked to contain each other so that she never became wholly accessible as a heterosexual object of desire. With *Pillow Talk*, Day did indeed become a new kind of sex symbol. Yet, while it glamorized her, muting her gender and sexual ambiguity, it did not resolve it. That ambiguity resurfaced in Jan's protection of her virginity, which can be understood as a resistance to initiation into heterosexuality. Thus the film's relationship to Cold War gender and sexual norms was more complicated than critics have acknowledged.[33] Like Calamity, Jan threatens to destabilize the dominant gender and sexual taxonomies, although this aspect of her identity remains much less marked.

The opening shots of *Pillow Talk* make clear that the role of Jan Morrow is not a typical one for Day. As the opening credits fade, a woman's bare leg, raised in the air, appears on the screen in close-up. The camera tracks back to reveal Day, in medium shot, adjusting her nylon stockings. She is wearing a pale-blue slip and sitting on the edge of her bed, humming the film's title song. She stands up, takes a robe out of the closet, and smoothes her hair in the mirror. This sequence of shots links her to the unidentified woman in the opening credits. As the credits begin rolling, a woman in a pale-blue nightgown appears on the left side of the screen. She is lying on her back in bed facing away from the camera, with her leg in the air, talking on the phone. She tosses a pillow toward the middle of the screen where the credits appear, and a man in pale-blue pajamas suddenly appears on the opposite side. Like the woman, he is lying on his back in bed facing away from the camera, talking on the phone. He too begins tossing pillows toward the middle of the screen. The lyrics of the title song, sung by Day, help to explain the meaning of their sexualized play. In the song's refrain, Day complains that she is tired of "hearing myself talk, talk, talk," and she wonders "how it would be / To have someone to pillow talk with me." The verse describes her frustrations as a single woman: "All I do is talk to my pillow / Talk to my pillow / Talk about the boy I'm gonna marry / Some day, somehow, some time." And it expresses her wish: "There must be a pillow-talkin' boy for me." In juxtaposing these two sequences, the film is careful to position Jan as both a subject and an object of desire. Although the shots of her dressing highlight her sexual desirability, they are preceded by the title sequence, which makes clear that it is her sexual fantasies, not Brad's, that will propel the film's narrative.

Pillow Talk was hardly the first of Day's films to emphasize her sex appeal or to treat her as an object-to-be-looked-at. *Teacher's Pet* (George Seaton, 1958) also sexually objectified the star, but in ways that were much more ambivalent. In the film, Day plays Erica Stone, a journalism professor who falls in love with Jim Gannon (Clark Gable), a famous city editor who pretends to be a student in her class so that he can woo her. Stone and Gannon have never met, and when Gannon attends the first class he is surprised by how attractive Stone is. When Stone enters the class and stands in front of the room, in long shot, she is wearing a black pencil skirt and fitted jacket that shows off her shapely figure. The film cuts to a reverse shot of Gannon, who is looking Stone up and down lasciviously. Stone, who does not know that Gannon is in the room, begins reading aloud the condescending letter, which he wrote in response to her invitation to address the class, in which he belittles the teaching of journalism. As he listens to her read the letter, Gannon realizes how old-fashioned his views sound, and he begins to squirm uncomfortably in his chair. Afraid that Stone will ask him who he is and discover that he is the author of the letter, he sneaks out of the room when she is not looking.

DORIS DAY AS A "NEW KIND OF SEX SYMBOL" IN *PILLOW TALK*.

In this way, the film punishes Gannon for sexually objectifying Stone. Before he can become involved with her, he must prove that he respects her
as an equal and that he no longer holds the views expressed in the letter.
In this scene Gannon functions as a diegetic substitute for the audience.
Teacher's Pet was the first film in which Day played a single, New York
career girl, and it anticipated the romantic comedies that became a staple
of Day's career after *Pillow Talk*. The audience was expected to share Gannon's surprise at Day's sexual attractiveness and to take a similar pleasure
in looking at her. But it was also, like Gannon, expected to limit that pleasure so that it did not conflict with Day's wholesomeness. Thus, where
Pillow Talk differed from the other films that emphasized Day's sex appeal
was in giving the audience license to objectify her. *Pillow Talk* has many
shots similar to the opening image of Day, and they are rarely mediated
by a male character whose looking is represented as transgressive.

At the same time, however, the audience does not have absolute license to objectify Day as Jan. The film is careful to make a distinction between her and other sexy, glamorous women. In the opening scene, when
Jan picks up the phone to make a call, the screen splits three ways. Brad
Allen, a Broadway composer who shares the line with Jan, appears on the
left side of the screen. He is seated at the piano composing a song and

Chapter Six

talking on the phone to one of his girlfriends, Eileen (Valerie Allen), who appears on the right side of the screen. Jan appears in the middle, literally as well figuratively coming between them. Eileen has on an orange negligee and is reclining seductively on a couch. When Jan realizes that Brad is on the line, she puts down the receiver. While he and Eileen engage in a kind of pillow talk, she puts on her robe and waits for them to hang up. But Brad begins singing "You Are My Inspiration," a song that he is composing for a Broadway show, and Jan picks up the receiver to listen. She rolls her eyes, indicating that she finds the lyrics insipid, then politely asks him to hang up so that she can make an "important call." When Eileen demands, "Who's that?," Brad replies, "The other half of my party line. Just ignore her and she'll go away." He then tells Jan, "I happen to consider this an important call." Jan exclaims in disbelief, "What, singing to a woman at nine o'clock in the morning?," which prompts an indignant Eileen to say, "It's none of your business what he does to me or when." A few minutes later Jan again attempts to make a call and again discovers that Brad is on the line talking to a woman, this time the French Yvette (Jacqueline Beer). Jan does not put down the receiver, but eavesdrops on the conversation, at once fascinated and repelled by its fatuousness. Yvette, who appears on the right side of the screen, is wearing a low-cut black negligee and is sitting seductively in a chair. When she asks if she can have dinner with Brad, he replies that he has six new songs to compose. Flirtatiously telling him that he has to keep up his strength, Yvette offers to come over and cook dinner for him, which makes Jan roll her eyes incredulously. Yvette asks him to sing "You Are My Inspiration," which he does, in French. Jan has finally had enough of their banter and demands that Brad hang up. When Yvette asks, "Who is that woman?," Brad replies, not incorrectly, "Some little eavesdropper on my party line. She's always listening in. It's how she brightens up her drab, empty life." Jan exclaims, "If I could get a call through once in a while, my life wouldn't be so drab!," and slams down the receiver.

These scenes mark Jan as sexually different. She is as sexy and glamorous as Eileen and Yvette, but she does not have the same interest in men and dating as they do, instead focusing on her career. The differences between Jan and the other two women could not be more striking. While they are at home still in their nightgowns talking on the phone to Brad, she is getting ready for a busy day at the office. Unlike Yvette, she would never have time to fix Brad dinner. Indeed, the only domestic activities in which we see her engage are making coffee and pouring tomato juice for her alcoholic cleaning lady, Alma (Thelma Ritter), who spends her afternoons eavesdropping on Brad's phone calls. Although Jan admits that her life is "drab" when she hangs up on Brad, she has no desire to lead the kind of life that Eileen and Yvette do. We know from the opening sequence that she would like to find a man with whom she can "pillow talk," but she is basically happy. As she tells Alma, "I have a good job. A lovely apartment. I go out with very nice men to the best places. The theater. The finest restaurants. What am I missing?" As Alma points out, if she has to ask the question, she must be missing something, but she is not interested in dating men like Brad Allen. Indeed, she does not understand why Eileen and Yvette are so attracted to him. Her reaction to him contrasts markedly with theirs. Whereas they listen with rapt attention as he flirts with them, Jan rolls her eyes and sighs heavily, indicating that she finds him foolish. Nor can she believe how easily they succumb to his come-ons. At the same time, the combination of fascination and repulsion with which she listens to him talk seductively to Yvette suggests that she is at least somewhat curious about how men and women negotiate sex.

Jan's differences from these other women render her identity illegible. Nobody believes that she can be happy living alone. By contrast, nobody ever questions Brad's happiness with the single life. He is a playboy bachelor. But there is no corresponding category for a sexually desirable, career-oriented woman like Jan, who is in her mid-thirties and has never been married.[34] When Jan finally complains to the phone company about Brad's monopolizing of the party line, she cannot make Mr. Conrad (Hayden Rorke), the official with whom she speaks, understand that she needs a private line so that she can make business calls. Because she is a woman, he thinks that the only emergency that would justify her having her own line would be pregnancy. Jan reminds him, "Mr. Conrad, being single, I'm not quite ready for that kind of emergency." Mr. Conrad does not take her complaint seriously until she calls Brad a "sex maniac." He immediately closes his office door and asks, "Has he used any objectionable language on the phone?," to which Jan replies, "No."

"Threats of any nature?"

"No."

"Has he made immoral overtures to you?"

"Well, not to me."

Mr. Conrad thinks that he has finally discovered the reason for Jan's complaint. He asks, "And you're bothered by this?" Confused by the question, Jan replies, "Yes. I mean, no. What do you mean *bothered*?" Mr. Conrad clarifies, "His carrying on with all these other women bothers you." Jan again struggles to make herself understood: "Mr. Conrad, please believe me, I don't care what he does. I just want him to stop doing it on my phone." But Mr. Conrad does not believe her. Because she is single, he assumes that Jan is unhappy that she does not have a man and that she wants Brad to talk to her the way he talks to other women.

Jan has even more difficulty making herself understood with Brad. Whenever they talk, he takes control of the conversation away from her by turning everything she says into a sexual double entendre. After the phone company sends a female investigator to his apartment to interview him, he calls Jan angrily, "You don't see me going down to the phone company and complaining about your affairs." She responds, "I don't have any affairs to complain about." He comments pointedly, "That figures." When Jan asks what he means, he explains, "Well, obviously you're a woman who lives alone and doesn't like it." Jan insists that she does like living alone, but he responds, "Look, I don't know what's bothering you but don't take your bedroom problems out on me!" Exasperated, she exclaims, "I have no bedroom problems. There's nothing in my bedroom to bother me." He snickers, "Oh, that's too bad." In this way, Brad reduces Jan to a stereotypical spinster. Like Mr. Conrad, he assumes that she is eavesdropping because she has no other sexual outlet and thus finds his conversations titillating. During a later, more heated exchange, Brad enjoins her, "Stop living vicariously in what you think I do. There are plenty of warm rolls in the bakery. Stop pressing your nose against the window." Even Alma refuses to believe that Jan likes living alone. When she overhears Jan tell Brad that she likes being single, Alma remarks, "If there's anything worse than a woman living alone, it's a woman saying she likes it." Jan has no way of articulating her social and sexual difference. No matter what she says or does, the other characters continue to view her in terms of the negative stereotypes about single women. Not surprisingly, in the face of this constant lack of social affirmation, Jan begins to doubt herself. After Brad accuses her of taking out her "bedroom problems" on him, she walks into her bedroom, sits down at her vanity table, peers into the mirror, and repeats "bedroom problems" three times, each time with more emphasis. Perhaps Brad and Alma are right: living alone and focusing on her career are not as enjoyable as she thinks.

Although in emphasizing the illegibility of Jan's identity, the film acknowledges that in the 1950s women were expected to define themselves in terms of domesticity and motherhood, it does not itself adopt this view. Rather, it validates Jan's difference from other women. One of the most remarkable aspects of the film is its negative representation of heterosexuality, which privileges Jan's point of view. In the film, women are expected to derive satisfaction from relationships that not only privilege male sexual fantasy, but also require them to give up their autonomy and control. In this context, Jan's lack of interest in dating seems totally understandable. Early in the film, the juxtaposition of two scenes of heterosexual seduction—one successful, the other failed—illustrates how heterosexuality subordinates women. In the first of these scenes, Brad and Maria (Julia Meade), a nightclub performer, are sitting on the couch in Brad's apartment, drinking champagne in medium shot. As they begin to kiss passionately, Brad reaches behind Maria and flips a switch. The lights grow dim, the stereo begins playing sultry music, and the door to the apartment locks. The film then dissolves to a long shot of a sports car parked in a secluded spot by the side of the road. We hear a woman yelp, and the camera tracks in to reveal Jan struggling with Tony Walters (Nick Adams), the son of one of her clients, who is forcing his attentions on her. Tony, who is a senior at Harvard, has offered Jan a ride from Scarsdale, where she was attending a party thrown by his mother, and he attempts to take advantage of her on the way. It is not until Jan holds up her fist menacingly and says, "I've never belted a Phi Beta Kappa before!," that he agrees to take her home. The juxtaposition of these two scenes serves to reinforce Jan's difference from other women. Although Brad is more subtle than Tony, his methods for getting women into bed are no less coercive. He seduces Marie in the same way that he has seduced Eileen and Yvette: by singing her the song "You Are My Inspiration" and by claiming that he wrote it especially for her. The only difference between the two scenes is that whereas Marie complies with Brad's sexual fantasy, Jan resists Tony's. Jan does not want to give up her sexual autonomy. Unlike Marie and the other women whom Brad dates, she wants to participate in heterosexuality on her own terms. Thus her protection of her virginity should be understood as a form of sexual agency.[35]

Jan's desire to maintain her autonomy and control helps to explain why she does not see through Brad's masquerade as Rex Stetson. Brad resorts to the masquerade when he sees Jan at a nightclub and discovers that she is not the stereotype that he imagined but is as sexually attractive as the women he usually dates. He knows that she will never go out with him if she finds out that he is her nemesis, Brad Allen. Brad's impersonation of a Texas oilman is not very convincing; not only does he do a bad job of imitating a Southern accent, but he falls in and out of it. Moreover, as himself, Brad goes so far as to warn Jan that Rex is a phony. Shortly after Rex takes Jan home from the nightclub where they meet, Brad calls her: "Don't let that yokel act fool you. This ranch hand Romeo is just trying to lure you into the nearest barn." But Jan never suspects that Rex is a fabrication. Because he resembles exactly the kind of man that she has fantasized about falling in love with, she has a vested interest in believing he is real. When she and Rex take a cab back to her apartment from the nightclub, Rex looks out the window at the buildings passing by and says implausibly, "All those buildings filled with people kind of scares a country boy like me." Jan muses in voice-over, "Isn't that sweet. So unpretentious and honest. What a relief after a couple of monsters like Tony Walters and that Brad Allen." Later, when he refuses her invitation to come into her apartment for a cup of coffee, instead saying goodnight at the door, she remarks, again in voice-over, "It's so nice to meet a man you feel you can trust." (Ironically, just then Brad is thinking how much easier it will be to get her into bed than he had thought: "Five or six dates ought to do it.") Rex represents the promise of a different kind of heterosexuality, one that does not require Jan to mold herself to his sexual fantasy. Instead, he molds himself to hers. After they have dinner, the following night, he takes her up to his hotel room, but he does not make a pass at her. She does not realize that his behavior is part of an elaborate ploy to seduce her, but interprets it as a sign that he is different from other men. Before they leave the room, she apologizes for suspecting his motives: "I should have known that you weren't like others. . . . Can you forgive me?" In other words, unlike the other characters, Rex mirrors Jan's social and sexual difference, and thus affirms rather than negates her identity.

Rex's difference from other men raises the question of whether Jan's desire can be properly understood as heterosexual, given the construction of heterosexuality in the film. The type of man Jan fantasizes about proves sexually ambiguous: Rex's sexual reticence may mean that he respects her, or it may mean that he is not attracted to women. At one point, Brad calls Jan to goad her: "Admit it, your western gentleman turned out to be a prairie wolf." Jan responds, "It may surprise you, Mr. Allen, to learn that not all men end a sentence with a proposition," then boastfully reveals that Rex has not yet made a pass at her. Brad wonders aloud if Rex is even "worse" than he thought. When Jan asks what he means, he answers evasively, "There are some men who just, uh, well, they're very devoted to their mother. You know the type that, uh, likes to collect cooking recipes, exchange bits of gossip." Jan understands the type of man that he means and exclaims, "What a vicious thing to say!" But rather than hanging up, she remains on the line. Brad advises her, "Don't you think you better make sure?" She replies, "You're sick!," and finally slams the receiver down. The fact that she continues to listen indicates that she herself has begun to have doubts about Rex. Perhaps the type of behavior that she looks for in a man is incompatible with heterosexuality.

Rex seems to confirm her doubts later that evening when she takes him to one of her favorite bars, and he begins to act effeminate. He asks her what it is like working with "all those colors and fabrics and all," takes a sip of his drink with his pinkie in the air, and tasting some dip, remarks that he would like to have the recipe for his mother. Jan decides that she does need to make sure about Rex's sexuality, and she asks him if he finds her attractive. He kisses her for the first time, dispelling her doubts. In marking Rex as sexually ambiguous, the film calls attention to the non-normativity of Jan's desire. Jan cannot take for granted that the kind of relationship that she has fantasized about is heterosexual, but must prove it. Jan and Rex decide to go away with each other for the weekend, and when Jan returns home to pack, she calls Brad: "Mr. Allen, just so you'll realize how wrong you are about Rex Stetson, he has just asked me to go away with him for the weekend." She wants Brad to know that her relationship with Rex is "normal," that it is not so different from other relationships. But it is not exactly true that Rex has asked her to go away with him, as Brad knows. Rex was too shy to ask, so Jan has had to propose it herself. As she later admits in voice-over in the scene in which they drive to Connecticut, "I practically tricked him into taking me." If Jan's relationship with Rex were "normal," she would not misrepresent what happened between her and Rex, nor would she need to prove to her nemesis Brad that Rex likes women.

As Steven Cohan has argued, Brad's masquerade as Rex calls attentions to the sexual indeterminacy of the category of the bachelor in the 1950s.[36] Brad and Rex appear to embody opposing characteristics. Brad is sophisticated, self-assured, and sexually aggressive, while Rex is unpolished, bashful, and sexually restrained. Moreover, Brad seduces women, whereas Rex maintains a respectful distance from them. But the differences between the two bachelors are less clear-cut than this comparison suggests. Bachelorhood had a sexually ambiguous meaning in the 1950s: it might indicate that a man did not want to limit his sexual options by settling down and getting married, or it might indicate that he was a "mama's boy," a latent homosexual who remained fixated on his mother. The fact that Brad and Rex are the same man highlights how easily the first meaning could slide into the second. The tensions and contradictions in Hudson's image only reinforced the potential for slippage between Brad and Rex. Like Brad, he was known as a playboy, one of Hollywood's most eligible bachelors, who dated several women simultaneously.[37] But like Rex, he was also rumored to be homosexual and had a widely publicized devotion to his mother.

The film attempts to stabilize the differences between Rex and Brad in part through its representation of Jonathan (Tony Randall), a Broadway producer who is Brad's best friend as well as one of Jan's clients. Jonathan acts as a foil for Brad.[38] He embodies more clearly than Brad the ambiguities of bachelorhood. He has been married four times, is seeing a psychotherapist, and blames his problems with women on his domineering mother. Moreover, he is in love with Jan and tries to convince her to marry him, but she is not sexually attracted to him and thinks of him as no more than a friend. The film foregrounds the differences between the two bachelors in the scene in which Jonathan tells Brad that he is in love with Jan and wants to marry her. Jonathan urges Brad to settle down because "there is nothing in this world so wonderful, so fulfilling as coming home to the same woman every night." But Brad, who has not yet seen Jan, associates marriage with castration, and he proclaims loftily, "Jonathan, before a man gets married, he's, uh, like a tree in a forest. He, he stands there, independent, an entity unto himself, and then, he's chopped down, his branches are cut off, he's stripped of his bark, and he's thrown into the river with the rest of the logs." Jonathan might agree with Brad if he were not in love with Jan, and he responds emphatically, "No, no. If this girl weren't something extra special, then maybe I'd agree with you. But with Jan, you look forward to having your branches cut off." In highlighting the differences between Brad and Jonathan, this scene seems intended to stabilize Brad's gender and sexual identities. As a man who looks forward to the castration of marriage, Jonathan appears to have more in common with Rex than Brad does. Like Rex, Jonathan occupies an unstable position in relation to heterosexuality, thereby helping to deflect attention from the possibility that Brad does too. But if Brad needs a gender and sexual foil, then perhaps he has more in common with Jonathan and Rex than he acknowledges.

Jonathan serves a similar function with respect to the relationship between Brad and Jan. In comparison with Jonathan's history of failed heterosexuality, Jan's and Brad's relationship appears normative. When Jan finally discovers that Brad has been masquerading as Rex as a ploy to get her into bed, she refuses to have anything to do with him. In treating her the way he does other women, he has undermined Jan's identity. But in the course of the masquerade, Brad realizes that he loves Jan and wants to marry her. Alma convinces him that he can win Jan back if he hires her to redecorate his apartment. Jan uses the job as an opportunity to take revenge, redecorating the apartment in lurid colors and garish furnishings, so that it resembles a parody of the bachelor pad. When Brad discovers what she has done, he breaks into her apartment, drags her out of bed, and carries her in her pajamas through the streets of Manhattan, back to his apartment. Throwing her onto the bed that, bordello-like, dominates the living room, he tells her, "So far as I'm concerned you can stay here and charge admission." Jan finally realizes that he wanted her to redecorate the apartment because he wants to marry her. When he reaches for the door, she prevents him from leaving the apartment by flipping a switch: the lights grow dim, a pink player piano begins playing a ragtime version of "You Are My Inspiration," and the front door locks. In this way, Jan reasserts her control. She takes on the role of the playboy bachelor, but without the element of coercion. The scene's final shot is a close-up of Jan looking up at Brad seductively from the bed.

The film ends with a coda, but, significantly, does not show Jan domesticated. Instead, three months after Brad and Jan get married, Brad visits Jonathan's office to tell him the good news that he and Jan are expecting a baby. As he approaches the office, a doctor and a nurse grab hold of him and begin to drag him down the hall. Struggling to break free, he tells them, "You don't understand. I'm going to have a baby!" The doctor, who is an obstetrician, exclaims, "Of course you are!" The possibility that Brad might be pregnant has been a running gag in the film ever since Brad slipped into the obstetrician's office and complained about having an upset stomach to avoid running into Jan as she is coming out of Jonathan's office. In returning to the gag, the coda indicates that Jan has with Brad the kind of relationship that she had with Rex. Brad's gender and sexual ambiguity ("I'm going to have a baby!") collapses once and for all the distinction between him and Rex. In the course of masquerading as Rex, Brad has taken on his identity. Thus *Pillow Talk*'s ending is as ambiguous as *Calamity Jane*'s. Although, unlike Calamity and Hickok, Jan and Brad do not share the same gender identity, neither is their relationship normatively heterosexual. Brad has come to occupy a feminine position in relation to Jan, which indicates that their relationship entails a gender and sexual reversal.

This reversal suggests that *Pillow Talk* did not mark as great a departure for Day as Hunter imagined when he approached her about starring in it. Although the role of Jan helped to contain Day's masculinity by glamorizing her, it drew on the gender and sexual ambiguity of her persona. Jan's relationship with Brad affirms her social and sexual difference by allowing her to participate in heterosexuality on her own terms. Brad's transformation into Rex indicates that he has molded himself to Jan's sexual fantasy. Jan thus occupies a masculine position in relation to him, although it is not marked as such by any alteration of her gender presentation, which remains resolutely feminine. This resurfacing of Day's masculinity, however muted, helps to explain why *Pillow Talk* did not wholly succeed in transforming her into a sex symbol. Although it was the first of Day's films that encouraged audiences to objectify her sexually, it did not wholly stabilize her relationship to heterosexuality. On the one hand, Jan's protection of her virginity was totally consistent with Day's wholesomeness. On the other hand, it corroborated the star's taxonomic illegibility, or queerness, for her chasteness marks her refusal to participate in heterosexuality normatively. For this reason, Jan's relationship to Cold War gender and sexual taxonomies was almost as problematic as Calamity's. Although Jan's queerness is much less marked than that of the other character, her desire for a relationship that does not require her to subordinate her fantasies is inconsistent with the norms of heterosexuality as they are represented in the film. But just as the wholesome elements of Day's image worked to contain Calamity's masculinity so that it did not appear deviant, so, too, did they work to contain Jan's transgression of Cold War gender and sexual norms. As a result, *Pillow Talk* appeared to ratify rather than challenge those norms.

....

KILLING OFF THE FEMME

The Haunting

In *The Haunting* (1963), a classic horror movie directed by Robert Wise, Julie Harris plays Eleanor Lance, a tense, high-strung woman who accepts an invitation to participate in a psychic experiment at Hill House, a supposedly haunted mansion in remote New England. As a ten-year-old girl, Eleanor had a violent encounter with a poltergeist, who showered her home with rocks for three days, and Dr. Markway (Richard Johnson), the anthropologist who has organized the Hill House experiment, hopes to assemble a group of people "touched by the supernatural," who will stimulate the "strange forces at work there." Built some ninety years before by Hugh Crain, a "misfit who hated people and conventional ideas," Hill House is the site of four women's deaths, which Dr. Markway recounts in an opening voice-over. Those who died were Crain's two wives; his daughter, Abigail, who lived to old age in the house; and Abigail's paid companion, who committed suicide after inheriting the house from her former mistress. Eleanor has spent all of her adult life taking care of her mother, a bedridden invalid who died two months before she received Dr. Markway's invitation, which she eagerly accepts as a chance for a "vacation." When she arrives at Hill House, she discovers that only one other person has accepted Dr. Markway's invitation: Theodora (Claire Bloom), a chic, sophisticated woman from Greenwich Village, who as Richard Dyer has noted embodies the stereotype of the predatory lesbian.[1] Theodora has extrasensory perception, which recalls the "radar-like communication" that Jess Stearn in *The Grapevine* claimed enabled lesbians to spot other lesbians. Theodora recognizes in Eleanor a "kindred spirit" and, being attracted to her, hopes to seduce her.

The Haunting's exploration of perverse female desire reflects the shift in the homophobic deployment of the category of the lesbian that has been the primary focus of *Cold War Femme*. In the Cold War era, the femme displaced the butch as the lesbian whose aberrant sexuality posed the greatest threat to existing social arrangements. Produced after the 1961 revision of the Production Code, which allowed discreet and restrained treatments of homosexuality, *The Haunting* provides a much more explicit representation of lesbian desire than the other movies examined herein.[2] Theodora openly expresses her desire for Eleanor from the moment they meet. When Eleanor introduces herself, assuring Theodora, "We're going to be great friends," Theodora replies sarcastically, "Like sisters?" She clearly wants to be more than Eleanor's friend. Later in the movie, after a terrifying encounter with the supernatural, Dr. Markway tells the women that he wants them to sleep in the same room, and Theodora exclaims, "You're the doctor!," as she eagerly leads Eleanor away by the arm. The movie underscores the lesbian subtext of the two women's relationship by attributing to them contrasting gender styles. Eleanor appears prim and proper in plain silk blouses and tweed skirts. She also wears a frilly nightgown in several scenes. By contrast, Theodora's wardrobe codes her as a butch. At various points in the movie, she wears a polka-dot tie, a pair of slacks, and a masculine-looking bathrobe. She also tells Eleanor to call her by her nickname, Theo. After Theo makes several attempts to seduce her, Eleanor experiences lesbian panic, denouncing Theo in language that echoes the association of lesbianism with the category of the "unnatural": "You're the monster of Hill House." But the movie does not endorse this view of Theo's identity.[3] On the contrary, in attributing extrasensory perception to her, it gives Theo a privileged knowledge of Eleanor's thoughts and feelings, as well as of the supernatural happenings in the house—a knowledge which, as Patricia White has pointed out, far exceeds that of Dr. Markway.[4] Indeed, Theo has more understanding of Eleanor's desire than Eleanor herself does.

In denouncing her as a "monster," Eleanor displaces onto Theo her own "unnatural" sexuality. Indeed, it is Eleanor who emerges as the real monster of Hill House. The movie attributes to her a privileged relation to the supernatural. Unlike Theo and the others, she stimulates the "strange forces" in the house. When she and Theo have a terrifying encounter with the supernatural while searching the house for Dr. Markway and Luke (Russ Tamblyn), the future heir of the house, who has agreed to participate in the experiment despite his refusal to believe in ghosts, Theo remarks with a shudder, "It wants you, Nell. The house is calling you." Moreover, when Luke discovers "Help Eleanor come home" written on one of the walls in the hallway, Eleanor becomes hysterical, and

Theo attempts to calm her by explaining, "Maybe something in the house finds you a kindred spirit, maybe thinks you have more understanding and sympathy than the rest of us." In associating her with the supernatural, the movie marks Eleanor's sexuality as "unnatural."[5] Dr. Markway constantly confuses the category of the "supernatural" with the category of the "unnatural," thus indirectly linking the haunting of Hill House with lesbianism. Early in the movie, Dr. Markway, attempting to persuade the current owner of the house to let him conduct the experiment, informs her that he intends to take with him people "involved one way or another with the abnormal" (rather than, more properly, the "paranormal"). Moreover, he later asks Theo and Eleanor if they have heard the "unsavory stories" circulating about Hill House, which discouraged the other people from accepting his invitation to participate in the experiment, and he describes the house as "diseased," "sick," and "deranged," and repeatedly claims that it was "born evil." In a scene that reinforces the association between the house and aberrant female desire, Eleanor asks Dr. Markway to explain the haunting, and he replies, "Don't ask me to give a name to something which hasn't got a name," indirectly invoking lesbianism, the "love that dare not speak its name." This construction renders Eleanor's sexuality monstrous and "abnormal." Eleanor refuses to "come home," that is, to acknowledge her desire for Theo. Thus, her desire returns in the form of the haunting, terrifying her and the others. .

Despite its homophobic treatment of its heroine's sexuality, however, *The Haunting* cannot be assimilated to the Cold War construction of the lesbian. Dr. Markway emerges as a stand-in for the experts who explained lesbianism in terms of the mother's failure to provide her daughter with a "design for femininity." In his opening voice-over, Dr. Markway describes Hill House in terms that echo Freud's notorious claim in *The Question of Lay Analysis* that "the sexual life of adult women is a 'dark continent' for psychology."[6] Dr. Markway views Hill House as an "undiscovered country waiting to be explored," which suggests that his interest in it as an object of study conceals a desire to solve the "riddle" of perverse female sexuality by uncovering its "laws." Despite his research, however, he never obtains the key to Eleanor's psyche. Indeed, he consistently misreads her desire. For example, in the movie's final scene, in which Eleanor, while fleeing the others, crashes her car into a tree and dies, Dr. Markway interprets the accident as confirmation of his belief that Hill House is haunted, and he pompously declares, "There was something in the car with her, I'm sure of it. Call it what you like but Hill House is haunted.

It didn't want her to leave, and her poor bedeviled mind wasn't strong enough to fight it. Poor Eleanor!" But Theo rejects this interpretation and provides an alternative construction of Eleanor's desire, which does not deprive her of sexual agency: "Maybe not 'poor Eleanor.' It was what she wanted, to stay here. She had no place else to go. The house belongs to her now, too. Maybe she's happier." In this way, the movie indirectly challenged the discourse of female homosexuality that circulated in American society during the Cold War era. In associating Eleanor's sexuality with the supernatural, the movie suggests that it defies explanation. As a feminine woman who has made a lesbian object choice, her desire cannot be attributed to a pathological identification with masculinity. Rather, it requires an explanation that acknowledges her difference from the butch Theo.

The movie's deviation from the Cold War construction of the lesbian surfaces more fully in its refusal to contain Eleanor's desire. In the Cold War era movies tended to adopt one of two strategies for containing the threat the femme allegedly posed to the dominant social order. Some movies, like *All about Eve*, masculinized the femme's identity by drawing on an older model of sexuality to mark her as a lesbian. In suggesting that the femme's femininity rendered her lesbianism invisible by disguising her identification with masculinity, these movies assimilated the femme's desire to the Cold War discourse of female homosexuality, which attributed the development of lesbian identities to a pathological rejection of femininity. Other movies, like *Marnie*, contained the femme's desire by ultimately realigning it with the institutions of heterosexuality. Rather than attribute the heroine's perverse sexuality to a rejection of femininity that glossed over the differences between her and the butch, these movies instead rendered her lesbianism "artificial" by attributing it to a traumatic childhood experience. Also drawing on an older model of sexuality, these movies assumed that the feminine woman who made a lesbian object choice was less deviant than the masculine women who did and thus could reorient her desire. In adopting these strategies, Hollywood cinema refused to acknowledge the femme's difference from both the butch and the straight woman. *The Haunting* adopts a different strategy: it kills off its heroine. It thereby indirectly validated the new system of sexual classification, which privileged object choice over gender identity. Eleanor's femininity neither masks an identification with masculinity, nor indicates that she can be incorporated into the institutions of heterosexuality.

Unlike many of the heroines we have encountered in this book,

Eleanor's attempt to realign her sexuality with the law fails. She displaces her desire for Theo onto Dr. Markway, whose paternalistic interest in her she mistakes for love. But in so doing, she replaces an accessible object of desire with an inaccessible one. She does not realize that Dr. Markway has a wife (Lois Maxwell), until she shows up unexpectedly at Hill House to inform him that newspaper reporters are on his trail and to persuade him to abandon his experiment, of which she disapproves. Mrs. Markway's appearance precipitates a crisis in which Eleanor imagines that she wants to take her place in the house. Mrs. Markway disappears into the house after being terrified by a supernatural experience in the nursery, the "cold, rotten heart" of the house where she has insisted on spending the night, and she gets lost searching for her husband. Eleanor increasingly takes on Hill House's "sick" and "deranged" identity, indirectly confirming the perversity of her desire. In one of her voice-overs, which punctuate the movie, she remarks that she has begun to disappear into the house "inch by inch." When Dr. Markway insists that she leave the house while he and the others remain behind to search for his missing wife, she exclaims, "I'm the one who's supposed to stay. She's taken my place." But Hill House cannot incorporate the normative Mrs. Markway, and it ejects her. By contrast, Eleanor's death in the final scene insures that she retains her place in the house as a "kindred spirit." Eleanor crashes her car into the tree when Mrs. Markway—who in a fluttering white nightgown looks like a ghost—frightens her by darting across the road, and she swerves to avoid hitting her. Despite her normative gender identity, Eleanor cannot be incorporated into the dominant social order.

But even as it acknowledges Eleanor's difference from both Theo and Mrs. Markway, *The Haunting* provides a psychoanalytic explanation of her "abnormal" sexuality. Eleanor's history bears an uncanny resemblance to that of Abigail and her paid companion. After Hugh Crain dies abroad, Abigail continues to inhabit the nursery, which suggests that his death arrests her development by preventing her from resolving the Oedipus complex. She dies an old woman in the nursery when her companion has a tryst with one of the local "farmhands" on the veranda and fails to hear her when she knocks her cane against the wall. The tryst emerges as a violation of the companion's homosocial bond with her mistress. After Abigail's death, the companion lives on in the house in "complete solitude," and haunted by her role in her mistress's death she eventually commits suicide by hanging herself from the railing of the circular staircase in the library. Abigail's death has the same impact on the companion as her father's death had on her. It arrests the companion's development by turning her away from heterosexual romance. This representation of the companion's relationship with her mistress reinforces the association between lesbianism and the supernatural in the movie. The nursery emerges as a site of perverse female desire, Hill House's "cold, rotten heart," which explains Mrs. Markway's terror when she attempts to occupy it. The representation also provides an explanation for Eleanor's deviant sexuality by drawing a parallel between her and the companion. Eleanor feels guilty about her mother's death and increasingly identifies with the companion. Like Abigail, Eleanor's mother pounded on the wall of her room when she needed her. The night she died, Eleanor ignored her pounding and went back to sleep. Eleanor's identification with the companion suggests that her guilt about her mother's death has arrested her development; hence her desire for other women.

This treatment of Eleanor's sexuality suggests that the feminine woman who made a lesbian object choice posed an even greater threat to American society than the Cold War construction of the lesbian indicated. In the Cold War era, Hollywood movies tended to promote lesbian panic by underscoring the femme's ability to pass as a "normal" woman. Reinforcing the association between lesbianism and communism in Cold War culture, these movies attempted to show that the femme's resemblance to the straight woman enabled her to spread her "abnormal" sexuality throughout society while escaping detection. By contrast, in insisting on her difference from the butch and the straight woman, *The Haunting* attempted to show that the femme threatened to destabilize the binary construction of gender and sexuality. As her choice of the paternalistic Dr. Markway as a father substitute indicates, despite her identification with femininity, Eleanor cannot resume her Oedipal journey, which her relationship with her mother has interrupted. Nor does her death in the final scene contain her "monstrous" desire. Her closing voice-over confirms Theo's belief that Hill House now belongs to her, as well as to the other female ghosts who haunt it. Echoing Dr. Markway's opening voice-over, Eleanor informs the viewer, "We who walk here walk alone," as an image of Hill House appears on the screen. In this way, *The Haunting* showed that in trying to repress the femme's difference as a subject of desire, the Cold War construction of the lesbian had failed to counteract the threat she posed to American society. At once similar to and different from the butch and the straight woman, the femme continued to haunt the normative construction of American womanhood.

NOTES

INTRODUCTION: RECLAIMING THE "LOST SEX"

1. For a history of the Daughters of Bilitis, see Gallo, *Different Daughters*. See also Adam, *Rise of a Gay and Lesbian Movement*.

2. Stearn, *The Grapevine*, 15. Hereafter all citations refer to this edition and are included in parentheses in the text.

3. For a genealogy of this discourse, see Terry, *An American Obsession*, 268–328.

4. On this aspect of Cold War homophobia, see especially D'Emilio, *Sexual Politics, Sexual Communities*; Johnson, *The Lavender Scare*; Smith, "National Security and Personal Isolation"; Dean, *Imperial Brotherhood*, 63–96; and Terry, *An American Obsession*, 329–52.

5. Stearn, *The Grapevine*, cover.

6. The scholarship on anticommunist discourse is immense. Some important examples are Caute, *The Great Fear*; Schrecker, *Many Are the Crimes*; and Dean, *Imperial Brotherhood*.

7. Quoted in Terry, *An American Obsession*, 330.

8. See in particular Johnson, *The Lavender Scare*, 162–63. See also Corber, "Cold War Femme."

9. I include my earlier work on Cold War homophobia. See in particular Corber, *In the Name of National Security*. In making this critique, I do not want to minimize the significance of previous scholarship on Cold War homophobia. Rather, I want to emphasize the need to locate the Cold War construction of the lesbian in twentieth-century U.S. women's history, as I attempt to do in this introduction. For an important exception to the imbalance in the scholarship, see Terry, *An American Obsession*. Terry does an excellent job of tracking the shifting construction of the lesbian in twentieth-century American culture. Where my analysis differs from hers is in showing how that shifting construction worked to produce a sexually ambiguous female femininity that underlay much of the sexual paranoia in Cold War cultural production.

10. For an important discussion of the sexological understanding of the feminine woman who made a lesbian object choice, see Chauncey, "From Sexual Inversion to Homosexuality."

11. It is important to point out that throughout the postwar period women

continued to attend movies more often than men. On Hollywood's cultivation of female audiences in the postwar period, see Klinger, *Melodrama and Meaning*, 36–68; and Byars, *All that Hollywood Allows*, 1–22.

12. For an especially astute discussion of the representation of lesbianism in classical Hollywood cinema, see Patricia White's *Uninvited*. White shows how the Production Code's regulation of the sexual content of Hollywood movies worked to produce rather than repress lesbian desires and identities. My project differs from White's in that it focuses on Hollywood cinema's deployment of two conflicting models of lesbianism in the Cold War era and how that deployment rendered female femininity sexually illegible.

13. Most of the work on gender and sexual mobility in classical Hollywood cinema has focused on the queering of masculinity. For an important example of this work, see Cohan, *Masked Men*. By contrast, I attend to classical Hollywood cinema's queering of femininity, its transformation of femininity into a powerfully ambiguous signifier of sexual identity.

14. Motion Picture Producers and Distributors of America, "The Motion Picture Production Code of 1930," 333.

15. For an astute and nuanced discussion of the coding of lesbians in classical Hollywood cinema, see White, *Uninvited*. See also Russo, *The Celluloid Closet*; Weiss, *Vampires and Violets*; and Barrios, *Screened Out*.

16. Adlai Stevenson, "A Purpose for Modern Woman," 30–31. Hereafter all citations refer to this edition and are included in parentheses in the text.

17. I discuss the Cold War crisis of masculinity in *Homosexuality in Cold War America*.

18. For an important discussion of companionate marriage, see Simmons, *Making Marriage Modern*, 105–37. See also Smith-Rosenberg, *Disorderly Conduct*, 245–96; and Bailey, *From Front Porch to Back Seat*, 25–56.

19. Lundberg and Farnham, *Modern Woman*, 237. Hereafter all citations refer to this edition and are cited in parentheses in the text.

20. Important discussions of momism include Rogin, *Ronald Reagan, the Movie*, 236–71; May, *Homeward Bound*, 100–118; and Feldstein, *Motherhood in Black and White*, 62–85.

21. Feldstein, *Motherhood in Black and White*, 41–42.

22. Wylie, *Generation of Vipers*, 212, 213. Hereafter all citations refer to this edition and are included in parentheses in the text.

23. Strecker and Lathbury, *Their Mothers' Daughters*, 10. Hereafter all citations refer to this edition and are included in parentheses in the text.

24. On the dominance of psychoanalytic discourse in the Cold War era, see Terry, *An American Obsession*, 297–328.

25. On the homophobic backlash against the New Woman, see Duggan, *Sapphic Slashers*, 245–96.

26. For a detailed discussion of the New Woman, see Franzen, *Spinsters and Lesbians*. See also Smith-Rosenberg, *Disorderly Conduct*, 245–96.

27. Dell, *Love in the Machine Age*, 132.

28. For a detailed discussion of Havelock Ellis's theory of sexual inversion, see Smith-Rosenberg, *Disorderly Conduct*, 275–81. See also Weeks, *Sex, Politics, and Society*, 141–59.

29. Quoted in Smith-Rosenberg, *Disorderly Conduct*, 276.

30. Quoted in Smith-Rosenberg, *Disorderly Conduct*, 279.

31. Smith-Rosenberg, *Disorderly Conduct*, 53–76.

32. For a discussion of the flapper's emergence as a model of modern womanhood, see Simmons, *Making Marriage Modern*, 139–59. See also Smith-Rosenberg, *Disorderly Conduct*, 245–96; Bailey, *From Front Porch to Back Seat*, 25–56; and Franzen, *Spinsters and Lesbians*, 107–32.

33. On mass cultural "fantasy bribes," see Jameson, "Reification and Utopia in Mass Culture."

34. For a discussion of "flapper marriage" as a variant of the companionate model, see Simmons, *Making Marriage Modern*, 139–59.

35. On the transformation of the domestic sphere, see Simmons, *Making Marriage Modern*, 105–39. See also Bailey, *From Front Porch to Back Seat*, 13–56; Franzen, *Spinsters and Lesbians*, 107–32; and Smith-Rosenberg, *Disorderly Conduct*, 281–96.

36. On the transformation of the New Woman into an "old maid" and potential lesbian, see Franzen, *Spinsters and Lesbians*, 107–32, and Smith-Rosenberg, *Disorderly Conduct*, 245–96.

37. For a discussion of Davis's remarkable survey, see Terry, *An American Obsession*, 126–32, 134–38.

38. Katharine Bement Davis, *Factors in the Sex Life of Twenty-Two Hundred Women*, 246. Hereafter all citations refer to this edition and are cited in the text.

39. See Franzen, *Spinsters and Lesbians*, 133–58. See also Kennedy and Davis, *Boots of Leather, Slippers of Gold*, 323–71.

40. See Breines, *Young, White, and Miserable*, 1–24.

41. On these social changes, see ibid.; May, *Homeward Bound*, 100–142; and Meyerowitz, *Not June Cleaver*.

42. On this aspect of white, middle-class femininity in postwar American society, see Breines, *Young, White, and Miserable*, 1–24.

43. For a discussion of the Daughters of Bilitis as an example of the difficulty postwar lesbians had establishing and sustaining alternative institutions, see Gallo, *Different Daughters*.

44. See Franzen, *Spinsters and Lesbians*, 133–58.

45. For a discussion of these hearings, see Johnson, *The Lavender Scare*, 101–18, and Terry, *An American Obsession*, 329–52.

46. Eisenhower's order signaled a troubling shift in focus from disloyalty to security, from acts to identities, which opened the door to purging employees on moral grounds. For a discussion of this shift, see Johnson, *The Lavender Scare*, 119–46; Terry, *An American Obsession*, 329–52; and Dean, *Imperial Brotherhood*, 97–168.

47. See Johnson, *The Lavender Scare*, 119–78.

48. Ibid., 147–78.

49. Ibid., 41–64.

50. See Dean, *Imperial Brotherhood*, 63–96, and Johnson, *The Lavender Scare*, 65–100.

51. Lait and Mortimer, *Washington Confidential*, 77.

52. See Johnson, *The Lavender Scare*, 147–78.

53. Ibid., pp. 119–46.

54. Ibid.

55. I have taken this language from Halperin, *How to Do the History of Homosexuality*, 104–37. Halperin does not show much interest in the history of lesbianism, but his analysis of the complex historical process that has produced the incoherence of the category of the (male) homosexual seems applicable to the category of the lesbian as well, and it has deeply influenced my understanding of the conflicting models of lesbian identity that circulated in Cold War culture.

56. Johnson, *The Lavender Scare*, 147–49.

57. Quoted in Noriega, "'Something's Missing Here!,'" 30.

CHAPTER ONE: REPRESENTING THE FEMME

1. Russo, *The Celluloid Closet*, 94.

2. Motion Picture Producers and Distributors of America, "The Motion Picture Production Code of 1930," 333.

3. Exemplary discussions of Code-era celluloid lesbians include Russo, *The Celluloid Closet*; Weiss, *Vampires and Violets*; and Barrios, *Screened Out*. For a particularly astute analysis of the censorship of "sex perversion" in classical Hollywood cinema, see White, *Uninvited*. Unlike Russo, Weiss, and Barrios, White argues that the Production Code was *productive*, not repressive, in the sense that it produced specific representations of gay and lesbian identities and sexualities. In her Foucauldian analysis, the Code set the perimeters within which movies could represent homosexuality and lesbianism.

4. As to her alleged lesbianism, Bankhead told fellow actress Louise Brooks: "I only became a Lez because I needed the publicity—I had to get a job. . . . In the 20s and 30s, a Lesbian was tops in desirability, especially with a girlfriend as a side dish" (quoted in Weiss, *Vampires and Violets*, 24).

5. Rogin, *Ronald Reagan, the Movie*, 236–71.

6. On this aspect of the Cold War, see especially Johnson, *The Lavender Scare*, and Terry, *An American Obsession*, 329–52. See also Corber, *In the Name of National Security*.

7. On this aspect of the Cold War, see especially Johnson, *The Lavender Scare*, and Terry, *An American Obsession*, 329–52. See also Corber, *In the Name of National Security*.

8. D'Emilio, *Sexual Politics, Sexual Communities*, 40–53.

9. For a discussion of Blick's testimony and its role in provoking the gay and lesbian panic of the Cold War era, see Johnson, *The Lavender Scare*, 79–89.

10. Lesbians were much less likely to have been arrested on morals charges than were gay men, who often cruised for sex in public and risked arrest by undercover police officers who entrapped them in parks and public restrooms. See Johnson, *The Lavender Scare*, 79–89.

11. U.S. Senate, Committee on Expenditures in the Executive Departments, *Employment of Homosexuals and Other Sex Perverts in Government*, 81st Cong., 2d sess., 1950, S. Rep. 241, 2.

12. Ibid.

13. Ibid., 4.

14. I elaborate the role of the Kinsey reports in speading this fear more fully in *Homosexuality in Cold War America*, 1–19.

15. Kinsey, Pomeroy, and Martin, *Sexual Behavior in the Human Male*, 37.

16. Ibid., 130.

17. Ibid., 129.

18. Kinsey, Pomeroy, Martin, and Gebhard, *Sexual Behavior in the Human Female*, 35.

19. Many of these experts denounced Kinsey for contributing to the spread of world communism by normalizing homosexuality, and congressional leaders pressured the National Research Council to cut off his funding, which it did in 1954. For more on Kinsey's blacklisting, see Terry, *An American Obsession*, 348–49.

20. For example, Edmund Bergler, a prominent psychologist, contradicted Kinsey by insisting that despite how common homosexuality was, it was nevertheless a mental illness. But he did not challenge Kinsey's findings about lesbian activity among women, which he associated with women's "pathological" rejection of their prescribed roles, a growing trend in American society since the 1920s. See Bergler, *Homosexuality*.

21. Interestingly, queer studies has perpetuated the disparity in attention paid to these two forms of lesbian identity. Until recently, queer work on gender focused almost exclusively on female masculinity, the exemplary study being Judith Halberstam's *Female Masculinity*. Although male femininity and femme femininity have not received the same critical reflection and theoretical elaboration, there have been important exceptions. See Rose and Camilleri, *Brazen Femme*;

Hemmings, "Out of Sight, Out of Mind?" and "'All My Life I've Been Waiting for Something . . .'"; Hart, "Living Under the Sign of the Cross"; Nestle, "The Fem Question"; and Martin, "Sexuality without Genders and Other Queer Utopias."

22. One reason that it is important not to collapse these histories is that the female sexual invert is also the antecedent of the female-to-male transsexual. See Halberstam, *Female Masculinity*, 75–110.

23. For an important discussion that situates female sexual inversion in relation to Victorian ideologies of femininity, see Chauncey, "From Sexual Inversion to Homosexuality." See also Newton, "The Mythic Mannish Lesbian."

24. For an astute analysis of the threat that female masculinity poses to patriarchal social arrangements, see Halberstam, *Female Masculinity*, 1–43.

25. On the sexological understanding of the feminine woman who made a lesbian object choice, see Chauncey, "From Sexual Inversion to Homosexuality"; Halberstam, *Female Masculinity*, 75–110; Vicinus, "'They Wonder to which Sex I Belong'"; and Smith-Rosenberg, *Disorderly Conduct*, 274–85.

26. Ellis, *Sexual Inversion*, 133. This edition of *Sexual Inversion*, the first volume of Ellis's series *Studies in the Psychology of Sex*, is based on the printing from 1906.

27. For important discussions of the emergence of sexual object choice as the organizing principle of sexuality, see Chauncey, "From Sexual Inversion to Homosexuality" and, more fully, *Gay New York*, 99–127.

28. Kennedy and Davis, *Boots of Leather, Slippers of Gold*, 323–71.

29. For a good discussion of the Code-era visual conventions that Hollywood developed to represent lesbians, see Barrios, *Screened Out*, 145–66.

30. For a discussion of Ritter's sexually ambiguous star image, see White, *Uninvited*, 176–77.

31. Ibid., 176.

32. For important analyses of the homoerotics of female spectatorial pleasure, see Stacey, "Desperately Seeking Difference" and "Feminine Fascinations"; Fuss, "Fashion and the Homospectatorial Look." Stacey's analysis of *All about Eve* in "Desperately Seeking Difference" is problematic because she understands Eve's lesbianism as a stage through which she passes on her way to developing a normative heterosexual identity (54–57). This analysis ignores the film's final scene, which makes it clear that Eve's development is anything but normatively heterosexual.

33. On this aspect of *All about Eve*'s reception, see Staggs, *All about "All about Eve"*, 219–21.

34. I discuss Lydecker as a killer fairy in *Homosexuality in Cold War America*, 55–78. On the Code-era visual codes developed by Hollywood to represent gay men, see Russo, *Celluloid Closet*, 3–60; Barrios, *Screened Out*, 167–82; and Dyer, *The Matter of Images*, 52–72.

35. Halperin, *How to Do the History of Homosexuality*, 109. Although Halperin limits his analysis to male homosexuality, his claim about the complex histori-

cal process underlying the production of "the homosexual" seems applicable to *All about Eve*, since it contains two irreconcilable ways of understanding the relationship between gender identity and object choice. The category of "the homosexual" is incoherent in part because it includes women as well as men who make a homosexual object choice, though, oddly, Halperin fails to consider this.

36. Ibid. Eve Kosofsky Sedgwick makes this distinction in *Epistemology of the Closet*, 86.

37. Halperin, *How to Do the History of Homosexuality*, 109.

38. Staggs, *All about "All about Eve"*, 217–31.

39. Ibid., 218.

40. Ibid., 241.

CHAPTER TWO: LESBIAN UNINTELLIGIBILITY

1. On Wyler's and Hellman's discussion about remaking *The Children's Hour*, see Herman, *A Talent for Trouble*, 411–17. See also Martinson, *Lillian Hellman*, 282–83.

2. On the censorship of Hellman's play, see White, *Uninvited*, 21–28. See also Noriega, "'Something's Missing Here!'" Noriega points out that several reviewers noted that *These Three* was an adaptation of Hellman's controversial play, thus enabling audiences to interpret the film against the grain of censorship, and that the movie opened while *The Children's Hour* was still on Broadway.

3. Hellman, *Six Plays by Lillian Hellman*, 71. Hereafter all references to the original version of Hellman's play are to this edition and are cited in parentheses in the text.

4. On the critical success of *These Three*, see Herman, *A Talent for Trouble*, 142–48. See also White, *Uninvited*, 23–34, and Noriega, "'Something's Missing Here!'" 24–25. Many reviewers thought that the movie was significantly better than the play.

5. Quoted in Noriega, "'Something's Missing Here!,'" 30.

6. Quoted in Hellman, *Scoundrel Time*, 93. Hellman's memoir discusses in detail her blacklisting by the studios following her HUAC testimony. See also Martinson, *Lillian Hellman*, 239–86.

7. See Herman, *A Talent for Trouble*, 413–17, and Martinson, *Lillian Hellman*, 282–83. For a discussion of Hays's work on the script, see Rapf, "'A Larger Thing.'"

8. Bosley Crowther, "The Screen: New 'Children's Hour,'" *New York Times*, 15 March 1962, 28.

9. Quoted in Herman, *A Talent for Trouble*, 417.

10. Hellman reinforced the play's political topicality by casting Kim Hunter in the role of Karen. Hunter had been blacklisted for supporting left-wing political causes. See Martinson, *Lillian Hellman*, 268–70.

11. Thomas Dash, "*The Children's Hour*," *Women's Wear Daily*, 19 December 1952, 32.

12. Many reviewers complained that the film's representation of lesbian panic was historically implausible. For example, Bosley Crowther stated, "It is incredible that educated people living in an urban American community today would react as violently and cruelly to a questionable innuendo as they are made to do in this film" ("The Screen: New 'Children's Hour,'" *New York Times*, 15 March 1962, 28). But in so doing they glossed over the Cold War antilesbian witch hunts.

13. Erhart, "'She Could Hardly Invent Them!'" Erhart does not situate this treatment of lesbian identity in relation to Cold War homophobia.

14. Smith-Rosenberg, *Disorderly Conduct*, 53–76.

15. For a historical account of this trial, see Faderman, *Scotch Verdict*. See also Moore, "'Something More Tender Still than Friendship.'"

16. See, for example, Tuhkanen, "Breeding (and) Reading."

17. Roughead, *Bad Companions*, 117. Hereafter all references are to this edition and are cited in parentheses in the text.

18. Quoted in Bryer, *Conversations with Lillian Hellman*, 25.

19. Mary Titus also argues, in "Murdering the Lesbian," that as a professional woman writer Hellman was deeply invested in the play's themes. But Titus is interested in how Hellman's choice of material may have reflected her own lesbian desire, whereas I simply want to suggest that as a professional woman the playwright was implicated in the backlash against the New Woman, one of the play's subtexts.

20. On the practice of chumming, see in particular Vicinus, "Distance and Desire"; Sahli, "Smashing"; and Rupp, "'Imagine My Surprise.'" See also Duggan, "The Trials of Alice Mitchell"; and Coyle and Van Dyke, "Sex, Smashing, and Storyville in Turn-of-the-Century New Orleans."

21. Ellis, *Sexual Inversion*, 44.

22. Quoted in Titus, "Murdering the Lesbian," 221.

23. For more on this backlash, see D'Emilio and Freedman, *Intimate Matters*, 202–21; Smith-Rosenberg, *Disorderly Conduct*, 245–96; Duggan, "The Trials of Alice Mitchell"; Inness, *The Lesbian Menace*, 33–51; and Chauncey, "From Sexual Inversion to Homosexuality."

24. For more on this aspect of the homophobic construction of female homosocial bonds, see Duggan, "The Trials of Alice Mitchell," 82–84.

25. For a detailed discussion of the cultural work that the companionate model of marriage performed, see Simmons, *Making Marriage Modern*, 105–39.

26. On the transformation of the New Woman into "old maid," see Simmons, *Making Marriage Modern*, 138–77; Smith-Rosenberg, *Disorderly Conduct*, 245–96; and Franzen, *Spinsters and Lesbians*, 79–106.

27. Quoted in Smith-Rosenberg, *Disorderly Conduct*, 283.

28. For a discussion of the impact of Gautier's novel on popular understandings of lesbianism, see Faderman, *Surpassing the Love of Men*, 264–68.

29. Hellman was eager to adapt the play for the screen and persuaded the producer Samuel Goldwyn to buy the screen rights, despite the objections of the Production Code Administration, by insisting, "It's not about lesbians. It's about the power of a lie. I happened to pick what I thought was a very strong lie," which suggests that she had few qualms about heterosexualizing its plot. Quoted in Herman, *A Talent for Trouble*, 141.

30. For an important discussion of *These Three* as a woman's film, see White, *Uninvited*, 26–28. White argues convincingly that the censorship of the movie did not wholly succeed in repressing the play's lesbian theme, which returned in the film's refusal to explicitly name the accusation against Martha and Joe. In this context, it would be interesting to speculate about the impact that Miriam Hopkins's screen image may have had on the movie's reception with audiences. Given rumors that Hopkins was a lesbian which circulated in Hollywood and on Broadway, Martha's lesbianism, repressed in the movie, returned in the casting of Hopkins, who in her public reputation had a problematic relation to the institutions of heterosexuality. For a discussion of the rumors about Hopkins, see Quirk, *Fasten Your Seat Belts*, 194–99, and Mayne, *Cinema and Spectatorship*, 133–36. But I am more interested here in how the movie reinscribed the very homophobic construction of sentimental women's culture it sought to disavow.

31. "Review of *These Three*," *Variety*, 25 March 1936, 15.

32. Most of McCrae's films prior to *These Three* were romantic comedies, which he made while under contract to MGM. It was only later in his career, in the 1940s and 1950s, that he became more closely associated with another genre, the western.

33. In the play, it is Karen who speaks these lines; in reassigning them to Martha, Hellman magnifies Mary's violation of the female world of romantic friendships.

34. For a detailed discussion of Hellman's revisions of the play, see Spencer, "Sex, Lies, and Revisions."

35. Hellman, *The Children's Hour*, 21. Hereafter all references to the 1952 version of the play are to this edition and are included in parentheses in the text.

36. Walter Kerr, "*The Children's Hour*," *New York Herald Tribune*, 9 December 1952, 18.

37. George Freedley, "Off Stage—and on," *Daily Telegraph*, 26 December 1952, 3.

38. It is worth noting that Wyler's casting reinforced these gender differences. MacLaine lacked Hepburn's glamorous screen image, and Wyler's choice of MacLaine to play Martha indicates the way in which the older model of sexuality continued to shape the representation of the lesbian in Hollywood cinema. Apparently Martha's lesbianism barred her from embodying the glamorous femininity promoted by Hollywood; only the heterosexually marked Karen could.

39. In her analysis of the movie, Erhart overlooks this scene, which complicates

her argument about Mary's role in the discursive production of Martha's lesbian-ism. The addition of this scene intensified the movie's political topicality by shift-ing the focus away from Mary's malevolence, which all of the earlier versions of the play highlighted, to the role of gossip, innuendo, and rumor.

40. Russo, *The Celluloid Closet*, 139; Erhart, "'She Could Hardly Invent Them!,'" 92–95; Noriega, "'Something's Missing Here!,'" 31–32; and White, *Uninvited*, 24.

41. Erhart also comments on the possibilities of lesbian identity and iden-tification opened up by the scene ("'She Could Hardly Invent Them!,'" 100). But she overlooks the way in which the scene simultaneously affirms Cold War sexual epistemology by encouraging the viewer to speculate about Karen's sexual identity.

CHAPTER THREE: RECUPERATING FEMME FEMININITY

1. Universal Studios' coinage of the term "sex mystery" for *Marnie* may have reflected the difficulty of assigning it to any one genre. The movie is part woman's film, part film noir, part murder mystery, and part romance.

2. I have taken these quotations from Universal Studios' recently released DVD of *Marnie*, which reproduces the posters, as well as several publicity stills for the film, as part of "The *Marnie* Archives."

3. Hitchcock discussed the significance of the casting with the French direc-tor François Truffaut during their extensive interviews in the 1960s. See Truffaut, *Hitchcock*, 325–28.

4. Stearn, *The Grapevine*.

5. Ibid., 10.

6. Knapp, "The Queer Voice in *Marnie*."

7. For a discussion of Mrs. Danvers's coding as a lesbian, see Russo, *The Cellu-loid Closet*, 46–48. See also White, *Uninvited*, 64–72.

8. The scholarship on the female gothic is vast. Some influential examples are Doane, *The Desire to Desire*; Modleski, *The Woman Who Knew Too Much*, 43–72; and Walsh, *Women's Films and Female Experience, 1940–50*. See also White, *Uninvited*, 61–93, for an important critique of the psychoanalytic approach of this scholarship and its repression of lesbianism.

9. Hitchcock directed a more typical example of the female gothic, *Suspicion*, also starring Fontaine, one year after *Rebecca*, in 1941. In it, Fontaine played Lina, the "ugly duckling" daughter of a famous military officer who after a whirlwind romance marries a notorious gambler and ladies' man, Johnny (Cary Grant). Shortly after they have set up house, she discovers that Johnny has been fired for embezzling money from his employer, a relative, and she begins to suspect him of plotting to poison her so he can collect on her life insurance.

10. *Rebecca* has been central to the feminist analysis of the construction of

female subjectivity in classical Hollywood cinema. See, for example, Doane, *The Desire to Desire*, 174–77; Modleski, *The Woman Who Knew Too Much*, 43–56; and de Lauretis, *Alice Doesn't*, 151–55. See also White, *Uninvited*, 64–68. None of this work, which approaches *Rebecca* from a psychoanalytic perspective, has shown any interest in locating the movie in its historical context. But as I have pointed out elsewhere, approaching Hitchcock's movies from a psychoanalytic perspective is circular, given their tendency to mobilize a psychoanalytic discourse to "explain" the sexuality of their heroes and heroines. See Corber, *In the Name of National Security*, 58–60. In linking *Rebecca* to the backlash against the female world of romantic friendships, I hope to elucidate the "gothic" form of female homosocial bonding Fontaine encounters at Manderley. The psychoanalytic approach to the movie does not fully explain why contemporary female audiences found its representation of female experience so compelling.

11. In an important critique of the feminist approach to *Rebecca*, White argues that it has repressed the lesbian connotations of Fontaine's paranoid relationship with Mrs. Danvers. According to White, Fontaine represses her lesbian desire by displacing it onto Mrs. Danvers, who she then experiences as persecuting her. See White, *Uninvited*, 72–75. See also Berenstein, "Adaptation, Censorship, and Audiences of Questionable Type" and "'I'm Not the Sort of Person Men Marry.'"

12. Quoted in Berenstein, "Adaptation, Censorship, and Audiences of Questionable Type," 18.

13. Berenstein, "'I'm Not the Sort of Person Men Marry,'" 87.

14. It is important to point out that in coding her as a lesbian, the movie draws on Daphne du Maurier's much more explicit representation of Rebecca as a lesbian. The novel constantly masculinizes Rebecca. For example, Maxim tells the heroine that when he confronted Rebecca in the boathouse the night he killed her, "she looked like a boy in her sailing kit, a boy with a face like a Botticelli angel" (du Maurier, *Rebecca*, 282). This is only one instance among many in the novel where Maxim's descriptions of his former wife suggest that his attraction to her had a homoerotic component, which the screen adaptation does not explore.

15. See Berenstein, "'I'm Not the Sort of Person Men Marry,'" 86.

16. Modleski, *The Woman Who Knew Too Much*, 57–72.

17. Both White and Berenstein rightly challenge Modleski's reading of the movie, which attributes lesbian desire to an unresolved Oedipus complex and in so doing reproduces a homophobic construction of lesbian identity. As both White and Berenstein point out, the movie represents neither Rebecca nor Mrs. Danvers as maternal figures for Fontaine. Rebecca in particular emerges as a sexually powerful woman whose refusal to accede to a heteronormative construction of womanhood transforms her into an object of desire for both Mrs. Danvers and Fontaine. See Berenstein, "'I'm Not the Sort of Person Men Marry,'" 89–91, and White, *Uninvited*, 66–67.

18. Modleski mistakenly reads this declaration not as Fontaine's panicked asser-

tion of her sexual difference from Mrs. Danvers but as a sign of her successful completion of her Oedipal task. See Modleski, *The Woman Who Knew Too Much*, 51.

19. See in particular Modleski, *The Woman Who Knew Too Much*, 48–50, and Berenstein, "I'm Not the Sort of Person Men Marry," 92.

20. Berenstein also discusses the importance of Fontaine's voice-over in disrupting the movie's heterosexual resolution. See Berenstein, "'I'm Not the Sort of Person Men Marry,'" 95.

21. Hitchcock made *Marnie* after a series of movies many critics consider masterpieces of Hollywood filmmaking: *Vertigo* (1958), *North by Northwest* (1959), *Psycho* (1960), and *The Birds* (1963). By contrast, *Marnie* is generally considered one of Hitchcock's least successful movies. Unlike his earlier "masterpieces," it was both a critical and a box-office failure. Critics usually attribute this reception to Hitchcock's style of filmmaking, in particular his use of cinematic techniques (painted backdrops, rear-screen projections, and so on), which by 1964 had become outmoded. For more on this view of the film, see Mogg, "Defending Marnie—and Hitchcock." But I think the film's outmoded representation of lesbianism provides a more compelling explanation of its disappointing reception. With the consolidation of a system of sexual classification that privileged object choice over gender identity, Marnie's "cure" in the final scene must have seemed implausible to many viewers.

22. See Kaplan, *Motherhood and Representation*. For Kaplan's discussion of Marnie's relationship with Bernice, see *Motherhood and Representation*, 119–22.

23. For a discussion of this aspect of the Cold War construction of the lesbian, see Terry, *An American Obsession*, 315–28.

24. For a particularly pernicious example of this homophobic discourse, see "Lesbianism: The Biological and Psychological Treason," in Strecker and Lathbury, *Their Mothers' Daughters*, 158–67.

25. For a different reading of Marnie's coding as a lesbian, see Knapp, "The Queer Voice in *Marnie*."

26. White, *Uninvited*, 94–119. See also Berenstein, "Adaptation, Censorship, and Audiences of Questionable Type," 21–32.

27. For many critics, the suffusion of the screen by the color red to signal Marnie's traumatic flashbacks provides another example of the movie's lack of formal sophistication, which they speculate alienated viewers and explains its critical and box-office failure. For an interesting counter-interpretation of this visual technique, see McElhaney, "Touching the Surface."

28. For an interesting discussion of the safe's function as a kind of lesbian fetish, see Knapp, "The Queer Voice in *Marnie*," 12–14.

29. The consolidation of the new system of sexual classification explains why Marnie's lesbianism remains coded, despite the fact that the film was made after the revision of the Production Code in 1960. The more explicit treatment of Marnie's lesbianism, which the new Code would have permitted, would have ren-

dered her incorporation into the institutions of heterosexuality even more implausible. In the postwar era, object choice increasingly trumped gender identity in determining a person's sexual classification. Thus Marnie's desire for other women needs to remain latent; otherwise, she cannot be "cured" of her lesbianism by reliving the repressed traumatic experience that has supposedly caused it.

30. It is important to point out that Marnie's rejection of marriage and motherhood reinforced her coding as a lesbian. In the 1950s lesbianism was often seen as sign or "symptom" of women's "maladjustment" to a dehistoricized and undertheorized "society." The homophobic deployment of the category of lesbian pathologized women's resistance to the domestication of their roles and identities. In representing Marnie as "sick," the movie participated in this discourse. For a discussion of this aspect of the Cold War construction of the lesbian, see Terry, *An American Obsession*, 297–314.

31. In her essay "*Marnie*," Corinn Columpar also discusses Bernice's prostitution as a form of resistance to the heterosexual economy of exchange.

32. Bernice's prostitution may have coded her as a lesbian. In *The Grapevine*, Stearn claims that many prostitutes were lesbian and that they expressed their hatred of men by making them pay for sexual relations that were not reciprocal (54–57). Certainly many viewers may have seen Bernice's "man-hating" as a sign that she was latently lesbian, in accordance with the implication, in Strecker's and Lathbury's *Their Mothers' Daughters*, that many mothers who brought up their daughters to hate men were latently lesbian. See also Terry, *An American Obsession*, 317–19.

CHAPTER FOUR: JOAN CRAWFORD'S PADDED SHOULDERS

1. I have drawn this account from the following sources: Hoopes, *Cain*, 350–53; Thomas, *Joan Crawford*, 135–39; Alexander Walker, *Joan Crawford*, 145–47; Quirk and Schoell, *Joan Crawford*, 125–32; James C. Robertson, *The Casablanca Man*, 86–91.

2. On Crawford's star image, see in particular Allen and Gomery, *Film History*, 175–86, and Pamela Robertson, *Guilty Pleasures*, 87–100. See also Herzog and Gaines, "'Puffed Sleeves before Tea-Time.'"

3. Quoted in Thomas, *Joan Crawford*, 136.

4. On this aspect of Crawford's persona, see in particular Herzog and Gaines, "'Puffed Sleeves before Tea-Time.'" See also Allen and Gomery, *Film History*, 175–86, and Pamela Robertson, *Guilty Pleasures*, 87–100.

5. Herzog and Gaines, "'Puffed Sleeves before Tea-Time.'"

6. Quoted in Alexander Walker, *Joan Crawford*, 147.

7. Quoted in Thomas, *Joan Crawford*, 137.

8. Quoted in Allen and Gomery, *Film History*, 181.

9. Herzog and Gaines, "Puffed Sleeves before Tea-Time."

10. Allen and Gomery, *Film History*, 183.

11. For more on the Letty Lynton dress and its influence on women's fashion, see Herzog and Gaines, "'Puffed Sleeves before Tea-Time.'"

12. On Crawford's appeal to working-class women, see Allen and Gomery, *Film History*, 175–86; Pamela Robertson, *Guilty Pleasures*, 87–100; and Herzog and Gaines, "'Puffed Sleeves before Tea-Time.'"

13. Pamela Robertson, *Guilty Pleasures*, 105–6.

14. Ibid., 99–100.

15. On this aspect of camp, see ibid., 95–97, and Ross, *No Respect*, 135–70. See also Babuscio, "Camp and the Gay Sensibility."

16. See, for example, Kreidl, *Nicholas Ray*, 43.

17. See Wilmington, "Nicholas Ray's *Johnny Guitar*," and Kreidl, *Nicholas Ray*, 43–59.

18. Quoted in Wilmington, "Nicholas Ray's *Johnny Guitar*," 23.

19. Ray's recollections about the movie should be taken with a grain of salt. In addition to misrepresenting Crawford's politics, he also claimed that the movie was shot in Barcelona, not the Arizona desert, and that it divided the Spanish city down the middle politically. Kreidl does not question these recollections but repeats them as facts. See Kreidl, *Nicholas Ray*, 48–50.

20. See Charney, "Historical Excess," and Wilmington, "Nicholas Ray's *Johnny Guitar*." See also Peterson, "The Competing Tunes of *Johnny Guitar*," 5–6.

21. See especially, Charney, "Historical Excess," and Wilmington, "Nicholas Ray's *Johnny Guitar*." See also Peterson, "The Competing Tunes of *Johnny Guitar*."

22. Several scholars have pointed out this difference. See Charney, "Historical Excess"; Peterson, "The Competing Tunes of *Johnny Guitar*"; and Pamela Robertson, *Guilty Pleasures*, 109–14.

23. See, for example, Nelson, "*Mildred Pierce* Reconsidered"; Cook, "Duplicity in *Mildred Pierce*"; Janet Walker, "Feminist Critical Practice"; Williams, "Feminist Film Theory"; and Walsh, *Women's Films and Female Experience, 1940–1950*, 129–32.

24. For a particularly interesting take on this split structure, see Pamela Robertson, "Structural Irony in *Mildred Pierce*." Roberston is one of the few critics who have noted Mildred's masculinization, which she discusses at length. See also White, *Uninvited*, 101, 109.

25. Cook, "Duplicity in *Mildred Pierce*."

26. James C. Robertson, *The Casablanca Man*, 91.

27. Walsh, *Women's Films and Female Experience, 1940–50*, 131.

28. Hoopes, *Cain*, 339.

29. It is worth noting that in the novel neither Mildred's success nor her desire for her daughter masculinizes her. I discuss the differences between the novel and the movie in "Joan Crawford's Padded Shoulders," 9–14.

30. See Hoopes, *Cain*, 348–49.

31. *Mildred Pierce* was the only one of Cain's novels that did not center on a murder, and the only one that had an omniscient narrator. For more on the differences between *Mildred Pierce* and Cain's crime fiction, see Corber, "Joan Crawford's Padded Shoulders," 9–14.

32. White, *Uninvited*, 109.

33. On the studio's publicity campaign for the movie, see Alexander Walker, *Joan Crawford*, 148.

34. The most fully elaborated version of this argument is Haralovich, "Too Much Guilt Is Never Enough for Working Mothers." See also Cook, "Duplicity in *Mildred Pierce*"; Williams, "Feminist Film Theory"; and Pamela Robertson, "Structural Irony in *Mildred Pierce*."

35. For more on this aspect of postwar American culture, see especially May, *Homeward Bound*. See also Meyerowitz, *Not June Cleaver*.

36. Cain, *Mildred Pierce*, 16. Hereafter all references are to this edition and will be cited in parentheses in the text.

37. See Cook, "Duplicity in *Mildred Pierce*"; Janet Walker, "Feminist Critical Practice"; and Pamela Robertson, "Structural Irony in *Mildred Pierce*."

38. For a detailed discussion of the function of supporting characters in classical Hollywood cinema, see in particular White, *Uninvited*, 136–93. See also Roof, *All about Thelma and Eve*, 1–22.

39. Eve Kosofsky Sedgwick, *Between Men*, 21–27.

40. For more on Crawford's fallen-woman pictures, see Pamela Robertson, *Guilty Pleasures*, 90–100. On the fallen-woman picture more generally, see Jacobs, *The Wages of Sin*.

41. Pamela Robertson, *Guilty Pleasures*, 89.

42. Pamela Robertson argues persuasively that contemporary lesbian viewers may have understood Vienna's alternation between masculine and feminine gender presentations as an alternation between butch and femme roles. Robertson, *Guilty Pleasures*, 111–14. I am more interested here in how Vienna's performances of masculinity and femininity rendered her gender performance sexually illegible.

43. Pamela Robertson, *Guilty Pleasures*, 111.

44. See Charney, "Historical Excess," 30; Peterson, "The Competing Tunes of *Johnny Guitar*," 11–13; and Pamela Robertson, *Guilty Pleasures*, 111–14.

45. "Cinema: The New Pictures," *Time*, 14 June 1954, 106.

46. For a discussion of Mrs. Danvers as a coded lesbian, see White, *Uninvited*, 64–72, and Berenstein, "'I'm Not the Sort of Person Men Marry.'" Adding to the similarities between the two coded lesbians, Emma's riding habit bears a striking resemblance to the nunlike garb Mrs. Danvers wears throughout Hitchcock's film.

47. Kass, "*Johnny Guitar*," 27.

48. "Cinema: The New Pictures," 106.

49. Bosley Crowther, *"Johnny Guitar,"* *New York Times*, 28 May 1954, 19.

50. Review of *Johnny Guitar*, *Variety*, 5 May 1954, 6.

51. Kass, *"Johnny Guitar,"* 27.

52. Virginia Graham, "Cinema," *Spectator*, 4 June 1954, 678.

53. Charney, "Historical Excess," 25–26.

54. Quoted in Kreidl, *Nicholas Ray*, 50.

CHAPTER FIVE: REMAKING BETTE DAVIS

1. For a detailed account of Brown's dismissal, see Robbins, *The Dismissal of Miss Ruth Brown*.

2. On the role of Brown's civil-rights activism in her dismissal, see ibid., 45–75.

3. For a detailed account of Taradash's difficulty making *Storm Center*, see ibid., 128–53.

4. Taradash persuaded Mary Pickford to star in *Storm Center*, which she hoped would be her comeback movie, but she eventually dropped out after the gossip columnist Hedda Hopper, who supported the Hollywood blacklist, pressured her to do so. Davis faced similar pressure from a crusading Marin County housewife, Anne Smart, who orchestrated a campaign to "clean up" California's public libraries. Smart appealed to Davis as a "mother" not to appear in *Storm Center*, which she claimed was procommunist propaganda, but Davis responded that she hoped her children would be proud of her for making the movie. For a detailed account of the campaign against the making of *Storm Center*, see ibid., 143–47.

5. *Storm Center* is the only movie Davis made in which her rivalry over a child was with the father instead of the mother. This revision of the maternal scenario so closely associated with her persona seems significant. Whether intentionally or not, it obviated the lesbian construction of female rivalry which Davis's motherhood cycle made possible. Obviously, such a construction would have complicated the movie's critique of McCarthyism by enabling viewers to make a connection between the maternal scenario underlying Hull's relationship with Freddie and the antilesbian witch hunts.

6. The films in the cycle are *The Old Maid*; *All This and Heaven Too*; *The Great Lie*; *Now, Voyager*; and *Old Acquaintance*. For a detailed discussion of this cycle and its role in shaping Davis's persona, see Britton, "A New Servitude" and *Katharine Hepburn*; and White, *Uninvited*, 111–35. See also Laplace, "Producing and Consuming the Woman's Film, 1910–1940," 138–66.

7. For a detailed discussion of *The Old Maid* and its relation to the later films in the cycle, see Britton, *Katharine Hepburn*, 71–80, and White, *Uninvited*, 114–19. Britton argues persuasively that the later films basically constitute sequels to *The Old Maid*.

8. For a detailed discussion of the cycle's queer representation of motherhood, see White, *Uninvited*, 111–35, and Britton, "A New Servitude," 32–59.

9. For more on this aspect of the cycle, see White, *Uninvited*, 111–35, and Britton, "A New Servitude," 32–59.

10. White, *Uninvited*, 134.

11. Davis made one other fallen-star film, early in her career: *Dangerous* (Alfred E. Green, 1936), for which she received her first Academy Award for Best Actress. For an interesting discussion of how Davis's fallen-star pictures shaped her persona, see Beckman, *Vanishing Women*, 153–88.

12. The screenwriters Katherine Albert and Dale Eunson, who wrote the script for *The Star*, claimed that they modeled Maggie Elliot on Joan Crawford. The movie makes several references to Crawford's career. For example, like Crawford, who had to make a screen test for *Mildred Pierce*, Maggie must make one for *The Fatal Winter*, and Maggie's hairdo during the test recalls Mildred's after her rise to success. For Albert's and Eunson's claims about the source of their screenplay, see Considine, *Bette and Joan*, 248–50. Considine claims incorrectly that at the end of the screen test Maggie repeatedly says to the crew, "Bless you!," supposedly one of Crawford's trademark sayings. Beckman repeats the claim (*Vanishing Women*, 216). But *The Star* also makes several references to Davis's career, which suggests that Davis also provided a model for Maggie. For example, in the opening scene Maggie walks past the auction house where her personal effects are being auctioned off. She stops and looks at a publicity still, supposedly of her as a young star, but actually of Davis as Judith Traherne in *Dark Victory* (Edmund Goulding, 1939). Also like Davis, Maggie had her own production company at the height of her career, before she became "box office poison." Finally, *The Star* exploited Davis's association with a misogynistic construction of female rivalry.

13. Riviere, "Womanliness as Masquerade."

14. *Stella Dallas*'s ambiguous ending has generated an enormous amount of feminist criticism, and I do not mean to gloss over the complexity of Stella's sacrifice, which enables her to escape a maternal destiny, as well as to realize her class ambitions vicariously. Feminist commentary on Stella's sacrifice includes Kaplan, "The Case of the Missing Mother"; Williams, "'Something Else Besides a Mother'"; Jacobs, *The Wages of Sin*, 133–38; and White, *Uninvited*, 101–8.

15. I agree with White that Kit comes closer to the "horizon" of lesbian identity than any of Davis's other characters in the motherhood cycle, because of her masculine gender style combined with her unmarried status. See White, *Uninvited*, 131. I would add, however, that Kit's proximity to the contemporary signifiers of lesbian identity also depends on Millie's performance of an excessive femininity, which in rendering her gender style sexually ambiguous, links it to femme identity.

16. The rivalry between Davis and Hopkins has become part of Hollywood lore and even deeply informed their personas. See, for example, Quirk, *Fasten Your Seat Belts*, 194–99, and Considine, *Bette and Joan*, 138–41. As Judith Mayne has pointed out, this lore has introduced a homoerotic component into Davis's asso-

ciation with female rivalry, as the rivalry between Davis and Hopkins is usually explained in terms of Hopkins's rumored lesbianism. See Mayne, *Cinema and Spectatorship*, 135–38. But what interests me most in this discourse is how it introduced a misogynistic and homophobic narrative of female homosocial desire into the construction of Davis's persona, which countered the one in the motherhood cycle.

17. Quoted in Sikov, *Dark Victory*, 216.

18. Quoted in Considine, *Bette and Joan*, 140.

19. Bette Davis, *The Lonely Life*, 188.

20. On the construction of Davis's persona early in her career at Warner Bros., see Schatz, "'The Triumph of Bitchery.'"

21. For an account of the studio's lawsuit against Davis, see Sikov, *Dark Victory*, 84–97. As Sikov points out, Davis's combative relationship with the studio allowed her to bypass its publicity machine and exert at least some influence over the shaping of her persona. See also Schatz, "'The Triumph of Bitchery,'" 20–21.

22. Quoted in Britton, *Katharine Hepburn*, 78. This view of Davis was widespread. For example, Carl Laemmle Jr., the head of production at Universal Studios, where Davis began her Hollywood career, famously said that the young actress had "about as much sex appeal as Slim Summerville," and when she first started at Warner Bros., the director Michael Curtiz described her as a "Goddamned nothing no good sexless son of a bitch!" (quoted in Sikov, *Dark Victory*, 38 and 47, respectively).

23. For a discussion of how Davis's "bitch" roles rendered her persona incompatible with the institutions of heterosexuality, see Britton, *Katharine Hepburn*, 76–78. See also White, *Uninvited*, 111–35, and Schatz, "'The Triumph of Bitchery.'"

24. Schatz argues persuasively in "'The Triumph of Bitchery'" that the contradictions in Davis's performance style worked to take the edge off these roles and to render them sympathetic by ascribing vulnerability to the characters.

25. In a provocative article on *Mr. Skeffington* (Vincent Sherman, 1944), Martin Shingler argues that Davis, who did not like her appearance, was uncomfortable playing such roles and tended to sabotage them by exaggerating her performance style so as to expose normative femininity as a masquerade. See Shingler, "Masquerade or Drag?" Shingler's argument may overstate Davis's authorship of her movies and overlooks her promotion of a misogynistic and homophobic construction of female homosocial desire, which suggests that her view of gender was more conflicted and less feminist than his argument allows for.

26. Quoted in Sikov, *Dark Victory*, 192.

27. The costume designer Norma Koch, who won an Academy Award for her work on the movie, claimed that Davis's costume in this scene "had to be [Jane's] idea of sexy. . . . I deliberately made the dress a half-size too small, so she would

look like one of those old chorus girls coming apart at the seams" (quoted in Considine, *Bette and Joan*, 299–300).

28. Mayne points out that Davis's association with female rivalry offscreen was as contradictory as her association with it on-screen. For example, Davis's friendship with Mary Astor during the filming of *The Great Lie* countered the narrative of her rivalry with Hopkins on the sets of *The Old Maid* and *Old Acquaintance*, and seemed to affirm the construction of female homosocial bonds in the motherhood movies. Ironically, Sandra's and Maggie's rivalry in *The Great Lie* depended on Davis's and Astor's close collaboration. The two actresses thought that the script for the movie was trite and rewrote the sequence of scenes in the Arizona desert. See Mayne, *Cinema and Spectatorship*, 136–41.

29. On Davis's performance style and its strengths in conveying the psychological complexity of the characters she played, see Britton, *Katharine Hepburn*, 77–78.

30. Quoted in Quirk, *Fasten Your Seat Belts*, 254.

31. Sherman was not happy with Davis's "tricks" and attempted to dissuade her from wearing the mask and speaking in a falsetto, but she threatened to walk off the set if he interfered with her performance. See Sikov, *Dark Victory*, 231–37, and Leaming, *Bette Davis*, 197–200.

32. On Wyler's threat, see Leaming, *Bette Davis*, 125–35, and Sikov, *Dark Victory*, 115–23. Davis's biographers agree that during the filming of *Jezebel* Wyler taught the star how to gain control over her gestural performance style and in so doing enabled her to give one of the subtlest performances of her career.

33. Quoted in Leaming, *Bette Davis*, 179. Wyler objected in particular to the rice powder Davis insisted on wearing to make herself look older. The ensuing conflict anticipated the one between Davis and Sherman four years later, when she insisted on wearing a mask in *Mr. Skeffington*.

34. It is important to point out that the movie's camp effect also depended on its over-the-top treatment of themes that were inextricably linked to Davis's persona (female rivalry, spinsterhood, maternal desire, and so on). Like Davis's campy performance, this treatment undercut the movie's attempt to contain the star's persona by transforming the type of woman's picture that consolidated her stardom in the 1940s into a horror movie.

35. Quoted in Ringgold, *The Films of Bette Davis*, 174–75.

CHAPTER SIX: DORIS DAY'S QUEER NORMATIVITY

1. Quoted in Hotchner, *Doris Day*, 200.

2. Quoted in ibid.

3. Quoted in ibid., 194.

4. Quoted in ibid., 200.

5. Quoted in ibid., 200.

6. McGee, *Doris Day*, 152.

7. *Please Don't Eat the Daisies* was based on Jean Kerr's bestselling account of the ups and downs of her life with the theater critic Walter Kerr.

8. Kennedy and Davis, *Boots of Leather, Slippers of Gold*.

9. Stacey asked filmgoers about their memories of their favorite stars and used the results to develop an important theory of female spectatorship. See Stacey, *Star-Gazing*.

10. Quoted in Stacey, *Star-Gazing*, 203. Whereas some of the women who responded to Stacey's advertisements identified with Day, others seem to have desired her. Veronica Millen, for example, also considered Day one of her favorite stars: "I thought she was fantastic, and joined her fan club, collected all the photos and info I could find. I saw *Calamity Jane* 45 times in a fortnight and still watch all her films avidly. My sisters all thought I was mad *going silly* on a woman . . . but I just thought she was wonderful" (quoted in Stacey, *Star-Gazing*, 138; emphasis added).

11. Clarke and Simmonds, *Move Over Misconceptions*, 1.

12. Quoted in McGee, *Doris Day*, 26.

13. Merk, "Travesty on the Old Frontier," 22.

14. Ibid.

15. For example, in her very last film, *With Six You Get Eggroll* (Howard Morris, 1968), Day played Abby McLure, a widow who owns and operates a lumberyard with her adolescent son. In early scenes at the lumberyard, she wears masculine-looking clothes and a hard hat.

16. This aspect of the film was especially apparent in Day's appearance. In the opening scene, for example, Jane/Day is wearing a baggy pair of blue jeans, a plaid cotton shirt, a man's white undershirt, and sneakers. It was also apparent in her voice. Simmonds points out in her contribution to the British Film Institute dossier that "as an instrument for conveying her thoughts and feelings on screen, Day uses her voice more than any other part of her body" ("The Girl Next Door," 7). Although Day did not lower her voice for *It Happened to Jane*, as she did for *Calamity Jane*, her voice is unusually brassy in the film and helps to convey Jane's masculine qualities. On Day's alteration of her voice for *Calamity Jane*, see Hotchner, *Doris Day*, 131.

17. Quoted in McGee, *Doris Day*, 122.

18. Quoted in ibid., 145.

19. Quoted in ibid., 145.

20. These were Frank Sinatra in *Young At Heart* (Gordon Douglas, 1955); Louis Jordan in *Julie* (Andrew Stone, 1956); Clark Gable in *Teacher's Pet* (George Seaton, 1958); Rock Hudson in *Pillow Talk* (Michael Gordon, 1959), *Lover Come Back* (Delbert Mann, 1962), and *Send Me No Flowers* (Norman Jewison, 1964); Cary Grant in *That Touch of Mink* (Delbert Mann, 1962); James Garner in *The*

Thrill of It All (Norman Jewison, 1963) and *Move Over, Darling* (Michael Gordon, 1963); Rod Taylor in *Do Not Disturb* (Ralph Levy, 1965) and *The Glass Bottom Boat* (Frank Tashlin, 1966); and Brian Keith in *With Six You Get Eggroll* (Howard Morris, 1968).

21. On *Calamity Jane* as a star vehicle for Day, see Hotchner, *Doris Day*, 131; McGee, *Doris Day*, 23; and Clarke and Simmonds, *Move Over Misconceptions*, 47.

22. Quoted in Clarke and Simmonds, *Move Over Misconceptions*, 47.

23. Clarke and Simmonds, *Move Over Misconceptions*, 40.

24. This is one of the few instances in a Day film where there is even a hint that the male character experiences her masculinity as castrating.

25. See especially Savoy, "'That Ain't All She Ain't,'" and Merk, "Travesty on the Old Frontier," 22–25. See also Bell-Metereau, *Hollywood Androgyny*, 90–91, and Halberstam, *Female Masculinity*, 209–10.

26. See especially Savoy, "'That Ain't All She Ain't,'" 172–73. For Savoy, the scene comments ironically on what he calls the "rigidity" of butch-femme roles in the 1950s even as it registers the normalization of Calamity's gender presentation.

27. Ibid., 170–71.

28. Savoy argues that this scene stages a warning to Calamity about her cross-dressing *as a man* (ibid., 152). But I am arguing that the scene stages a warning about her cross-dressing *as a woman*, which can only lead to social calamity, as it does later in the film. The film does not privilege anatomical sex in the way that Savoy's analysis implies that it does.

29. According to Savoy, the song's lyrics "announce the epistemology of the lesbian closet" (ibid., 166). But I am proposing that the scene's homoerotic overtones are much queerer. If the song's lyrics announce an epistemology of anything, it is that of the gay male closet. Because of her cross-dressing and because she is singing about Hickok, Calamity resembles a gay man more than a butch lesbian.

30. On the role of *Calamity Jane* in opening up Day's persona to a lesbian construction, see White, *Uninvited*, 38–39.

31. Quoted in Hotchner, *Doris Day*, 197.

32. This may explain why critics have overlooked the way in which *Calamity Jane* affirms Calamity's masculinity. They have approached the film, whether consciously or not, through the lens of the wholesome elements of Day's image.

33. See especially Fuchs, "Split Screens."

34. Steven Cohan has argued that Jan anticipated the "liberated," single, career girl—the female counterpart of the playboy bachelor—that Helen Gurley Brown wrote about in her bestselling book, *Sex and the Single Girl* (1962). But as he himself acknowledges, the women Brown wrote about were in their early twenties. What sets Jan apart from other women is that she is already in her thirties and has never married, despite her sexual desirability. In fact, all of the women Brad dates seem well beyond the age of the "Cosmo girl." See Cohan, *Masked Men*, 278–80.

35. Cohan argues that Jan is not a virgin. As evidence, he cites Jan's voice-over in the scene in which she and Rex drive to the country for the weekend. In that scene, Jan tells herself, "You know you've gone out with a lot of men in your time, but this—this is the jackpot." See Cohan, *Masked Men*, 279. But after she discovers that Brad has been masquerading as Rex as part of a ploy to get her into bed, Jan tells Jonathan tearfully, "I'm so ashamed. I've never done anything like this before. I thought we were going to get married!" At the very least, this suggests that Jan was going to have sex with Rex only because she thought they would be getting married.

36. Cohan, *Masked Men*, 287–90. See also Fuchs, "Split Screens," 230–33.

37. For a discussion of the sexual ambiguity of Hudson's image, see Meyer, "Rock Hudson's Body"; Cohan, *Masked Men*, 295–303; and Klinger, *Melodrama and Meaning*, 97–129.

38. For an excellent discussion of Jonathan's complex function in the film, see Cohan, *Masked Men*, 290–95.

CONCLUSION: KILLING OFF THE FEMME

1. Dyer comments in particular on the leopard-spotted coat with black leather trim that Theo is wearing when she arrives at Hill House ("Seen to Be Believed," 18).

2. Despite the 1961 revision, the Production Code continued to result in censorship of the treatment of lesbianism in Hollywood cinema. For example, the Production Code Administration objected to a scene in the script in which Theo paints Eleanor's toenails, even as it acknowledged that the scene complied with the Code's new set of categories for judging movies: "We doubt that we could approve a picture under the Code in which a woman, with Lesbian intentions, is indulging in physical intimacies with, or bedroom proximities to another woman, even though these things are done with *tact and refinement*" (quoted in White, *Uninvited*, 229; emphasis added). In the movie version of the scene, Eleanor paints her own toenails while Theo lounges on the bed in her pajamas, drinking brandy.

3. Vito Russo misreads the movie's homophobic discourse of female homosexuality, which as I argue here centers not on Theo, but on Eleanor, who embodies the stereotype of the sexually repressed spinster. Russo argues that Theo "gets her psychosexual jollies by hugging Julie Harris and blaming it on ghosts" (*The Celluloid Closet*, 158).

4. White, *Uninvited*, 80–82.

5. White argues compellingly that the supernatural functions in the movie as a strategy of representation that transforms lesbian desire into homophobic fear (*Uninvited*, 82–88). White's reading of the movie has deeply influenced my own, but I think she overlooks the significance of the gender differences between Theo and Eleanor. I argue that the movie's exploration of perverse female desire reflects

the obsession with the feminine woman who made a lesbian object choice that pervaded Cold War culture. Whereas Theo's aberrant desire can be explained in terms of an inverted gender identity, Eleanor's cannot. Thus she emerges as the focus of the movie's homophobic discourse of lesbianism.

6. Freud, *The Standard Edition of the Complete Psychological Works of Sigmund Freud*, 212. White, too, points out the Freudian echo (*Uninvited*, 80).

BIBLIOGRAPHY

Adam, Barry. *Rise of a Gay and Lesbian Movement*. New York: Twayne, 1995.

Allen, Robert C., and Douglas Gomery. *Film History: Theory and Practice*. New York: Knopf, 1985.

Babuscio, Jack. "Camp and the Gay Sensibility." *Gays and Film*, ed. Richard Dyer, 40–57. London: British Film Institute, 1980.

Bailey, Beth. *From Front Porch to Back Seat: Courtship in Twentieth-Century America*. Baltimore: Johns Hopkins University Press, 1988.

Barrios, Richard. *Screened Out: Playing Gay in Hollywood from Edison to Stonewall*. New York: Routledge, 2003.

Beckman, Karen. *Vanishing Women: Magic, Film, and Feminism*. Durham, N.C.: Duke University Press, 2003.

Bell-Metereau, Rebecca. *Hollywood Androgyny*. 2d ed. New York: Columbia University Press, 1993.

Berenstein, Rhona J. "Adaptation, Censorship, and Audiences of Questionable Type: Lesbian Sightings in *Rebecca* (1940) and *The Uninvited* (1944)." *Cinema Journal* 37.3 (spring 1998): 6–37.

———. "'I'm Not the Sort of Person Men Marry': Monsters, Queers, and Hitchcock's *Rebecca*." *CineAction* 29.3 (fall 1992): 82–96.

Bergler, Edmund. *Homosexuality: Disease or Way of Life?* New York: Hill and Wang, 1957.

Breines, Wini. *Young, White, and Miserable: Growing up Female in the Fifties*. Chicago: University of Chicago Press, 1992.

Britton, Andrew. *Katharine Hepburn: The Thirties and After*. Newcastle upon Tyne, U.K.: Tyneside Cinema, 1984.

———. "A New Servitude: Bette Davis, *Now, Voyager*, and the Radicalism of the Woman's Film." *CineAction* 26–27 (1992): 32–59.

Bryer, Jackson R., ed. *Conversations with Lillian Hellman*. Jackson: University Press of Mississippi, 1986.

Byars, Jackie. *All that Hollywood Allows: Rereading Gender in 1950s Melodrama*. Chapel Hill: University of North Carolina Press, 1991.

Cain, James M. *Mildred Pierce*. 1941. Reprint, New York: Vintage, 1989.

Caute, David. *The Great Fear: The Anti-Communist Purges under Truman and Eisenhower*. New York: Simon and Schuster, 1978.

Charney, Leo. "Historical Excess: *Johnny Guitar*'s Containment." *Cinema Journal* 25.4 (summer 1990): 23–34.

Chauncey, George. "From Sexual Inversion to Homosexuality: The Changing Conceptualization of Female 'Deviance.'" *Passion and Power: Sexuality in History*, ed. Kathy Peiss and Christina Simmons, with Robert A. Padgug, 87–117. Philadelphia: Temple University Press, 1989.

———. *Gay New York: Gender, Urban Culture, and the Making of the Gay Male World, 1890–1940*. New York: Basic, 1994.

"Cinema: The New Pictures." *Time*, 14 June 1954, 106.

Clarke, Jane, and Diane Simmonds, eds. *Move Over Misconceptions: Doris Day Reappraised*. London: British Film Institute, 1980.

Cohan, Steven. *Masked Men: Masculinity and the Movies in the Fifties*. Bloomington: Indiana University Press, 1995.

Columpar, Corinn. "*Marnie*: A Site/Sight for the Convergence of Gazes." *Hitchcock Annual* 10 (2002): 51–73.

Considine, Shaun. *Bette and Joan: The Divine Feud*. New York: E. P. Dutton, 1989.

Cook, Pam. "Duplicity in *Mildred Pierce*." *Women in Film Noir*, ed. E. Ann Kaplan, 68–82. London: British Film Institute, 1978.

Corber, Robert J. "Cold War Femme: Lesbian Visibility in Joseph L. Mankiewicz's *All about Eve*." *Gay and Lesbian Quarterly* 11.1 (2005): 1–22.

———. *Homosexuality in Cold War America: Resistance and the Crisis of Masculinity*. Durham, N.C.: Duke University Press, 1997.

———. *In the Name of National Security: Hitchcock, Homophobia, and the Political Construction of Gender in Postwar America*. Durham, N.C.: Duke University Press, 1993.

———. "Joan Crawford's Padded Shoulders: Female Masculinity in *Mildred Pierce*." *Camera Obscura* 21.2 (spring 2006): 1–31.

Corber, Robert J., and Stephen Valocchi, eds. *Queer Studies: An Interdisciplinary Reader*. Malden, Mass.: Blackwell, 2003.

Coyle, Katy, and Nadiene Van Dyke. "Sex, Smashing, and Storyville in Turn-of-the-Century New Orleans: Reexamining the Continuum of Lesbian Sexuality." *Carryin' on in the Lesbian and Gay South*, ed. John Howard, 54–73. New York: New York University Press, 1997.

Davis, Bette. *The Lonely Life: An Autobiography*. New York: G. P. Putnam, 1962.

Davis, Katharine Bement. *Factors in the Sex Life of Twenty-Two Hundred Women*. New York: Harper and Brothers, 1929.

Dean, Robert D. *Imperial Brotherhood: Gender and the Making of Cold War Foreign Policy*. Amherst: University of Massachusetts Press, 2001.

De Lauretis, Theresa. *Alice Doesn't: Feminism, Semiotics, Cinema*. Bloomington: Indiana University Press, 1984.

Dell, Floyd. *Love in the Machine Age: A Psychological Study of the Transition from Patriarchal Society*. New York: Farrar and Rinehart, 1930.

D'Emilio, John. *Sexual Politics, Sexual Communities: The Making of a Homosexual Minority in the United States, 1940–1970*. Chicago: University of Chicago Press, 1983.

D'Emilio, John, and Estelle Freedman. *Intimate Matters: A History of Sexuality in America*. New York: Harper and Row, 1989.

Doane, Mary Ann. *The Desire to Desire: The Woman's Film of the 1940s*. Bloomington: Indiana University Press, 1987.

Duggan, Lisa. *Sapphic Slashers: Sex, Violence, and American Modernity*. Durham, N.C.: Duke University Press, 2000.

———. "The Trials of Alice Mitchell: Sensationalism, Sexology, and the Lesbian Subject in Turn-of-the-Century America." *Queer Studies: An Interdisciplinary Reader*, ed. Robert J. Corber and Stephen Valocchi, 73–87. Malden, Mass.: Blackwell, 2003.

du Maurier, Daphne. *Rebecca*. New York: Harper, 2006.

Dyer, Richard. *The Matter of Images: Essays on Representations*. London: Routledge, 1993.

———. "Seen to Be Believed: Some Problems in the Representation of Gay People as Typical." *Studies in Visual Communication* 9.2 (spring 1983): 2–19.

Ellis, Havelock. *Sexual Inversion*. Honolulu: University Press of the Pacific, 2001.

Erhart, Julia. "'She Could Hardly Invent Them!': From Epistemological Uncertainty to Discursive Production in *The Children's Hour*." *Camera Obscura* 35 (1995): 85–106.

Faderman, Lillian. *Scotch Verdict: Dame Gordon vs. Pirie and Woods*. New York: William Morrow, 1983.

———. *Surpassing the Love of Men: Romantic Friendship and Love between Women from the Renaissance to the Present*. New York: William Morrow, 1981.

Feldstein, Ruth. *Motherhood in Black and White: Race and Sex in American Liberalism, 1930–1965*. Ithaca, N.Y.: Cornell University Press, 2000.

Franzen, Trisha. *Spinsters and Lesbians: Independent Womanhood in the United States*. New York: New York University Press, 1996.

Freud, Sigmund. *The Standard Edition of the Complete Psychological Works of Sigmund Freud*. Vol. 20. Ed. James Strachey. London: Hogarth, 1955.

Fuchs, Cynthia J. "Split Screens: Framing and Passing in *Pillow Talk*." *The Other Fifties: Interrogating Midcentury American Icons*, ed. Joel Foreman, 224–53. Urbana: University of Illinois Press, 1997.

Fuss, Diana. "Fashion and the Homospectatorial Look." *Critical Inquiry* 18.2 (spring 1992): 713–37.

Gallo, Marcia. *Different Daughters: A History of the Daughters of Bilitis and the Rise of the Lesbian Rights Movement*. Berkeley, Calif.: Seal Press, 2007.

Halberstam, Judith. *Female Masculinity*. Durham, N.C.: Duke University Press, 1998.

Halperin, David M. *How to Do the History of Homosexuality*. Chicago: University of Chicago Press, 2004.

Haralovich, Mary Beth. "Too Much Guilt Is Never Enough for Working Mothers: Joan Crawford, *Mildred Pierce*, and *Mommie Dearest*." *Velvet Light Trap* 29 (1992): 43–52.

Hart, Lynda. "Living Under the Sign of the Cross: Some Speculations on Femme Femininity." *Butch/Femme: Inside Lesbian Gender*, ed. Sally R. Munt, 214–24. London: Cassell, 1998.

Hellman, Lillian. *The Children's Hour*. New York: Dramatists Play Service, 1981.

———. *Scoundrel Time*. New York: Little, Brown, 1976.

———. *Six Plays by Lillian Hellman*. New York: Random House, 1979.

Hemmings, Clare. "'All My life I've Been Waiting for Something . . .': Theorizing Femme Narrative in *The Well of Loneliness*." *Palatable Poison: Critical Perspectives on* The Well of Loneliness, ed. Laura Doan and Jay Prosser, 179–96. New York: Columbia University Press, 2001.

———. "Out of Sight, Out of Mind? Theorizing Femme Narrative." *Sexualities* 2.1 (winter 1999): 451–64.

Herman, Jan. *A Talent for Trouble: The Life of Hollywood's Most Acclaimed Director*. New York: Da Capo, 1995.

Herzog, Charlotte C., and Jane M. Gaines. "'Puffed Sleeves before Tea-Time': Joan Crawford, Adrian, and Women Audiences." *Stardom: Industry of Desire*, ed. Christine Gledhill, 74–91. New York: Routledge, 1985.

Hoopes, Roy. *Cain: The Biography of James M. Cain*. Carbondale: Southern Illinois University Press, 1982.

Hotchner, A. E. *Doris Day: Her Own Story*. New York: William Morrow, 1976.

Inness, Sherrie A. *The Lesbian Menace: Ideology, Identity, and the Representation of Lesbian Life*. Amherst: University of Massachusetts Press, 1997.

Jacobs, Lea. *The Wages of Sin: Censorship and the Fallen Woman Film, 1928–1942*. Madison: University of Wisconsin Press, 1991.

Jameson, Fredric. "Reification and Utopia in Mass Culture." *Signatures of the Visible*, 9–34. New York: Routledge, 1992.

Johnson, David K. *The Lavender Scare: The Cold War Persecution of Gays and Lesbians in the Federal Government*. Chicago: University of Chicago Press, 2004.

Kaplan, E. Ann. "The Case of the Missing Mother: Maternal Issues in Vidor's *Stella Dallas*." *Heresies* 16 (1983): 81–85.

———. *Motherhood and Representation: The Mother in Popular Culture and Melodrama*. London: Routledge, 1992.

Kass, Robert. "*Johnny Guitar*." *Catholic World*, June 1954, 27.

Kennedy, Elizabeth Lapovsky, and Madeline D. Davis. *Boots of Leather, Slippers of Gold: The History of a Lesbian Community*. New York: Penguin, 1994.

Kinsey, Alfred C., Wardell B. Pomeroy, Clyde E. Martin, and Paul Gebhard. *Sexual Behavior in the Human Female*. Philadelphia: Saunders, 1953.

Kinsey, Alfred C., Wardell B. Pomeroy, and Clyde E. Martin. *Sexual Behavior in the Human Male*. Philadelphia: Saunders, 1948.

Klinger, Barbara. *Melodrama and Meaning: History, Culture, and the Films of Douglas Sirk*. Bloomington: Indiana University Press, 1994.

Knapp, Lucretia. "The Queer Voice in *Marnie*." *Cinema Journal* 32.4 (summer 1993): 6–23.

Kreidl, John Francis. *Nicholas Ray*. Boston: Twayne, 1977.

Lait, Jack, and Lee Mortimer. *Washington Confidential*. New York: Crown, 1951.

Laplace, Maria. "Producing and Consuming the Woman's Film, 1910–1940." *Home Is Where the Heart Is: Studies in Melodrama and the Woman's Film*, ed. Christine Gledhill, 138–66. London: British Film Institute, 1987.

Leaming, Barbara. *Bette Davis*. New York: Cooper Square, 2003.

Lundberg, Ferdinand, and Marynia Farnham. *Modern Woman: The Lost Sex*. New York: Harper and Brothers, 1947.

Martin, Biddy. "Sexuality without Genders and Other Queer Utopias." *Femininity Played Straight: The Significance of Being Lesbian*, 71–94. New York: Routledge, 1996.

Martinson, Debora. *Lillian Hellman: A Life with Foxes and Scoundrels*. New York: Counterpoint, 2005.

May, Elaine Tyler. *Homeward Bound: American Families in the Cold War Era*. New York: Basic, 1988.

Mayne, Judith. *Cinema and Spectatorship*. London: Routledge, 1993.

McElhaney, Joe. "Touching the Surface: Marnie, Melodrama, Modernism." *Alfred Hitchcock Centenary Essays*, ed. Richard Allen and Sam Ishii Gonzales, 87–105. London: BFI Publishing, 1999.

McGee, Garry. *Doris Day: Sentimental Journey*. Jefferson, N.C.: McFarland, 2005.

Merk, Mandy. "Travesty on the Old Frontier." *Move Over Misconceptions: Doris Day Reappraised*, ed. Jane Clarke and Diane Simmonds, 21–28. London: British Film Institute, 1980.

Meyer, Richard. "Rock Hudson's Body." *Inside/Out: Lesbian Theories, Gay Theories*, ed. Diana Fuss, 259–88. New York: Routledge, 1991.

Meyerowitz, Joanne, ed. *Not June Cleaver: Women and Gender in Postwar America, 1945–1960*. Philadelphia: Temple University Press, 1994.

Modleski, Tania. *The Woman Who Knew Too Much: Hitchcock and Film Theory*. New York: Methuen, 1988.

Mogg, Ken. "Defending Marnie—and Hitchcock." *Hitchcock Annual* 10 (2002): 72–83.

Moore, Lisa. "'Something More Tender Still than Friendship': Romantic Friendship in Early Nineteenth-Century England." *Feminist Studies* 18.3 (fall 1992): 513–28.

Motion Picture Producers and Distributors of America. "The Motion Picture Production Code of 1930." *The Movies in Our Midst: Documents in the Cultural History of Film in America*, ed. Gerald Mast, 321–33. Chicago: University of Chicago Press, 1983.

Nelson, Joyce. "*Mildred Pierce* Reconsidered." *Film Reader* 2 (1977): 65–70.

Nestle, Joan. "The Fem Question." *Pleasure and Danger: Exploring Female Sexuality*, ed. Carole S. Vance, 232–41. London: Pandora, 1989.

Newton, Esther. "The Mythic Mannish Lesbian: Radclyffe Hall and the New Woman." *Signs* 9.2 (spring 1984): 557–75.

Noriega, Chon. "'Something's Missing Here!': Homosexuality and Film Reviews during the Production Code Era, 1934–1962." *Cinema Journal* 30.1 (winter 1990): 20–41.

Peterson, Jennifer. "The Competing Tunes of *Johnny Guitar*: Liberalism, Sexuality, Masquerade." *Cinema Journal* 35.3 (spring 1996): 3–18.

Quirk, Lawrence J. *Fasten Your Seat Belts: The Passionate Life of Bette Davis*. New York: William Morrow, 1990.

Quirk, Lawrence J., and William Schoell, *Joan Crawford: The Essential Biography*. Lexington: University of Kentucky Press, 2002.

Rapf, Joanna E. "'A Larger Thing': John Michael Hayes and *The Children's Hour*." *Postscript* 9.1–2 (winter–spring 1989–1990): 38–52.

Ringgold, Gene. *The Films of Bette Davis*. New York: Citadel, 1966.

Riviere, Joan. "Womanliness as Masquerade." 1929. Reprinted in *Formations of Fantasy*, ed. Victor Burgin, James Donald, and Cora Kaplan, 35–44. London: Methuen, 1986.

Robbins, Louise S. *The Dismissal of Miss Ruth Brown: Civil Rights, Censorship, and the American Library*. Norman: University of Oklahoma Press, 2000.

Robertson, James C. *The Casablanca Man: The Cinema of Michael Curtiz*. New York: Routledge, 1993.

Robertson, Pamela. *Guilty Pleasures: Feminist Camp from Mae West to Madonna*. Durham, N.C.: Duke University Press, 1996.

———. "Structural Irony in *Mildred Pierce*; or, How Mildred Lost Her Tongue." *Cinema Journal* 30.1 (fall 1990): 42–54.

Rogin, Michael Paul. *Ronald Reagan, the Movie: And Other Episodes in Political Demonology*. Berkeley: University of California Press, 1987.

Roof, Judith. *All about Thelma and Eve: Sidekicks and Third Wheels*. Urbana: University of Illinois Press, 2002.

Rose, Chloe Brushwood, and Anna Camilleri, eds. *Brazen Femme: Queering Femininity*. Vancouver: Arsenal Pulp, 2002.

Ross, Andrew. *No Respect: Intellectuals and Popular Culture*. New York: Routledge, 1989.

Roughead, William. *Bad Companions*. New York: Duffield and Green, 1931.

Rupp, Leila. "'Imagine My Surprise': Women's Relationships in Mid-Twentieth

Century America." *Hidden From History: Reclaiming the Gay and Lesbian Past*, ed. Martin Duberman, Martha Vicinus, and George Chauncey, 395–410. New York: Meridian, 1989.

Russo, Vito. *The Celluloid Closet: Homosexuality in the Movies*. Rev. ed. New York: Harper and Row, 1987.

Sahli, Nancy. "Smashing: Women's Relationships before the Fall." *Chrysalis* 8 (1979): 17–27.

Savoy, Eric. "'That Ain't All She Ain't': Doris Day and Queer Performativity." *Out Takes: Essays on Queer Theory and Film*, ed. Ellis Hanson, 151–82. Durham, N.C.: Duke University Press, 1999.

Schatz, Thomas. "'The Triumph of Bitchery': Warner Bros., Bette Davis, and *Jezebel*." *Wide Angle* 10.1 (spring 1988): 17–29.

Schrecker, Ellen. *Many Are the Crimes: McCarthyism in America*. Princeton, N.J.: Princeton University Press, 1999.

Sedgwick, Eve Kosofsky. *Between Men: English Literature and Male Homosocial Desire*. New York: Columbia University Press, 1985.

———. *Epistemology of the Closet*. Berkeley: University of California Press, 1990.

Shingler, Martin. "Masquerade or Drag? Bette Davis and the Ambiguities of Gender." *Screen* 36.3 (fall 1995): 179–92.

Sikov, Ed. *Dark Victory: The Life of Bette Davis*. New York: Henry Holt, 2007.

Simmonds, Diane. "The Girl Next Door." *Move Over Misconceptions: Doris Day Reappraised*, ed. Jane Clarke and Diane Simmonds, 6–11. London: British Film Institute, 1980.

Simmons, Christina. *Making Marriage Modern: Women's Sexuality from the Progressive Era to World War II*. New York: Oxford University Press, 2009.

Smith, Geoffrey S. "National Security and Personal Isolation: Sex, Gender, and Disease in the Cold-War United States." *International History Review* 14 (1992): 307–37.

Smith-Rosenberg, Carroll. *Disorderly Conduct: Visions of Gender in Victorian America*. New York: Oxford University Press, 1985.

Spencer, Jenny S. "Sex, Lies, and Revisions: Historicizing Hellman's *The Children's Hour*." *Modern Drama* 47.1 (spring 2004): 44–65.

Stacey, Jackie. "Desperately Seeking Difference." *Screen* 18.3 (fall 1987): 48–61.

———. "Feminine Fascinations: Forms of Identification in Star-Audience Relations." *Stardom: Industry of Desire*, ed. Christine Gledhill, 141–63. London: Routledge, 1991.

———. *Star-Gazing: Hollywood Cinema and Female Spectatorship*. London: Routledge, 1994.

Staggs, Sam. *All about "All about Eve": The Complete Behind-the-Scenes Story of the Bitchiest Film Ever Made*. New York: St. Martin's, 2000.

Stearn, Jess. *The Grapevine: A Report on the Secret World of the Lesbian*. New York: MacFadden, 1965.

Stevenson, Adlai. "A Purpose for Modern Woman." *Women's Home Companion*, September 1955, 30–31.

Strecker, Edward A., and Vincent T. Lathbury. *Their Mothers' Daughters*. Philadelphia: J. B. Lippincott, 1956.

Terry, Jennifer. *An American Obsession: Science, Medicine, and Homosexuality in Modern Society*. Chicago: University of Chicago Press, 1999.

Thomas, Bob. *Joan Crawford: A Biography*. New York: Simon and Schuster, 1978.

Titus, Mary. "Murdering the Lesbian: Lillian Hellman's *The Children's Hour*." *Tulsa Studies in Women's Literature* 10.2 (summer 1991): 215–32.

Truffaut, François. *Hitchcock*. New York: Simon and Schuster, 1983.

Tuhkanen, Mikko. "Breeding (and) Reading: Lesbian Knowledge, Eugenic Discipline, and *The Children's Hour*." *Modern Fiction Studies* 48.4 (winter 2002): 1001–40.

Vicinus, Martha. "Distance and Desire: English Boarding School Friendships, 1870–1920." *Signs* 9.4 (winter 1984): 600–622.

———. "'They Wonder to which Sex I Belong': The Historical Roots of the Modern Lesbian Identity." *Lesbian Subjects: A Feminist Studies Reader*, ed. Martha Vicinus, 233–60. Bloomington: Indiana University Press, 1996.

Walker, Alexander. *Joan Crawford: The Ultimate Star*. New York: Harper and Row, 1983.

Walker, Janet. "Feminist Critical Practice: Female Discourse in *Mildred Pierce*." *Film Reader* 5 (1982): 164–72.

Walsh, Andrea. *Women's Films and Female Experience, 1940–50*. New York: Praeger, 1984.

Weeks, Jeffrey. *Sex, Politics, and Society: The Regulation of Sexuality since 1800*. London: Longman, 1989.

Weiss, Andrea. *Vampires and Violets: Lesbians in Film*. New York: Penguin, 1993.

White, Patricia. *Uninvited: Classical Hollywood Cinema and Lesbian Representability*. Bloomington: University of Indiana Press, 1999.

Williams, Linda. "Feminist Film Theory: *Mildred Pierce* and the Second World War." *Female Spectators: Looking at Film and Television*, ed. E. Deirdre Pribam, 12–30. New York: Routledge, 1988.

———. "'Something Else Besides a Mother': *Stella Dallas* and the Maternal Melodrama." *Cinema Journal* 24.1 (winter 1984): 2–27.

Wilmington, Michael. "Nicholas Ray's *Johnny Guitar*." *Velvet Light Trap* 12 (spring 1974): 19–25.

Wylie, Philip. *Generation of Vipers*. Champaign, Ill.: Dalkey Archive, 1996.

INDEX

Robert J. Corber is a professor and the director of the
Women, Gender, and Sexuality Program at Trinity
College. He is the author of *Homosexuality in Cold War
America: Resistance and the Crisis of Masculinity* (1997),
*In the Name of National Security: Hitchcock, Homophobia,
and the Political Construction of Gender in Postwar
America* (1993), and co-editor of *Queer Studies:
An Interdisciplinary Reader* (2003).

....

Library of Congress Cataloging-in-Publication Data
Corber, Robert J., 1958–
Cold war femme : lesbianism, national identity, and
Hollywood cinema / Robert J. Corber.
p. cm.
Includes bibliographical references and index.
ISBN 978-0-8223-4928-0 (cloth : alk. paper)
ISBN 978-0-8223-4947-1 (pbk. : alk. paper)
1. Lesbianism in motion pictures. 2. Cold War—
Social aspects—United States. 3. Women in popular
culture—United States. I. Title.
PN1995.9.L48C673 2011
791.43′6526643—dc22
2010028811